JOHN STEINBECK

A Study of the Short Fiction

Twayne's Studies in Short Fiction

Gordon Weaver, General Editor
Oklahoma State University

John Steinbeck, 1961.
Courtesy of the Steinbeck Library, Salinas, CA.

JOHN STEINBECK

A Study of the Short Fiction

R. S. Hughes
University of Hawaii

TWAYNE PUBLISHERS • BOSTON

A Division of G. K. Hall & Co.

Twayne's Studies in Short Fiction Series, No. 5
Editorial Assistant to Gordon Weaver: Stephanie Corcoran

Copyediting supervised by Barbara Sutton.
Book design by Janet Zietowski.
Book production by Gabrielle B. McDonald.
Typeset in 10/12 Times Roman by Williams Press, Inc.

Printed on permanent/durable acid-free paper
and bound in the United States of America.

Library of Congress Cataloging-in-Publication Data

Hughes, R.S., 1948—
John Steinbeck: a study of the short fiction / R.S. Hughes.
    p. cm.—(Twayne's studies in short fiction; TSSF 5)
Bibliography: p. 198
Includes index.
ISBN 0-8057-8302-4
1. Steinbeck, John, 1902-1968—Criticism and interpretation.
I. Title.   II. Series.
PS3537.T3234.Z7147   1988
813'.52—dc19
                                                    88-19967
                                                    CIP

For Charlene

*In the midst of
winter, I finally
learned that there
was in me an
invincible summer.*

—Albert Camus

Contents

Preface

John Steinbeck wrote short stories for nearly forty years, winning virtually every major prize and honor for mastery of the form. His unique spirit of place—the "Steinbeck Country" on the central coast of California—imbues his stories with the special flavor of the American West. The ranches, farms, small towns, and seaside villages in his tales, and the earthy, simple people who inhabit them, reflect this ruggedly beautiful landscape. Yet beneath the tranquil surface of his California idylls, Steinbeck probes into the secret lives of his characters, revealing complex and disturbing human problems.

During his career, Steinbeck explored a variety of story types, including sketches, parables, allegories, beast fables, and even science fiction. He also attempted various styles; his best known is a crisp, graphic prose that renders his native California with picturelike accuracy. Though few critics would argue that his canon is uniformly brilliant, Steinbeck created a number of short story masterpieces. Comparing him favorably to Chekhov, André Gide concludes, Steinbeck wrote "nothing more perfect, more accomplished, than certain of [his] short stories." Indeed, "The Chrysanthemums," "Flight," *The Red Pony,* and others rank among the finest stories of Steinbeck's era, and they continue to be read and enjoyed today.

John Steinbeck: A Study of the Short Fiction provides an introduction to Steinbeck's achievement in short fiction. Part 1 appraises his popular *Long Valley* stories, his uncollected tales of the 1940s and 1950s, and his short story cycle, *The Pastures of Heaven.* Part 2 contains a selection of letters in which Steinbeck candidly discusses his craft. And part 3 offers four critics' views on his short fiction, their topics ranging from his "strong women" to his provocative Jungian archetypes. In sum, parts 1, 2, and 3 constitute an overview of Steinbeck's short fiction—including analyses of individual stories, observations on story writing by the author himself, and a sampling of previously published criticism.

Preface

Several people have assisted me during the writing of *John Steinbeck: A Study of the Short Fiction.* Gordon Weaver, General Editor of *Twayne Studies in Short Fiction,* warmly encouraged and skillfully guided me through each stage of the project. Anne Jones and Liz Traynor, Twayne editors in Boston, responded promptly and fully to my occasional question. Carlton A. "Dook" Sheffield generously offered his insights into the short fiction of his lifelong friend. A. Grove Day, also a friend of Steinbeck, provided invaluable biographical and background information. Professor Joseph Kau, English Department Chair at the University of Hawaii at Manoa, kindly helped me arrange a Research Relations Fund grant and a one-semester leave. Finally, for that ineffable, yet essential, support every writer needs, I wish to offer my special thanks to Charlene and Nathan.

R. S. Hughes

University of Hawaii

THE SHORT FICTION:
A CRITICAL ANALYSIS

Steinbeck the Short Story Writer

Though today most readers remember John Steinbeck for such important novels as *The Grapes of Wrath* (1939), his achievement in short fiction is equally impressive. Mary Rohrberger has aptly said: "In the end . . . [Steinbeck's] reputation may rest on the short stories. As a novelist he is competent; as a short story writer, he can be superb." Other critics agree. Mordecai Marcus calls "The Chrysanthemums" "one of the world's great stories." Joseph Warren Beach compares Steinbeck's short fiction artistry with that of Chekhov and Anatole France. And Clifton Fadiman praises *The Red Pony* as a "masterpiece."[1] As for the popular success of his stories, Steinbeck won the O. Henry Memorial Award for prize stories four times. His work was also frequently honored in Edward J. O'Brien's *Best Short Stories* annuals and in O'Brien's ultimate of select anthologies, *50 Best American Short Stories, 1915–1939.*[2]

Steinbeck excelled in the short story for good reason. The form very likely appealed to him more than did the novel; his novels not infrequently began as short pieces and then simply expanded beyond their intended boundaries. As Steinbeck once explained to Mavis McIntosh: "I think that, when this is sent off [the novel *To a God Unknown* (1933)] I shall do some short stories. I always think I will and they invariably grow into novels, but I'll try anyway.[3] "The Raid" (1934), "Affair at 7, Rue de M——" (1955), and "How Mr. Hogan Robbed a Bank" (1956), for example, inspired *In Dubious Battle* (1936), *The Short Reign of Pippin IV* (1957), and *Winter of Our Discontent* (1961). "The Snake" (1935) was the precursor of *Cannery Row* (1945) and *Sweet Thursday* (1954). And "Breakfast" (1936) reappeared slightly altered in *The Grapes of Wrath* (1939). Steinbeck's preference for the short story also can be seen in the episodic structure of such early novels as *Tortilla Flat* (1935), in which each episode, says Arthur Voss, is sometimes a "virtually independent" story.[4]

Part 1. The Short Fiction: A Critical Analysis

Steinbeck wrote short fiction intermittently throughout his career. He did not drop the form once his reputation as a novelist was firmly established, as some critics contend.[5] Fourteen or more Steinbeck stories appeared, in fact, *after* he published his popular novels of the thirties. Moreover, Steinbeck seems to have used short fiction as his primary vehicle of stylistic experimentation when, in the 1950s, he tried to escape what he called the "straight jacket" of his customary style. "Affair at 7, Rue de M——" (1955), with its bizzare plot and atypical Gothic atmosphere, provides ample evidence of Steinbeck's experimental use of short fiction. He also attempted a Stone Age parable in "The Short-Short Story of Mankind" (1955) and an ironic exposé on the perfect crime in "How Mr. Hogan Robbed a Bank" (1956).

During his lifetime Steinbeck wrote more than 50 short stories (including those in *The Pastures of Heaven*). While 50 tales might not seem a large number for a story writer, in addition to these short pieces Steinbeck generated nearly thirty volumes of novels, nonfiction, and plays. D. H. Lawrence provides a parallel example. In addition to his novels, Lawrence published numerous volumes in other genres and, like Steinbeck, wrote 50 or 60 stories. Other twentieth-century writers in English, of course, have produced more stories than did either Steinbeck or Lawrence. Katherine Mansfield penned 88, William Faulkner more than 100, F. Scott Fitzgerald about 160, and the popular story teller O. Henry exceeded 250![6]

Though Steinbeck's fifty or so short stories may seem few compared to the career totals of these last writers, his canon of short fiction is actually far larger than is generally known. Most readers are only acquainted with Steinbeck's tales in *The Long Valley* and *The Pastures of Heaven,* totalling about twenty-five stories. Less well known are his dozen or so uncollected pieces published in *Collier's, Harper's, Reader's Digest,* the *Atlantic,* and other magazines. In addition, several college and apprentice stories have survived, including six in manuscript. Other tales are scattered among Steinbeck's war and travel dispatches, and still others appear as interchapters in such novels as *Cannery Row* and *The Grapes of Wrath.* Unfortunately, the uncollected and unpublished stories can be difficult to find. Until recently, most of the uncollected pieces could be read only in the periodicals of their original publication. This situation has been partially remedied by the appearance in Japan of *Uncollected Stories of John Steinbeck* (1986), which includes seven tales. Steinbeck's unpublished stories are still available for inspection only through their repositories: the Stanford, Harvard, and San Jose State University libraries. Thus, until a complete edition of Steinbeck's stories appears (not presently in the works), some of the uncollected and all of the unpublished texts will remain inaccessible to the general reader.[7]

John Steinbeck began telling stories early in his life. His childhood friends remember gathering in the basement of the Steinbeck's Salinas, California, home to hear John spin yarns of ghosts and leprechauns, of "spooks, sprites, and other invisible beings." As one friend, Max Wagner, recalls: "Storytelling was natural for him, I guess—not only spooky stuff but other kinds, too. And he made them all up." Steinbeck's knack for telling stories led him to commit his tales to writing. Late nights during his high school years he worked in his attic bedroom. As he told Dorothy Vera: "I used to sit in that little room upstairs . . . and write little stories . . . and send them out to magazines under a false name and I never put a return address on them. . . . I wonder what I was thinking of? I was scared to death to get a rejection slip, but more, to get an acceptance."[8]

As the maturing Steinbeck continued to pen stories, his confidence in his ability grew. After graduating from Salinas High School in 1919, he entered Stanford University, where he attended classes intermittently for six years. At Stanford, with his dream of becoming a writer clearly in view, he often skipped classes in order to read freely in the university library and compose his tales. Carlton A. "Dook" Sheffield, Steinbeck's college roommate and lifelong friend, remembers hearing the aspiring author read these pieces animatedly in their Encinas Hall room. When kind-hearted Dook was not around, Steinbeck sometimes wandered the building and prevailed upon other less-willing listeners. Although his program of independent reading and writing (and some course-work) moved him closer to fulfilling his dream, Steinbeck did not earn many credits toward graduation. In 1925, he left Stanford without a degree.[9]

After working briefly as a resort caretaker near Lake Tahoe in the Sierras, Steinbeck boarded a freighter bound for New York City, where he hoped to establish himself as a writer. But having spent his small savings wooing an attractive woman on a port call in Havana, Cuba, he arrived in Manhattan broke. He took a job on the construction site of Madison Square Garden wheeling 150-pound barrows of cement—heavy labor that left him too tired to write. His college friend A. Grove Day recalls that when the exhausted Steinbeck soon quit, his foreman said to the future Nobel Laureate: "I'm sorry to lose you, my boy. You've got the makings of a darn good day larborer." Fortunately for himself and for his future readers, Steinbeck knew his talents lay elsewhere.[10]

He finally did secure a writing job in New York, though not the kind he wanted. An influential uncle wrangled him a position as a newspaper reporter for the New York *American*. Already becoming a skilled storyteller, Steinbeck's problem on this new job was that he frequently failed to separate fact from fancy. He also became emotionally involved with his subjects, rather than maintaining a "professional" distance. As he showed later in his career, his forte in journalism was never straight news; rather, it was feature writing and human interest stories. Consequently, after a brief and indifferent performance as a reporter, he was fired by the *American,* on which occasion he quipped that having been canned by a Hearst newspaper, at last he had "some credentials as a writer."[11]

During and after his stint as a newspaper reporter, Steinbeck wrote short stories and tried to sell them. Accounts vary as to the exact number, though most critics estimate roughly a dozen. Since only six survive, several of these texts were evidently lost or destroyed. Although Steinbeck was briefly encouraged to submit a collection of stories by editor Guy Holt at the McBride publishing house, when Holt's replacement subsequently rejected the tales, Steinbeck lost hope. After struggling six months in near poverty and squalor, he left Manhattan without a publishing contract. "The City had beaten the pants off me," Steinbeck was later to say. "Whatever it required to get ahead, I didn't have."[12]

The early failure did not daunt him. Steinbeck returned to California and in time became a successful writer, more successful than he had ever imagined. And it was a short story that by most accounts launched his career—the 1933 publication of "The Red Pony." With the subsequent appearance of other stories and the novels *Tortilla Flat* (1935), *In Dubious Battle* (1936), and *Of Mice and Men* (1937), Steinbeck's fortunes dramatically rose. His growing popularity with readers during the 1930s (along with vicious attacks by a few critics) took him by surprise. As Jackson J. Benson points out, from the beginning Steinbeck wrote not for money or fame but for the sheer love of words and the pleasure of weaving words into stories. The joy he took in story telling buoyed him through a career of more than forty years, and ultimately brought him to Stockholm, where in 1962 he accepted the Nobel Prize for Literature.[13]

On his way to winning the Nobel Prize, Steinbeck came under the influence of many great and some lesser literary figures. One of the most profound influences on his own early tales was story writer and teacher Edith Ronald Mirrielees. According to Robert DeMott, in 1924 Steinbeck enrolled in Mirrielees's English 136 class, "Short Story Writing," at Stanford and "later remembered [it] as one of the best [courses] he ever took."[14] Mirrielees apparently helped the young writer in two ways: first, she suggested a method to assist him in the drawing of round and believable characters; and, second, since she was a stickler for careful editing, she encouraged him to develop a lean, disciplined style.

During one class meeting, Mirrielees read Steinbeck's "Fingers of Cloud" (1924), which had recently been published in the *Stanford Spectator*. Perhaps noting the flatness of its female protagonist, Gertie, Mirrielees suggested that Steinbeck try placing his characters in new and different circumstances invented entirely out of his imagination.[15] By putting his characters against an unfamiliar backdrop, she may have reasoned, Steinbeck would be better able to detect their lack of roundness and believability. Evidently he took her suggestion to heart, since in his next few stories he invented fantastic and surreal settings, bordering on the obscure. "Adventures in Arcademy" (1924), with its deliberately distorted portrait of Stanford campus life, provides an example. But once Steinbeck began portraying his native California realistically, the end result of Mirrielees's suggestions was to help him achieve such lifelike characters as Jody Tiflin in *The Red Pony* and Elisa Allen in "The Chrysanthemums."

Mirrielees also helped Steinbeck improve his stories by emphasizing careful editing. She was especially strict about wordiness and over ornamentation, which frequently hampered his early writing. As Steinbeck reported to a friend: "She does one thing for you. She makes you get over what you want to say. Her only vicious criticism is directed toward turgidity, and that is a good thing." According to Benson, Mirrielees's advocacy of a "lean, terse style" in the face of the young Steinbeck's effusiveness began "an internal critical battle [within him] that lasted for close to a decade." Benson believes that Steinbeck did not become a successful writer "measured in terms of sales or critical response" until he finally heeded Mirrielees's advice.[16] Perhaps in gratitude for her help, nearly forty years after he took her course Steinbeck wrote a preface to Mirrielees's *Story Writing* (1962), the revised version of a textbook she had been preparing when Steinbeck was her student (see part 2).

Since he was an avid reader, the popular writers who influenced the young Steinbeck were many, and were occasionally detrimental to his work. The difficulties we have today in reading Steinbeck's apprentice stories, for instance, can be attributed, in part, to fantasy writer James Branch Cabell (1879–1958). Robert DeMott's remark that at this stage in his career Steinbeck revealed "a profound subservience to popular literary models"[17] seems especially appropriate with regard to Cabell. Immensely popular during Steinbeck's formative years, Cabell had significant impact on Steinbeck's early work. His extended flights of fancy in "The Gifts of Iban" (1927), for example, reflect Cabell's influence. In drawing his setting, Steinbeck apparently borrowed from Cabell's popular novel *Jurgen* (1922) the fantasy backdrop Cabell calls "The Garden Between Dawn and Sunrise." Steinbeck's "brightly colored" forest in "The Gifts of Iban" is a twilight world or "half remembered dream,"[18] closely resembling that in Cabell's *Jurgen*. And Steinbeck's characters, especially the protagonist Iban, seem to be based on Cabell's chief character. In his unrequited love for the beautiful Cantha, Iban even manifests a primary trait of Cabellian heroes— a yearning for "a paragon of beautiful womanhood," who ultimately rejects him.[19] Thus, in the story's fantasy, as well as in its themes of rejection, loneliness, and the shattering of masculine dreams, Steinbeck's "The Gifts of Iban" echoes the work of James Branch Cabell.

Another lesser figure who influenced Steinbeck was also popular during Cabell's heyday. Donn Byrne (1889–1928), born ten years after Cabell, may have provided the literary model for Steinbeck's unpublished story "The Nail" (ca. 1924–26). Byrne's retelling of the Old Testament story of Sampson and Delilah in *The Changeling and Other Stories* (1923) is similar in conception and execution to Steinbeck's piece, which recounts the Judges story of Sisera and Jael, in which the Hebrew woman, Sisera, drives a tent nail into the head of the wounded Canaanite, Jael. Both Donn Byrne's and Steinbeck's tales involve a man and a woman of opposing nations and both depict how the man takes the woman into his confidence and is betrayed by her. While "The Nail" seems to show Byrne's influence, Steinbeck was not sufficiently moved by him to produce any further biblical dramatizations in this form. As Harry T. Moore says, while Steinbeck was a devotee of Donn Byrne (and Cabell) during his college years, "he violently repudiated them later." Steinbeck himself said in a 5 November 1929 letter, "I think I have swept all the Cabbelyo-Byrneish preciousness out for good."[20]

Besides Cabell and Byrne, Steinbeck emulated other, more enduring writers. Even before he entered Stanford, Steinbeck had dreamed of becoming another Jack London (1876–1916). A Californian of part Irish ancestry like Steinbeck himself, London wrote some eighteen collections of short fiction, and his work resembles Steinbeck's in several respects. Both writers share proletarian values, sketch graphic scenes from nature, and reflect Darwinian or biological views of life in their literary naturalism. No stories better illustrate the latter two similarities than London's "To Build a Fire" (1908) and Steinbeck's "Flight" (1938). Each tale features a vivid natural backdrop—London's frozen Yukon and Steinbeck's salt-bitten California coast. And each is naturalistic—a naive protagonist is initiated into the harsh, indifferent workings of nature and, as a result, dies.[21]

London's protagonist, simply called "the man" in "To Build a Fire," learns too late the harsh lessons of the Yukon. Venturing out on a seventy-five below zero day, he falls through a patch of ice and soaks his legs with freezing water. To stay alive, he must thaw out by a fire. But to build a fire in his numb condition becomes increasingly difficult and finally impossible. He struggles desperately to maintain his body heat, even plots to kill his dog in order to warm himself in its carcass. Reconciling himself to his fate, the man falls into a stupor and dies. His "big native husky," by contrast, manages, with the common sense of his breed, to survive, reflecting London's Darwinian view that the weak (or in this case, the foolhardy) perish while the strong endure.

Steinbeck's Pepé Torres in "Flight" similarly overestimates his ability to cope with nature—his own human nature (he is only nineteen) and nature as manifested in California's rugged Santa Lucia Mountains and the shadowy creatures who haunt them. When Pepé lets his knife fly during a drunken quarrel in Monterey, he sets in motion a chain of events leading almost lockstep to his death. Pepé's doom can be felt along every inch of his flight into the Santa Lucias. Just as London's protagonist at first desperately attempts to save his life, so too does Pepé flee on horseback into the mountains, trying to avoid the ominous "dark watchers," mysterious figures who seem to portend his death. Yet when he loses his horse, his rifle, and his supplies, Pepé, like London's protagonist in "To Build a Fire," faces death with resignation, if not calm dignity. Both London's and Steinbeck's initiates realize too late the foolishness of pitting their wills against the much stronger will of nature. Life for them operates on a purely physical basis, without even the faint suggestion of spiritual transcendence or redemption. Thus, the naturalistic thrust of each story is pervasive.

Born the same year as London, Sherwood Anderson (1876–1941) also influenced Steinbeck's way of story telling. Steinbeck's debt to Anderson, who left his mark on Hemingway, Faulkner, Wolfe, Caldwell, and Saroyan, as well,[22] is most clearly reflected in the similarities between Anderson's *Winesburg, Ohio* (1919) and Steinbeck's *The Pastures of Heaven* (1932). Both works are short story cycles depicting the distorted lives of inhabitants in a small community. Anderson's "grotesques," who fasten themselves so tenaciously to a single truth that it becomes a falsehood, resemble Steinbeck's self-deluded characters, who, conversely, create falsehoods about themselves and then parade them as truths. In Anderson's "Hands," for instance, Wing Biddlebaum is a former schoolmaster who is run out of a Pennsylvania town for innocently touching schoolboys. Wing accepts the erroneous "truth" that his gentle, expressive hands are dangerous, and he consequently withdraws from life. Similarly, in Steinbeck's *The Pastures of Heaven,* Shark Wicks is a small-time peach farmer who invents a bogus fortune, and this phony "truth" distances him from his neighbors. Because the imaginary truths of both Anderson's and Steinbeck's protagonists set them off from others, they frequently lack nourishing human contact and often turn in on themselves, making an unhealthy adjustment to life.

Anderson's probing into the secret lives behind the respectable facades of his characters finds its parallel in Steinbeck's stories outside of *The Pastures of Heaven* as well. We can see this parallel by comparing Anderson's "The Teacher," from *Winesburg, Ohio,* with Steinbeck's "The White Quail" (1935), collected in *The Long Valley.* The two stories deal with repressed sexuality and its psychological consequences—violence, in both cases. Anderson's Kate Swift is "The Teacher"—thirty and tormented by unfulfilled desires—who becomes enamored of her former student, George Willard. But Kate's sexual passion has for so long found no outlet in Winesburg that she seems unable to express it in healthy ways. Consequently, in the schoolroom she is "silent, cold, and stern," and the townspeople find something "biting and forbidding" about her. Although on several occasions she has tried to arouse young George, when one night in the office of the *Winesburg Eagle* he finally takes her in his arms, Kate with "two short little fists [begins] to beat on his face." After she runs off George Willard finds himself "swearing furiously."[23]

In Steinbeck's "The White Quail," repressed sexuality similarly leads to violence. An albino quail one day alights in Mary Teller's perfect garden, and Mary imagines it to be the very essence of herself. Thus, when the quail is threatened by a prowling cat, she orders her husband, Harry Teller, to poison the unwelcome feline. Harry says he will frighten it away instead with his BB gun, yet he shoots the quail, not the cat. Behind this surprise ending, as in Anderson's story, lies sexual frustration. Harry kills the quail because it symbolizes both Mary's obsession with her garden and, consequently, her aloofness toward her husband. The hungry cat, on the other hand, suggests the affection-starved Harry. Each night when Mary retires into her bedroom and Harry tries the locked door, his sexual frustration grows. Like Kate Swift in Anderson's "The Teacher," Harry's thwarted passion finally explodes.

Harry Thornton Moore, author of the first critical study on Steinbeck, argues that eventually Steinbeck's enthusiasm for Anderson faded and Steinbeck began to admire Ernest Hemingway and D. H. Lawrence. The question of Hemingway's influence on

Steinbeck is a difficult one; although in 1939 Steinbeck said of Hemingway, "I'm convinced that in many ways he is the finest writer of our time," Steinbeck purportedly feared Hemingway's influence and therefore avoided his works. I "didn't read him until about 1940," Steinbeck once told Peter Lisca. Benson notes that actually as many as ten years before this time, Steinbeck did read and admire at least one Hemingway short story, "The Killers" (1927). DeMott contends that by 1934, Steinbeck had also read *The Sun Also Rises* and the first four stories in *Men Without Women*. And late in the 1930s, Steinbeck was so impressed with a Hemingway story about the Spanish Civil War called "The Butterfly and the Tank" (1938) that he wrote him a complimentary letter, which led to the two authors' first meeting. Steinbeck's admiration of Hemingway, despite some professional jealousy, endured well into the 1960s. Thus, in 1962, upon the announcement of Steinbeck's winning the Nobel Prize for Literature, he told reporters that Hemingway's short stories were among his favorite writings.[24]

Not surprisingly, there are several similarities in the short fiction of the two authors, especially in style and characterization. Both writers developed prose styles with what Lisca calls "deceptively simple" surfaces. Benson has said that like Hemingway, "who talked about fiction in terms of an iceberg—only one-eighth of which shows above the surface—Steinbeck became convinced that there was a good deal more to his fiction than critics would ever be able to perceive." Steinbeck believed "that the full depth of his work might be *felt* by the sensitive, ordinary reader, but that the critic, working primarily by intellectual analysis, would tend to miss the full dimensions of it." Edmund Wilson, who complained that Steinbeck's stories were "almost entirely about plants and animals," provides an apt example of a critic who misread Steinbeck by reading him only on the surface.[25]

Both Steinbeck and Hemingway have been popular with readers, in part, for the apparent simplicity of their writing. Terse, Anglo-Saxon diction, abundant action, and almost photographic realism in both writers' work satisfy even the least discriminating reader's appetite for a well-told tale; yet beneath this surface action and realism, the more sophisticated reader can wrestle with questions of fate, death, love, and the meaning of existence. Due in part to their "deceptively simple" surfaces, Steinbeck and Hemingway produced a number of short story "icebergs," with meanings hidden deep below the surface. Hemingway's Nick Adams stories and his two-page masterpiece, "Hills Like White Elephants," certainly fall into this category. Similarly, a child can read and enjoy Steinbeck's *The Red Pony* stories, yet adults have been stimulated and challenged by them as well.

Turning to characterization, Steinbeck and Hemingway present fictional worlds that can be, in Mimi Gladstein's words, "onesidedly masculine." In Steinbeck's case, this is more often true in the novels than in the short fiction, where memorable female characters frequently appear. Both writers, however, do indeed focus on male companionship, especially pairs of men in what Lisca calls mentor-neophyte relationships.[26] Such male pairings can be found in Hemingway's "The Short Happy Life of Francis Macomber" and Steinbeck's "The Raid." Hemingway's neophyte Francis Macomber is a wealthy American hunting big game who learns to overcome fear by his association with the "great white hunter," Robert Wilson. Although Macomber at first bolts from a charging lion, later by observing Wilson—a model of courage—Macomber holds his ground when attacked by a wounded buffalo. Despite Macomber's "accidental" death (his wife, threatened by his new found courage, shoots him in the back of the head), for a few happy moments he masters fear.

In Steinbeck's "The Raid" (1934), courage is also the lesson neophyte Root learns from his mentor, veteran communist organizer, Dick. One night in a small California town, the two men prepare to hold a party meeting which Root (with good reason) fears will be raided by vigilantes. Worrying he may buckle under if attacked, Root seeks moral support from Dick—whose mastery of fear resembles that of Hemingway's "great white hunter." When the meeting is stormed, Root stands firm as a flying two-by-four grazes his head. Though both men are knocked unconscious, later in the hospital cell of a jail Dick congratulates Root for not running under fire.

The fact that Steinbeck and Hemingway sometimes present fictional worlds that are "one-sidedly" masculine is also reflected in both writers' depiction of women. In Hemingway's stories, dominating and unscrupulous women appear in various forms—the sexually manipulative younger woman, the powerful wife with money, and the emasculating "Terrible Mother."[27] Perhaps Hemingway's best-known female character of this type is the wife of Francis Macomber in "The Short Happy Life." Margot Macomber belittles, undercuts, cuckholds, and (as we have seen) ultimately shoots her husband. While Steinbeck portrays a wider variety of female characters in his short fiction than does Hemingway—including bright, capable, and energetic females ("strong women") frustrated by the limited roles accorded them in a patriarchial society—he does give us an occasional domestic tyrant (or "Terrible Mother") of the kind portrayed in some of Hemingway's Nick Adams stories. Emma Randall in "The Harness" so thoroughly dominates her husband, Peter, a successful Salinas Valley farmer, that he must escape on annual drunken sprees in the brothels of San Francisco. Emma is a sickly, tidy, childless woman who forces her apparently robust husband to wear a shoulder harness and stomach belt to improve his posture, thereby making him look "respectable." When she dies, although Peter sheds the symbols of her domination—the harness and belt—he remains her psychological slave. He keeps the house as spotlessly clean as if his wife were still alive and restrains his libidinous pleasures to his customary annual week in San Francisco. Thus, Emma's frightening power extends even beyond the grave.

While Steinbeck's admiration of Hemingway was of long standing, Richard F. Peterson says that D. H. Lawrence "had an intense effect upon" Steinbeck, but only "for a brief period of time." This brief period seems to have encompassed the early 1930s when Steinbeck wrote the bulk of his short stories. Critics have sometimes compared the short fiction of Steinbeck and Lawrence. Clifton Fadiman in the *New Yorker,* for instance, calls Steinbeck's stories "exceptionally sensitive" and notes that his "subtleties of feelings" remind one of Lawrence. Edmund Wilson also makes a similar comparison (though unfavorable to Steinbeck) between the two writers. Lawrence's influence on Steinbeck probably stems from the British author's last volume of short fiction, *The Woman Who Rode Away* (1928). Peterson says that several stories in the Lawrence collection that portray "frustrated" female characters "may have influenced the creation of those equally frustrated" women in Steinbeck's *The Long Valley.* Peter Lisca points to four *Long Valley* tales in particular: "The Chrysanthemums," "The

White Quail," "Johnny Bear," and "The Snake." In these four stories one can detect a Lawrencian sensitivity to female characters and a probing into their psychological and sexual natures.[28]

"The Chrysanthemums" (1937) provides an excellent example. Elisa Allen, the protagonist, resembles the lead character in Lawrence's title story from *The Woman Who Rode Away*. Both women are Californians in their midthirties who have become bored or frustrated with their marriages. And both, as a result, seek adventure. Lawrence's unnamed protagonist in "The Woman Who Rode Away" (1925) searches for wild Indians in the hills of Mexico and, unfortunately, finds them. The men of the Indian tribe confine her, strip off her clothes, touch her naked body, and then sacrifice her to their gods. Elisa Allen in "The Chrysanthemums" seeks adventure more vicariously through an itinerant pot mender who calls on the Allen's Salinas farm. Elisa romanticizes the man's vagabond life-style and responds erotically to his feigned interest in her chrysanthemums. She tears off some of her clothes, her breasts swells passionately, and she even reaches for the man's greasy trousers. The fixer charges Elisa for mending a few worthless old pots, and then thoughtlessly tosses away some chrysanthemum sprouts she has given him. Like the protagonist in "The Woman Who Rode Away," Elisa finds that what she has perceived as a romantic alternative to her stifling marriage turns out to be a destructive illusion.

Other female characters in Steinbeck and Lawrence shrink from sexual contact with men and instead identify with male power, or try to exert control in what Peterson suggests are traditionally male domains. This phenomenon is epitomized in Lawrence's "None of That" and Steinbeck's "The Snake." As the title of Lawrence's story, "None of That" suggests, protagonist Ethel Crane abhors physical contact with men, preferring instead the life of the imagination. Her immense attractiveness and wealth, however, allow her to string along various male suitors without becoming their mistress, until she meets a Mexican matador named Cuesta. Cuesta, whose profession entitles him to fight and kill bulls, embodies the very thing Ethel supposedly detests—raw physicality. Yet he becomes her object of desire because, as Peterson argues, Ethel identifies with Cuesta's power and brutal mastery over bulls. Just as Ethel identifies with the matador in "None of That," so too does the mysterious woman in Steinbeck's "The Snake" identify with a male rattlesnake. The tall, slim, black-eyed woman (whose stark appearance even suggests that of a snake) enters Dr. Phillips' Monterey, California, laboratory and asks to buy a male rattlesnake. Once the purchase is arranged, she wants to see her snake eat. Dr. Phillips reluctantly agrees, placing a white rat into the reptile's cage. As the snake poises to strike, Dr. Phillips notices that the woman seems to duplicate exactly its movements. Her sympathy with the snake (not to mention her snakelike appearance) suggests the same identification with male power and brutality Peterson finds in Lawrence's short fiction.[29]

In addition to Lawrence, Hemingway, Anderson, London, and the other writers mentioned above, Steinbeck's reading extended to Willa Cather (who, he said, wrote "the best prose in America"), Robert Louis Stevenson, Dostoyevsky, Tolstoy, Flaubert, Milton, and others.[30] Of American writers from his own generation, Steinbeck's favorites were Faulkner and, as we have seen, Hemingway. But while Steinbeck (like Faulkner) can be considered a regionalist with universal appeal, and while (like Hemingway) he frequently wrote in a terse, objective style, Steinbeck is a unique writer who has earned his own niche in the history of the American short story.

In surveys of short fiction, Steinbeck is most often categorized as a naturalistic writer, sometimes as a regionalist, and occasionally as a proletarian or social protest writer.[31] He is considered modern because of his techniques, especially his colloquial, conversational style and his Sherwood Anderson-like probing into the psychology of his characters. Although in some ways advanced for his time, Steinbeck was not an innovator in the short story form itself. While he experimented with various forms during his career, Steinbeck (unlike Anderson) did not greatly influence the development of the short story. What is unique about his stories is their spirit of place ("Steinbeck Country"), their earthy, simple characters who can be deceptively complex, and their poignant themes, which often strike at the heart of the human condition. Since Steinbeck wrote short fiction for nearly forty years, his style, technique, themes, and other features of his work evolved through the periods of his artistic apprenticeship, maturity, and last years, when some critics believe the quality of his work declined. Despite these inevitable changes in his art, some generalizations can be made about Steinbeck as a story writer.

Perhaps the most easily discernible feature of Steinbeck's short fiction is his "Steinbeck Country" settings—the region in and around Monterey County, California, consisting of Salinas and its long agricultural valley, the southern half of Monterey Bay, with its towns from Castroville to Carmel, and a host of sometimes isolated ranches and farms in the mountains and valleys and on the rugged Pacific coast down to Big Sur and beyond. These "Steinbeck Country" settings can be found in nearly all Steinbeck stories of the 1930s, whereas his tales of earlier and later decades have backdrops ranging from New York City ("East Third Street") to rural Mexico ("The Miracle of Tepayac") to London ("Reunion at the Quiet Hotel") to Paris ("Affair at 7, Rue de M——") to realms of pure fantasy ("The Gifts of Iban"). These latter settings reflect Steinbeck's many travels, as well as his brief residency in New York in the 1920s and then his more or less permanent stay there during the last twenty years of his life.

Characters in Steinbeck's short fiction are generally earthy, simple people who, beneath their unremarkable exteriors, often harbor complex human problems. Given the complexity of these characters, Stanley Young has praised Steinbeck's sensitivity and sympathy to human beings "on all levels of experience," while Edmund Wilson, as we have seen, has contrarily called Steinbeck's characters "rudimentary" and conceived and presented in animal, rather than human terms.[32] Women in Steinbeck's tales are typically housewives, school teachers, and occasionally prostitutes. While these female characters rarely have careers or financial resources of their own, they often possess hidden strengths that can emerge in moments of crisis. Male characters tend to be cattle ranchers, farmers, blue-collar workers, storekeepers, nostalgic old men, and adolescents embarked on the elusive quest for "manhood." Elisa Allen in "The Chrysanthemums" and Jody Tiflin in the four *Red Pony* stories provide examples of Steinbeck's most sensitively drawn female and male protagonists.

Steinbeck's plotting at its best can also be seen in these above-mentioned stories. In "The Chrysanthemums," Steinbeck develops a subtly complex plot whose surprise ending turns on and fully integrates the story's several levels of meaning. Similarly, in "The Gift," perhaps the finest tale in *The Red Pony,* all plot elements

17

are smoothly connected from the day Jody receives his gift pony to the day it dies. Despite these and other successes in short fiction, Steinbeck was sometimes criticised for contriving action and resorting to too obvious symbolism. Some tales in *The Pastures of Heaven* betray the first flaw, as when a motiveless practical joke by Bert Munroe (in chap. 7) leads to the expulsion of the enterprising, though disreputable, Lopez sisters from the pleasant valley. "The White Quail" betrays the second flaw, since the protagonist, Mary Teller, becomes too completely identified with the story's central symbol.[33] Steinbeck was frequently capable, however, of drawing thoroughly effective symbols, such as Elisa Allen's chrysanthemums.

The style Steinbeck is best known for is spare, crisp, and objective. His graphic, picturelike accuracy in depicting people and places in stories of the 1930s reflects his literary naturalism of this period. But the term "literary naturalist" does not fully define him. We can also find elements of fantasy and mysticism in his work, originating with his fondness for yarns of ghosts and leprechauns and his lifelong fascination wih the Arthurian legend. His characters generally speak in plain, simple English with some dialect indicating regional or ethnic flavor. He tends to structure stories in one of two ways: either they are loosely knit and episodic ("How Edith McGillcuddy Met R. L. Stevenson") or tight and dramatic ("The Chrysanthemums"). And his usual narrative point of view is third person, yet "Breakfast," "Johnny Bear," "Affair at 7, Rue M——," and some apprentice stories are written from the first-person perspective.

Variety is the best word to describe the generic types Steinbeck employed in short fiction. He experimented with sketches, parables, beast fables, and initiation stories, and even dabbled in fairy tales and science fiction. Variety also describes his numerous themes. Whereas he championed proletarian values in his novels of the 1930s, Steinbeck focused in his short stories of that era on the problems of individual human beings. A common theme in his short fiction, as we have seen, is frustration stemming from loneliness, isolation, blocked communication, or sexual repression, and these frustrations occasionally lead to violence. In his tales of the 1930s, respectability is also a recurrent theme; and in the forties and fifties Steinbeck deals with such topical themes as divorce

Steinbeck the Short Story Writer

and nuclear holocaust. With this introduction to Steinbeck's place in the history of the short story, and this look at the unique features of his work in the genre, we can now investigate in more detail the stories on which his reputation was built.

Scenes from "Steinbeck Country": *The Long Valley*

Fifteen of Steinbeck's finest and best-known stories are collected in *The Long Valley* (1938). The title of this collection somewhat misleadingly suggests that all fifteen take place in the "long" Salinas Valley. Yet fewer than a half dozen can be identified with this valley, and most of the remainder occur elsewhere in "Steinbeck Country."[1] "Flight" takes place on the Pacific coast just north of Big Sur, "The Snake" on Cannery Row in Monterey, *The Red Pony* stories near the Santa Lucia Mountains, and "The Murder" in the Corral de Tierra (setting of *The Pastures of Heaven*). Other stories range further from the Salinas Valley. "Breakfast" probably occurs in the San Joaquin or Sacramento Valley, and "The Raid" and "The Vigilante" are set in outlying small towns. By far the story most removed in time and place from the others is "Saint Katy the Virgin," which harks back to fourteenth-century Europe.

Although some critics have faulted him for including stories that do not seem to belong in *The Long Valley*, Steinbeck was not entirely to blame for the selection. In 1938 Covici-Friede, his publisher, was experiencing financial difficulties and needed another best-seller like *Of Mice and Men* (1937) to save the firm. Editor Pat Covici, therefore, "pressed" Steinbeck for a story collection immediately. Although he was surprised by Covici's sudden request (Steinbeck told Elizabeth Otis on 2 May 1938, "I didn't know that Pat was considering doing the short stories soon"), Steinbeck gathered together all his tales published during the 1930s (and the unpublished "Flight") for the volume. Too late to save Covici-Friede from bankruptcy, *The Long Valley* finally appeared in September 1938.[2]

In this chapter, I discuss each *Long Valley* story, generally following the order in which it appears in the volume. Certain tales with related themes or contexts are grouped together for analysis. The first three stories discussed below, for example— "The Chrysanthemums," "The White Quail," and "The Harness"—each take place in the Salinas Valley and probe the psychological consequences of unhappy or unhealthy marriages.

"The Chrysanthemums" (1937)

Among Steinbeck's fifty or more pieces of short fiction, no story has been more highly praised than "The Chrysanthemums." Steinbeck began writing it on 31 January 1934,[3] and by the time he finished in February of that year, he sensed that he had created a subtly powerful work. In a letter to George Albee, Steinbeck says: "I shall be interested to know what you think of the story, The Chrysanthemums. It is entirely different and is designed to strike without the reader's knowledge. I mean he reads it casually and after it is finished feels that something profound has happened to him although he does not know what nor how. It has had that effect on several people here."[4]

This subliminal quality sets the story apart. Critics have been responding favorably to "The Chrysanthemums" ever since Steinbeck composed it. Carol Henning Steinbeck, the author's first wife and perhaps most incisive critic of this period, said it was "the best of all [his] stories." Brian Barbour has praised it as Steinbeck's "most artistically successful story." Jackson J. Benson and Louis Owens consider the tale his "finest"; Roy S. Simmonds characterizes it as "one flowing surge of creativity." And Mordecai Marcus calls "The Chrysanthemums" "one of the world's great short stories."[5]

While its subtleties are difficult, if not impossible, to capture in retelling, "The Chrysanthemums" can be summarized as follows: One December afternoon on the Allen Ranch, a "grey-flannel fog" seals the Salinas Valley like a "closed pot."[6] Elisa Allen, a vigorous woman of thirty-five, works in her fenced garden powerfully cutting down chrysanthemum stalks. Her husband, Henry, having just sold thirty head of cattle, appears and suggests they dine out that evening. When Henry returns to the fields, a rickety wagon drawn by a horse and burro wobbles toward the house. The big, bearded driver introduces himself to Elisa as a pot mender. Although Elisa three times declines his services, she warms to him when he expresses interest in her chrysanthemums. He tells her that a lady on his route wants some chrysanthemums, and Elisa excitedly prepares several sprouts in a red pot. As she talks with the tinker, Elisa becomes empassioned and reaches toward his leg, almost touching it. Then she scurries behind the house to find two old, dented saucepans, which he repairs for fifty cents. After the tinker departs, the exuberant Elisa bathes, exults in her naked body before a mirror, and dresses for dinner. When Henry returns and marvels at how strong she looks, Elisa confides that she never before knew how strong. As they leave for dinner in their car, Elisa spots the chrysanthemum sprouts she had given the tinker lying in the road. He has thrown them away and kept the red pot. She begins to cry, but hides her tears from Henry.

Since "The Chrysanthemums" is arguably Steinbeck's finest short story, Simmonds notes that a "small critical industry has grown up around [it]." Benson believes that many critics have addressed themselves to this enduring tale because, "like most outstanding stories, 'The Chrysanthemums' can be taken a number of different ways." Despite variant interpretations of the story, one theme critics keep coming back to is frustration, stemming from the protagonist's unfulfilled or thwarted desires. Critics have differed, however, on the specific source of Elisa Allen's frustration. Richard Astro, Robert M. Benton, and Elizabeth McMahan suggest a poor marriage as its source. Brian Barbour and William V. Miller blame a combination of ambiguous spiritual and sexual problems. Warren French argues that Elisa's behavior reflects sublimated "maternal instincts"; and, similarly, Mordecai Marcus says that she longs to bear children (a notion refuted by McMahan). Benson sees in her a woman trying to find a creative, significant role in a male-dominated society; Charles A. Sweet calls her the "embryonic feminist." And finally, John H. Timmerman finds in Elisa the artist's frustration with an unappreciative society. What all these readings have in common is that they suggest, in Owens's words, the "repression of powerful human impulses," which leads, as we have seen, to frustration.[7]

Central to almost any reading of the story is the protagonist, Elisa Allen, whom Joseph Warren Beach calls "one of the most delicious characters ever transferred from life to the pages of a book." Elisa is a Steinbeck "strong woman." According to Marilyn H. Mitchell (see her essay in part 3), such strong women have "a strength of will usually identified" with men, as well as an "ambiguous combination of traditionally masculine and feminine traits."[8] Elisa is in her prime—strong, talented, energetic, eager, and handsome. Yet she lives on an isolated ranch, is married to a well-meaning but unexciting cattleman, and has no creative outlets beyond the confines of her house and garden. And since Henry Allen, a traditional male, is the couple's sole breadwinner, Elisa's contribution to their material comfort and well-being is seemingly undervalued by herself, if not by her husband.

According to Benson, Steinbeck probably based the character of Elisa Allen on his own first wife, Carol Henning Steinbeck. Like Elisa, Carol was a woman of considerable talent and energy who wore "masculine clothes" and was "strong, large-boned" and "handsome rather than pretty." At the time "The Chrysanthemums" was composed, the Steinbeck's (like the Allen's) had no children. Although when she first met John Steinbeck, Carol was training for a career in advertising, after their marriage she took a series of temporary jobs as they moved from place to place. Benson says that "The Chrysanthemums" "indicates very strongly that Steinbeck was aware of and sympathetic to" forces frustrating his wife.[9] Basing his reading of the story on these biographical insights, Benson concludes: "Of the forces aligned against Elisa's freedom to be what she is capable of being, perhaps the most subtly destructive are, on the one hand, the basic understandings held by society of a woman's presumed limitations—a force that seems to permeate the atmosphere of the story—and, on the other hand, the misguided sympathy and kindness offered by the husband. It is the latter that is so terribly defeating—what is the feminine equivalent of 'emasculating'?"[10]

Evidence in the story suggests that Elisa, reflecting Carol Henning Steinbeck, is talented and energetic—as well as frustrated. She cuts her chrysanthemum stalks with excessive energy; "her work with the scissors [is] over-eager, over-powerful." The stalks seem "too small and easy for her energy" (10). She has "strong," "terrier fingers," which destroy pests "before they get started." Even her gardening clothes suggest power: "heavy leather gloves," "clod-hopper shoes," "a man's black hat," and "a big corduroy apron with four big pockets" to hold gardening tools (10). Nearby behind the garden we see Elisa's "neat white farm house with red geraniums close-banked around it." The house looks "hard-swept" with "hard-polished windows, and a clean mud-mat on the front steps" (10). Everything about both the house and garden is orderly and immaculate—giving us clues as to how she spends her time.

We can also surmise that Elisa's marriage neither fills her time nor fulfills her desires. That she and Henry have less than complete rapport is evident from their first meeting in the story when Elisa "start[s]" at the sound of her husband's voice (11). And later, after she bathes and dresses for dinner, Elisa must "set herself" for his arrival; she [stiffens] and her face [grows] tight" (21). There is an unnatural or estranged quality to their relationship, so that at times they seem to be speaking different languages. When Henry puts on his "joking tone" and invites her to the fights in Salinas, for instance, Elisa takes him seriously, answering "breathlessly . . . 'No, I wouldn't like to go' " (12). For his part, Henry is "bewildered" by his wife's exuberance after her meeting with the tinker and then "complain[s]" when her spirits sink at the story's end (21, 23). He seems to have little understanding of her sensitive emotions.

While Steinbeck describes Elisa Allen with loving detail, he neglects to offer even a brief description of her husband. Henry Allen, a stereotypical rancher and husband, actually needs little introduction. A static, stock figure, he provides essential information about Elisa and acts as a measure of changes in her behavior. At the story's beginning, for example, he notes her unique talents as a gardener. " 'You've got a gift with things,' Henry observed. 'Some of those yellow chrysanthemums you had this year were ten inches across' " (11). Henry also helps us to chart the rise and fall of her spirits. After Elisa's encounter with the tinker, Henry says to her, "You look strong enough to break a calf over your knee, happy enough to eat it like a watermelon" (21–22). But later when her spirits flag on discovering the pot mender's insincerity, Henry says, "Now you're changed again" (23). Thus, during these scenes and at other times in the story, Henry's words help to define the character of Elisa.

Henry Allen, whether from lack of interest or obtuseness, never enters the special world of his wife's garden. Yet, while Henry remains outside, restrained (like the ranch animals) by "the wire fence that protected [it] from cattle and dogs and chickens" (11), the itinerant pot mender breaches her special world after only a few minutes' conversation with Elisa. " 'Come into the yard,' " she exclaims, and "the man came through the picket gate." (16).

Compared to Henry Allen, the tinker is, indeed, an exciting and romantic figure. A casual traveler, who "ain't in any hurry," and aims "to follow nice weather" (14), what a contrast his life provides to the fenced-in existence of Elisa. Perhaps because of his fluid style of living, he brings out Elisa's sense of her own confinement and unfulfilled desires. Although the tinker is ragged and unclean in appearance, he taps Elisa's dormant passion. When she speaks with him her "breast swell[s] passionately" and her "voice [grows] husky" (18). At the height of her desire, the impassioned Elisa erotically describes the night ("Every pointed star gets driven into your body. It's like that. Hot and sharp and—lovely") and her "hand [goes] out toward his legs" and "her hesitant fingers almost touch the cloth" of his trousers (18). Thus, although her staid husband provides a measure for Elisa's change, it is the tinker who becomes the impetus of that change.

Elisa's most abrupt transformation occurs when she discovers that the tinker has tossed away her chrysanthemum sprouts. "Far ahead on the road Elisa saw a dark speck. She knew" (22). When she spots this "dark speck," Elisa's new sense of well-being is dashed and she begins to weep. The story's carefully foreshadowed surprise ending hinges on these few words. Earlier we are given clues about the tinker's motives and his basic insincerity. After three failed attempts (using conventional persuasion) to sell Elisa his services, he finally notices her flowers. "What's them plants, ma'am?" he asks. Immediately, the "irritation and resistance melt[s] from Elisa's face" (15). By changing his tactics and feigning interest in her chrysanthemums, the manipulative fixer accomplishes his purposes—to make some money off a naive prospect. His insincerity is again underscored when Elisa reminds him before he leaves to keep the sand damp in the red pot. "Sand, ma'am . . . Sand?" he responds. " 'Oh, sure. You mean around the chrysanthemums. Sure I will.' He clucked his tongue" (20).

These foreshadowings attest to Steinbeck's finely crafted plot in "The Chrysanthemums." According to Barbour, Steinbeck "succeeds in organizing this story in a way he does nowhere else."[11] The chrysanthemums themselves, the story's central symbol, provide the structural underpinning of the plot. Early in the story the chrysanthemum stalks resemble phalluses, and Elisa's "over-eager" (10) snipping of them suggests castration. Then in the "rooting" bed (12) Elisa's inserting the "little crisp shoots" into open, receptive furrows of earth suggests sexual coition. Sometime later the sprouts become Elisa's children, when she explains lovingly to the pot mender how to care for them ("I'll tell you what to do" [17]). And Elisa's full-grown chrysanthemums, which are yellow and giant (measuring "ten inches across" [11]) may represent the fruition of her talent and energy—the beautiful blooms of her desperation. Because Steinbeck did not try (as he did in "The White Quail") to peg this symbol to a single, static idea, "The Chrysanthemums" is rich in ambiguity.

The story is rich in other ways as well. Characteristic of Steinbeck's short fiction of the 1930s, "The Chrysanthemums" contains vivid seasonal imagery, as well as colorful images of flowers, plants, and animals. The tale opens in a December "grey-flannel fog" (9), suggesting not only the lack of sunshine in winter but also the coldness and sterility of this pallid season. Cleverly suggesting the oppressive closeness of winter, Steinbeck has the fog seal the valley "like a lid" on a "closed pot" (9). This "pot" image (like the house and garden imagery discussed above) underscores Elisa's circumscribed existence. Although fog seals the Salinas Valley in greyness, the "yellow stubble fields [seem] to be bathed in pale cold sunshine" and the "thick willow scrub . . . [flames] with sharp and positive yellow leaves" (9). These bright, sunny yellows (including Elisa's chrysanthemums) in the midst of winter suggest Elisa's hope, rekindled by the tinker, for a more fulfilling life. That the fixer represents such hope to Elisa is made clear when she whispers as she watches the tinker leave: "That's a bright direction. There's a glowing there." (20). Elisa's garden itself can also be thought of as a paradise or Eden, with Elisa as the innocent Eve who falls prey to the wiles of the deceptive tinker. The tinker dresses in (Satanic or reptilian?) black, his eyes are dark and "full of brooding" and his hands are calloused and cracked—in "every crack a black line" (13–14).

Animal imagery also abounds in the story. Ernest W. Sullivan argues that one "cannot help being struck by the repeated association of unpleasant canine characteristics with the otherwise attractive Elisa Allen."[12] For starters, Elisa has "terrier fingers" (11), as we have seen, and she crouches "low like a fawning dog" (18) before the tinker. Elisa also raises her upper lip, "showing her teeth" (19), as would an angry dog. The correspondences between the people and their dogs in the story elucidate the human characters' behavior. The two ranch shepherds and the tinker's mongrel, though Sullivan argues to the contrary, reflect their respective masters. The Allens, like their shepherds, are a distinct breed, and (despite Elisa's foiled rebellion) they live conventional, domesticated lives; the tinker and his mongrel, on the other hand, are homeless strays who wander about looking for their next meal.

One final feature of the story that deserves our attention is Steinbeck's point of view—third-person objective. This restricted point of view—in which the narrator reports events "objectively" without entering into the minds of the characters—is especially important in regard to the protagonist. Much of Elisa Allen's appeal stems from the ambiguity of her actions, and that ambiguity is maintained because we can only surmise what she is thinking and feeling. Mary Teller in "The White Quail" is less interesting than Elisa precisely because Steinbeck too explicitly tells us what Mary is thinking, while Elisa remains a mystery.

"The Chrysanthemums," to summarize, is probably Steinbeck's ultimate masterpiece in short fiction. In it he illustrates the frustrating limitations placed on women (and men) by sex-stereotyped roles and by traditional attitudes about "normal" female and male behavior. The sympathetically drawn Elisa Allen ranks as the most memorable female protagonist in Steinbeck's short fiction. The story's narrative, with its carefully foreshadowed surprise ending, is his most finely wrought. And the richly suggestive symbol, Elisa's chrysanthemums, allows the story to sustain widely diverse readings. Considering these strengths, it is no wonder that Mordecai Marcus calls "The Chrysanthemums" "one of the world's great short stories."

"The White Quail" (1935)

"The White Quail" offers another psychologically penetrating view of an unsatisfying marriage. Robert M. Benton has argued, however, that " 'The White Quail' is somewhat less effective than 'The Chrysanthemums' because the symbolism is so explicit in this second [Long Valley] story."[13] Namely, Mary Teller's garden and the white quail become too obviously identified with her. As mentioned above, when Mary orders her husband to kill a gray cat that threatens the quail, Harry Teller instinctively shoots the quail instead of the cat. Although ashamed, Harry destroys the rare bird because it represents his aloof and untouchable wife. Stanley Renner explains Mary and Harry Teller's behavior in the story as "a dangerous sexual tension precipitated by a marriage patterned on idealized terms," where the wife is seen as "sexless, and inviolable" and the husband views his own sexuality as "unmentionably vile and shameful." This "growing but unacknowledged sexual tension," says Renner, is worked out symbolically through the garden and "the forces that threaten it."[14] These are the two poles in the story: at one extreme, Mary Teller, symbolized by her scrupulously tended garden and by the white quail; at the other, her frustrated husband, who seems allied with the "wild" brush (27) encroaching upon Mary's garden and with the hungry gray cat.

Harry Teller is one of several frustrated and/or lonely male characters in The Long Valley, along with Mike in "The Vigilante," Peter Randall in "The Harness," Jim Moore in "The Murder," and Dr. Phillips in "The Snake." Steinbeck himself was experiencing loneliness when he wrote "The White Quail." In the manuscript copybook containing the original draft of the story, he writes of having such feelings despite his marriage of several years.[15] While Steinbeck hoped his loneliness would make him more productive, that it bothered him is evidenced in the story by Harry Teller's pitiful last remark. "Oh, Lord, I'm so lonely!" (42). According to Steinbeck's jottings in the copybook, his wife, Carol, also felt lonely, given that during this period she sacrificed time normally devoted to her marriage and her own interests to nursing Steinbeck's ailing parents. This surrender of her time may have prompted Carol, like Mary Teller, to crave rigid control over her life, thus protecting herself, in Thomas Kiernan's words, from the "vicissitudes of an uncertain world."[16]

Since Mary is able to achieve the rigid control she desires, Marilyn H. Mitchell regards her as another Steinbeck "strong woman" (like Elisa Allen in "The Chrysanthemums"), with a "strength of will usually identified with the male" (see part 3). But Mary and Elisa "are trapped between society's definition of the masculine and the feminine," says Mitchell, "and are struggling against the limitations of the feminine." Both "must somehow express themselves meaningfully within the narrow possibilities open to women in a man's world," and both choose a garden in which to focus their energies; they undertake their projects, Mitchell argues, with a dedication "traditionally considered masculine."[17]

Through strength of will and subtlety, then, Mary Teller creates her perfect garden. After looking for five years, she chooses a husband who that future garden will "like" (13). Says Mitchell, to Mary the garden is "a 'child' whose 'step-father' she must carefully select with only a secondary interest in the man's desirability as a husband." Harry becomes a good prospect for Mary because of "his passivity and his income" and because he is attracted to her prettiness, while not comprehending her complex psychology. For this reason, Mary succeeds in "completely dominating him," says Mitchell, "for she skillfully cloaks her aggressive manipulation in feminine frailty." Thus when she locks him out of her bedroom to "prevent his getting at 'the me that's way inside,' " Harry merely feels "ashamed" of his sexual desire (36).[18]

Given Mary Teller's strength of will and subtle skill in manipulating her husband, Mitchell calls her "one of the most ruthless and egotistical of all Steinbeck's characters," a "virtual caricature of the selfish, castrating female who inspires animosity." And French finds her "the most unattractive woman in Steinbeck's fiction before the incredible Kate Trask of *East of Eden*." Other critics agree. Astro calls Mary a narcissist, since she is "so engulfed in private fantasies that her perception of nature is a mirror of her own distorted mind." Arthur L. Simpson says she resembles an artist so obsessed with her artistic creation that she excludes from her life human warmth and compassion. Fontenrose sees her as godlike, "eternally admiring" the "Platonic heaven, changeless and eternal" (her garden) she has created. And Owens calls her grandiose behavior "an attempt to construct an unfallen Eden in a fallen world, a neurotic projection of Mary's self." These critics' impassioned responses to the story suggest that while it is not the most successful of Steinbeck's *Long Valley* stories, "The White Quail" has a subtle, and perhaps profoundly disturbing, power.[19]

"The Harness" (1938)

Like "The White Quail," "The Harness" is another study of a marriage in which one spouse dominates the other. Owens argues that the story's protagonist, Peter Randall, resembles the repressed and frustrated husband of Mary Teller in the former tale. The "deep sexual and spiritual starvation" suffered by Harry Teller in his unsatisfying relationship with Mary foreshadows Peter Randall's perhaps even more psychologically unhealthy union with his wife, Emma. Randall also resembles Pat Humbert in *The Pastures of Heaven* (1932), who loses both his parents and, according to Timmerman, becomes chained to their ghosts "by a past that he cannot change and a present that he cannot control."[20]

"The Harness" features a unique double-surprise plot, the first surprise positioned early in the story, and the second at the end.[21] Peter Randall is introduced to us as "one of the most highly respected farmers of Monterey County," who "held his shoulders back as though they were braced, and he sucked in his stomach like a soldier" (111). Despite his fine posture and "grave and restrained" manner, within Peter neighbors detect a "force held caged" (111). This pent-up "force" precipitates the first surprise in the story.

Upon the death of his sickly, "skin-and-bones" wife (111), Peter begins "wailing like a crazy man" (115). After an embarrassing scene, Randall peels off his shirt to reveal a shoulder harness and stomach belt. They were his wife's idea. He vows to his neighbor, Ed Chapell, that after Emma's funeral he will never wear them again. "I tell you," he says to Chapell, "it's all over" (119). Chapell is "scandalized" (119) to learn that upstanding Peter Randall is, at heart, a slouchy, licentious man who spends annual riotous weekends in San Francisco. Randall begins to put his facade of conservatism and respectability behind him by planting forty acres of fragrant sweet peas, a financially risky venture Emma would have squelched.

The story's second surprise occurs in a San Francisco hotel where Ed Chapell later encounters the drunken Randall returning from the city's brothels. To Chapell's amazement, Randall explains, "I just had to come up to the city. I'd'a busted if I hadn't come up." (128–29). Though his risky crop succeeded beyond his expectations, Randall didn't enjoy the forty acres of sweet peas. "The whole time, all the year, I been worrying" (128). Although he has indulged himself in booze and brothels, Randall plans to atone to Emma by putting in the electric lights she had always wanted. While Randall renews his vow to never again wear the harness, Chapell realizes that his neighbor's enslavement to his wife goes much deeper than that. Emma still lives inside him. "She didn't die dead" (129), Randall admits.

This surprise conclusion, says Fontenrose, shows that "the supposed reality revealed behind an appearance of respectability and rural content now seems to be itself appearance; and the old appearance of respectability looks more like reality." Actually Peter Randall is neither merely a facade of respectability, nor a slouchy, libidinous man, but both. Yet he is unable to integrate these two sides of his personality, so he continues to live schizophrenically— a model Mason, farmer, and husband fifty-one weeks of the year, and an irresponsible sensualist the one remaining week. As we have seen, Randall suffers from what Owens calls a "deep sexual and spiritual starvation" and therefore compensates with his annual orgies.[22]

Behind Randall's "sexual and spiritual starvation" is his wife, Emma, whom Fontenrose finds "puritanical and pleasure-hating."[23] Emma is a middle-aged, "skinny bird of a woman," who becomes so sickly she drops in weight to "eighty-seven pounds" (111, 114). In keeping with her personality, Emma's farmhouse is immaculately "clean and dusted," with "thick cocoa-fiber mats" to keep dirt out. And since the Randalls have no children, their home remains "unscarred, uncarved, unchalked" (113). The dried-up, "tight" (114) appearance of Emma and the spick-and-span, even sterile, condition of her house suggest the atmosphere in which her husband, Peter, languishes.

Ed Chapell, an important minor character, is instrumental in revealing Peter Randall's true psychological condition. Chapell appears in the two surprise, or reversal, scenes—first, upon Emma's death when Randall discards his harness (and his apparently bogus respectability) and, second, when in the San Francisco hotel Randall reveals his continued bondage to his dead wife. In between these two scenes, Chapell also notes that Randall lives as a widower much as he had before Emma's death. Although Randall vows to "track dirt into the house," hire a "big fat housekeeper" (121), and never again to wind the "mournful" mantel clock, on a visit to the Randall home Chapell detects "no dirt on the floor" and hears the "mantel clock ticking away" (123–24). As for the housekeeper, Randall explains that he simply has never found time to hire one (126). Thus, even before Randall's admission that his dead wife "didn't die dead" (129), Chapell finds signs that reveal as much.

Peter Randall's almost total domination by his wife is suggested by the harness itself, which French calls the "physical symbol of his psychological enslavement." The sweet peas Randall plants— "forty acres of color and smell" (121)—provide a more subtle symbol, in Owens words, of Randall's "profound need for sensation." When he looks down on these "great squares of pink and blue," Randall inhales deeply with his "blue shirt open at the throat, as though he wanted to get the perfume down next to his skin" (125). Paradoxically, he cannot fully enjoy the sweet peas because Emma's haunting voice has worried him from the day of planting through the harvest. No wonder Steinbeck originally called Randall's story "The Fool."[24]

"Flight" (1938)

Like Peter Randall, Pepé Torres in "Flight" also appears to be a "fool," yet Pepé's untimely end results more from fate than foolishness. As mentioned above, Steinbeck frequently presents his characters from a biological, deterministic perspective. In "Flight," when Pepé Torres knifes a man in Monterey, the few remaining days of this nineteen-year-old protagonist are as predetermined as the rising and setting of the sun. He flees his pursuers in the rugged Santa Lucia Mountains (reflecting the story's original title, "Manhunt"). While trying to avoid the ominous "dark watchers," Pepé loses his food, water, and weapons; and his horse is shot out from under him. He crawls onward like an animal as bullets ricochet around him. Finally, as if reconciled to his death, he bows his head, weakly crosses himself, and ascends a mountain ridge, silhouetting himself against the sky. Instantly, a rifle cuts him down. He tumbles, starting a small avalanche, which ultimately covers his head.

Few, if any, of Steinbeck's short stories have been more often the subject of critical debate than "Flight." The first influential reading of the story came from Edmund Wilson. Complaining that Steinbeck assimilates "human beings to animals" (see previous section), Wilson singled out "Flight" as an example of this tendency. "[A] young Mexican boy," said Wilson, "is finally reduced to a state so close to that of the beasts that he is apparently mistaken by a mountain lion for another four-footed animal." Wilson's literal reading of the story was not challenged until nearly thirty years later when Peter Lisca discussed "Flight" in *The Wide World of John Steinbeck* (1958). Rather than denying Pepé's apparent regression to animal behavior, Lisca perceived the story as a moral allegory operating on two levels: first, the physical level involves Pepé's literal "separation from civilized man and his reduction to the state of a wild animal"; and, second, the symbolic level (moving in the opposite direction) shows "how man, even when stripped of all his civilized accoutrements . . . is still something more than an animal." On this second level, Lisca contends, Pepé faces his doom "not with the headlong retreat or futile death struggle of an animal, but with the calm and stoicism required by the highest conception of manhood."[25]

Since Lisca's comments in 1958, most criticism published on "Flight" has reflected either his or Wilson's views. Readings echoing Lisca's allegorical interpretation usually characterize Pepé's ordeal as an initiation into adulthood rather than as an irreversible march into doom. Dan Vogel sees Pepé as an "Everyman" and his flight as a "universal journey." Paul McCarthy characterizes this journey as "an impressive reworking of such traditional themes as the flight from society into the wild, the passage from innocence to experience, and the painful growth to maturity." And John Antico sees in it "the emergence of Man from the primeval darkness."[26]

Readings reflecting Wilson's literal interpretation, in contrast, often describe "Flight" as the tragic regression of a boy into an animal. French calls the story a naturalistic tragedy because, "although the reader may sympathize with Pepé, he should realize that the boy's position is logically hopeless." Walter K. Gordon says that "Flight" illustrates "man's moral deterioration and regression that inevitably results when he abandons responsibility for his actions." By running away, says Gordon, Pepé becomes "less than an animal rather than a man." And Chester F. Chapin suggests that Pepé, as a "pinhead," is incapable of moral regeneration.[27]

On the literal level, "Flight" is indeed a bleak story. The nineteen-year-old protagonist's doom becomes clear early in the tale. When Pepé starts his flight into the mountains, Mama Torres begins "the high, whining keen of the death wail. 'Our beautiful—

our brave,' " she cries. " 'Our protector, our son is gone.' " (54) That Pepé will soon die is indicated by this wail, and confirmed by his siblings, Rosy and Emilio. "Is he dead? Do you think he is dead?" Emilio asks. "He is not dead," Rosy explains. "Not yet" (55). Steinbeck underscores Pepé's fate by subtle images showing that he has been cut off forever from his childhood life on the Torres farm. When he comes to the canyon leading into the mountains, Pepé looks back to see the "houses . . . swallowed in the misty light," as the canyon closes in on him (55). Pepé himself becomes a misty figure, suggesting his impending death. "Long before he entered the canyon, he had become a grey, indefinite shadow" (54).

The "dark watchers" Pepé encounters along the trail also seem to portend his death. Black figures who haunt the Santa Lucias, the dark watchers suggest death by their stealthy nature and their unpredictable appearances along the trail. Dan Vogel calls them "the universal Nemesis"; John Antico says they "symbolize the death that is in store for Pepé"; and Louis Owens identifies them as the "pure idea of death." The dark watchers are plausibly dead persons themselves who haunt the living and remind them of their similar fate. William Jones argues that Pepé himself becomes a dark watcher when he rises upon a ridge—"black against the morning sky" (70)—at the story's end to meet his fate.[28] Once asked about these dark watchers, Steinbeck purportedly said: "I don't know who they are or what they represent. All I know is that the people around Monterey believe in them. As you know, there are certain small areas in the woods which animals avoid and will not cross. We don't know why, but we know such spots exist. I don't know who the dark watchers are."[29]

Assuming that Pepé's death is fated—as it clearly seems to be from the dark watchers and other evidence in the story—then we must face a disturbing paradox: Pepé reaches adulthood almost simultaneously with his death. From the beginning of the story Pepé claims he is a man, though Mama Torres disagrees. "Thou? A man? Thou art a peanut" (48). Yet when Pepé returns from Monterey, he is changed. His boyish looks gone, "in his eyes . . . [t]here was no laughter anymore, nor any bashfulness. They were sharp and bright and purposeful" (51). Mama Torres can see the difference. "Yes, thou art a man, my poor little Pepé. Thou art a man" (52). Pepé is "poor" because, in "Flight," becoming a man is synonymous with dying. Just as Pepé's father, the last man on the Torres farm, was struck down by a rattlesnake ten years earlier, so too Pepé, having now become a man, will die. M. R. Satyanarayana likens "Flight" to the Greek myth of Phaëthon, in which a son of Helios, when permitted to drive the chariot of the sun, is struck down with a thunderbolt by Zeus. Thus, in becoming a man, the boy dies (see part 3). The symbolic death of childhood is indeed a plausible reading of the story. Dan Vogel, for example, sees in Pepé's journey "the escape from the Mother, the divestiture of the father, and the death and burial of childhood."[30]

Pepé is, in fact, two different characters in the story—first a child and then an adult. Although the point at which Pepé is transformed from a boy into a man seems unequivocal (he returns from Monterey "changed" [51]), not all critics agree. John Antico argues that the true test of Pepé's manliness, and hence the proof of his manhood, occurs at the story's end when he rises dramatically on a mountain ridge to meet his death. Chester F. Chapin offers the more extreme view that Pepé never attains manhood, since his deficient intellect leaves him unequipped to cope with adult life. At whatever point Pepé's transformation occurs, Steinbeck is careful to present him sympathetically to the reader. Norman Friedman points out that Steinbeck excludes the Monterey knifing scene to "avoid showing his protagonist acting senselessly, without thought, and fatefully."[31] Pepé merely summarizes these events in one brief paragraph to Mama Torres (51–52), enabling us to understand why he must flee into the mountains, while not prejudicing us against him for his brutal act.

Steinbeck's care in crafting the story extends beyond his portrayal of the young protagonist, to the plot itself. "Flight" is divided into four sections, each marking one stage of Pepé's development. The first section presents the boyish Pepé and foreshadows "coming events," in Horst Groene's words, by "the extended scenic presentation" of Pepé's skillful knife throwing. When the second section begins (50) Pepé has already been catapulted into adulthood. As if to signify his maturity, Pepé dons his father's black coat and carries a rifle into the mountains. In the third section (55–61) Pepé demonstrates his maturity, according to Groene, since he "consumes food and water sparingly and keeps a watchful eye on the trail" (yet loses his knife). In the final section (61–70) he leaves behind his remaining supplies, including his other inheritances from his father (black coat and rifle), which Groene says "have been clearly established as symbols of manliness." Pepé then descends seemingly "to the level of animal existence." But this dehumanizing process "is reversed by Pepé's final gesture of manly grandeur and human dignity."[32]

While these four sections in the story indicate stages in Pepé's development, they also suggest the "universal journey" of men and women through life. When Pepé first enters the Santa Lucias, the trail is lush and green with the springlike freshness of youth. A stream runs "smoothly, glinting in the first morning sun," and "wild mint" grows along the edges (55–56). "Sentinel redwoods" guard the trail, "great round red trunks bearing foliage as green and lacy as ferns," with a "perfumed and purple light" (56). But soon this vernal beauty disappears. Suggesting the fading of youth and the approach of middle age, the redwoods become "smaller and their tops . . . dead, bitten dead where the wind reached them" (57). As Pepé ascends the trail the country grows "more rough and terrible and dry" (57). "[T]he bare rock mountaintops [are] pale and powder-dry under the dropping sun" (57–58)," evoking the advent of old age. Finally, when Pepé nears his death, the trail turns "waterless and desolate" (69). All he can see are "starving sage" and "broken granite" (69). His trek ends at "giant outcroppings" where "granite teeth [stand] out against the sky" (69). These are the "Jaws of Death," according to Owens, which swallow Pepé, making him finally one with nature.[33]

Pepé begins his flight healthy and alert and ends it enfeebled and unconscious. He has lost all his possessions, and departs this world essentially empty-handed. By the time of his death he can speak only with the "thick hiss" of a snake (70). Hilton Anderson points out several instances of such snake imagery in the story, especially as these parallel Pepé's moods and actions. Steinbeck uses this and other animal imagery, according to Edward J. Piacentino, "to define features of Pepé Torres' character or to accent some of the physical challenges he experiences during his flight for survival and the resulting psychological traumas of this ordeal."[34] Piacentino argues that Steinbeck establishes Pepé's innocence before his trouble in Monterey with images of "selected domestic farm animals" (chickens, cows, and sheep), and then later during his flight Steinbeck underscores the youth's "jungle-like struggle for survival" with "wild, potentially dangerous animals" (wildcats, mountain lions, rattlesnakes, buzzards) and the threats they pose to "weaker, smaller animals" (doves, quail, little does, small brown birds, etc.). This predator-prey relationship among animals closely parallels Pepé's own predicament after he commits murder and flees for his life.

Steinbeck employs other imagery to suggest Pepé's fate. The moon, a vivid white orb when Pepé begins his flight, follows him up the mountain slopes, and subsequently rises and descends during the three nights of his journey. Antoni Gajewski argues that when the moon rises, Pepé is vigorous and strong; when it descends, his strength wanes. Even the Torres farm echoes Pepé's fight for survival.[35] The rickety buildings cling precariously like "aphids on the mountain skirts," crouching low "as though the wind might blow them into the sea" (45). The harsh hand of nature can be seen in the "rattling, rotting barn . . . grey-bitten with sea salt" (45). This Jeffers-like landscape suggests hard, bitter struggle and foreshadows Pepé's ordeal in the barren, granite mountains.

Given the story's vivid action and carefully drawn landscape, Richard Astro argues that "Flight" "may be the most skillfully told tale" in *The Long Valley*. Lisca also ranks the story as "one of the best" in the collection, and praises its "firm prose style" and "crisp rendering of factual details" reminiscent of Hemingway. And French finds in "Flight" a "rare example of a Naturalistic story . . . an achievement matched among Steinbeck's longer works only by *In Dubious Battle*."[36]

These critics seem to agree that, stylistically, "Flight" is an extraordinary tale, perhaps because Steinbeck exercises unusual restraint in portraying each scene objectively. Since the third-person narrator remains outside the minds of the protagonist and other characters, external events are emphasized. Much of the story's mystery, ambiguity, and suspense stems from this effective third-person, objective stance. Steinbeck's deft handling of the narrative may explain why it is one of his most frequently anthologized stories and why F. W. Watt calls it "perfectly executed."[37] Despite this critical praise, Steinbeck's agents tried in vain to publish "Flight" prior to its 1938 appearance in *The Long Valley*, a plight barely escaped by the next story to be discussed, "The Snake."

"The Snake" (1935)

"So bizarre that Steinbeck could not get it published except in a local newspaper," "The Snake" was known even to its author as a "frightful" story and, according to Benson, seemed so "outrageous" to his literary agents that they returned it to him.[38] Steinbeck finally sold the tale (for "six months' use of a beautiful big bay" horse) to the Monterey *Beacon,* a newspaper run in conjunction with a stable. Thus, "The Snake," which marks the first fictional appearance of Ed Ricketts, did not reach a large audience until, like "Flight," it appeared in *The Long Valley* (1938).

Benson reports that "about a half dozen people feel certain that they witnessed the event in Ed Rickett's Cannery Row laboratory which was the genesis of the story."[39] In "About Ed Ricketts," Steinbeck claims he wrote the tale "just as it happened."

> A woman came in one night wanting to buy a male rattlesnake. It happened that we had one and knew it was a male because it had recently copulated with another snake in the cage. The woman paid for the snake and then insisted that it be fed. She paid for a white rat to be given it. Ed put the rat in the cage. The snake struck and killed it and then unhinged its jaws preparatory to swallowing it. The frightening thing was that the woman, who had watched the process closely, moved her jaws and stretched her mouth just as the snake was doing. After the rat was swallowed, she paid for a year's supply of rats and said she would come back. But she never did come back.[40]

While Steinbeck says he told the story "just as it happened," accounts of others who purportedly witnessed the same incident vary from his. Webster Street, for example, says that Ricketts (Dr. Phillips in the story) put the white mouse (not rat) in the snake's cage of the biologist's own volition and that the woman, "one of the dancers from a local vaudeville team that was passing though Monterey," had taken "a fancy to Ed" and was simply visiting in the lab. Street says "the sexy-looking dame" was "fascinated by the whole thing, but she didn't say a word" as she watched for "perhaps half an hour, until there wasn't anything left but the tail of this mouse hanging out of the snake." Afterward, "she just got up and left and we never saw her again."[41]

A. Grove Day, who also remembers seeing the incident, explains that the woman was actually playing with the white mouse (again, not rat) when she dropped and hurt it. Someone suggested they feed it to a rattlesnake Rickett's father had found on a golf course. Day recalls that when they did, the snake swallowed the mouse whole except for its tail, so that the rattler looked as if it were smoking a cigarette. The snake "took his time and everybody thought it was funny when the tail stuck out. Dr. Ricketts was probably the least concerned watcher." To Day's recollection, the woman, "possibly an actress type, maybe a blonde . . . , absolutely did not dress in dark clothes or have a snaky body, hair and eyes." Day concludes, "John invented a 'true' origin for this psycho story, as many writers often do."[42]

While Street's and Day's recollections of the incident are quite similar, Steinbeck's account departs significantly from those of his two friends. In Steinbeck's version, the woman is not an observer but the principal participant; she does not merely happen into the lab when the snake feeding occurs, but herself asks to see it take place; she also insists that the snake be a male; and rather than simply watching with fascination as the snake strikes and eats, she sympathetically undulates with its motions. These differences between Steinbeck's recollection of the incident and those of his two friends suggest, as Webster Street has said, that "John made a story out of it and gave it a lot of implications."[43]

It is these "implications" that constitute the principal difference between what apparently happened in Rickett's lab and the story called "The Snake" that Steinbeck created. For example, he very clearly makes the woman into a type (if not an archetype) rather than an individual human being. Paul McCarthy argues that this "snakelike primitive" woman is unbelievable because of Steinbeck's tendency to create such types "designed principally to express an idea, attitude, or emotion."[44] The woman's bizarre behavior (and its psychological implications) reveal Steinbeck's deliberate reshaping of the incident. And Dr. Phillips' admission when the puzzling woman departs, "I've read so much about psychological sex symbols . . . ," seems to be another attempt to shape the story and draw out implications.

As Charles E. May indicates in his provocative essay on "The Snake" (see part 3), the dark, mysterious woman seems indeed to be a "psychological archetype" who represents repressed instinctual and unconscious forces inside Dr. Phillips. The woman enters the lab and "symbolically embodies the sound of the sea" and hence, as the story's narrator characterizes it, the "deep pool of consciousness" (78).[45] Dr. Phillips, in fact, is unable to judge "whether the water sigh[s] among the piles or whether the woman sigh[s]" (83). She is also identified with the snake because of her snakelike appearance and motions. "A tall, lean woman," she wears a "severe dark suit" and has "straight black hair" and "black eyes . . . veiled with dust" (75, 78). She weaves as the snake weaves and becomes sleepy after it eats.

Identified with the sea, the woman brings to mind the Jungian collective unconscious—the mysterious, unfathomable depths of the "group psyche-memory," in Steinbeck's words. Her likeness to the snake, as mentioned in the previous section, can be taken as a Freudian identification with the phallus (significantly the woman insists on a *male* serpent); or, according to May, it can be seen in more androgynous, Jungian terms as both phallic and vaginal, since the snake not only phallically emits venom, but also swallows whole (*vagina dentata*) the white rat. The snake then (and hence the woman) becomes paradoxically a symbol of both maleness and femaleness.[46]

May argues that this "snake-woman or instinctual force has risen abruptly from the doctor's unconscious to confront him." She brings "the message of the mythic world" which he in his realm of "reason and science" has ignored.[47] This realm of Dr. Phillips is indicated by the "tight little building" he uses for his laboratory (73) and by the way he imposes order on his laboratory and its specimens. The alley cat he gases and embalms (75ff.) and the methodically timed starfish sperm and ova experiment (76ff.) he conducts are cases in point. And even though the scientist seems to have a harmonious relationship with these living creatures, he is nonetheless in control—until the mysterious woman appears.

That a Jungian reading of "The Snake" seems so apt is not surprising. During the early 1930s, when the idea for the story was probably incubating in Steinbeck's mind, Steinbeck, Ed Ricketts, and Joseph Campbell (a foremost authority on Jungian archetypes) read and discussed Jung in Ricketts' lab. Owens notes that Steinbeck was a "serious reader of Jung . . . and an acquaintance of Joseph Campbell" and that Steinbeck sometimes worked "deliberately with Jungian images."[48] In "The Snake," then, the "implications" Steinbeck has given the story are essentially Jungian. He has created an archetype in the dark woman and reinforced this archetype with the primordial atmosphere of Dr. Phillips' oceanfront laboratory. Sea waves wash incessantly against earthborn pilings, and the befuddled scientist, after encountering the woman, ponders "psychological sex symbols" (86).

In addition to this Jungian reading, the story has been approached in other ways, as well. Fontenrose calls it a "zoological garden of Eden" intruded upon by a "neurotic female devil." French also sees the woman as a temptress figure, and Reloy Garcia says she introduces the principle of evil into the scientist's world. Lisca argues that the woman's odd behavior can be attributed to frustration, probably of a sexual nature. And Bernard Mandelbaum contends that the events of the story are actually only the dream of Dr. Phillips.[49] Whether a dream or waking nightmare, "The Snake" rightfully has been called "frightful," "outrageous," and "bizarre."

"The Raid" (1934)

"The Snake" is one of many *Long Valley* tales that prompts Joseph Fontenrose to say, "It is surprising how seldom the depression and its problems make themselves felt" in these stories. Fontenrose concludes that " 'The Raid' alone is concerned with contemporary troubles." Although two other *Long Valley* tales ("The Vigilante" and "Breakfast"), in fact, also spring from such contemporary events, "The Raid" most clearly reveals the troubled depression years. When Steinbeck composed this story a whole new social context was taking shape around him. According to Benson, "The thirties in California had brought not only the Depression but also an era of severe labor strife." While labor conflicts occurred on California's docks and in its packing sheds and fields, Benson reports that the struggles of migrant farm workers would especially "have a profound effect on the direction of Steinbeck's career." Indeed, three of Steinbeck's most successful novels, as Benson indicates, emerged from this milieu: *In Dubious Battle* (1936), *Of Mice and Men* (1937), and *The Grapes of Wrath* (1939).[50]

41

Part 1. The Short Fiction: A Critical Analysis

Published two years before *In Dubious Battle* (and probably conceived as an episode for that novel), "The Raid" provides the first indication of Steinbeck's interest in California's farm-labor movement and its organizers. According to Benson, Steinbeck happened upon the subject almost by accident. Tipped off by a friend that two communist organizers were hiding out in Seaside (near Monterey), Steinbeck paid the destitute fugitives for their stories. From their firsthand accounts of California's labor unrest, as well as from information he gathered elsewhere, Steinbeck intended to write an "autobiography" of a strike leader. Steinbeck's plans quickly changed when his literary agent, Mavis McIntosh, urged him, in Benson's words, to "use his material as the basis for a novel instead." This was the beginning of *In Dubious Battle* and probably of "The Raid," as well.[51]

The lead pair of characters in the novel (Jim and Mac) and in the story (Root and Dick) are very similar, having different names but essentially the same relationship. And both pairs are based on the same labor activists Steinbeck had met in the fields and in the homes of sponsors and friends. A possible model for Root in "The Raid" is novice strike organizer Cicil McKiddy, a twenty-four-year-old Dust Bowl migrant at the time Steinbeck knew him. According to Benson, McKiddy had volunteered to help in the farm-labor movement—then spearheaded by the Communist party—when he found himself in the midst of the cotton strike of 1933. Ella Winter, a labor sympathizer, remembers McKiddy characteristically wearing "a turtle-neck blue sweater," just as Root does in "The Raid." Root's mentor, Dick, is probably modeled on one or more "canny" party veterans, such as Pat Chambers or Shorty Alston, who had organized strikes in the San Joaquin and Imperial valleys.[52]

The mentor-neophyte relationship of Dick and Root in "The Raid," as mentioned in the previous section, resembles such male pairings found in several Hemingway stories. In Steinbeck's tale, neophyte Root learns steadfastness from the veteran communist organizer, Dick. Amidst the smell of "fermenting fruit" (95) from strike-closed packing plants, Root and Dick prepare to hold a meeting one dark night in a deserted building. The frightened Root tacks up party posters and sets out leaflets. Both men then wait until long after the appointed meeting time. Root's fears about a possible raid intensify when a man appears warning that vigilantes are coming. Worrying he may bolt under pressure, Root looks to the veteran Dick as a model of courage. Consequently, when a mob storms the building, Root is able to stand firm.

M. R. Satyanarayana (in his essay included in part 3) calls "The Raid" a "sociological initiation," in which a youth is initiated into "an altogether new social order." Satyanarayana argues that Root goes through various "rites of passage" in the story's four numbered sections: "(1) the hero's severance from the mother, (2) the revelation of the mystery of adult experience, (3) the ordeal, and (4) the symbolic death and rebirth." "Thrown out by the father for his radical views," says Satyanarayana, Root has already been severed from his mother before the story begins. Soon Dick reveals to Root the "magic formula" (party slogan) for standing firm in adversity. "The men of little spirit must have an example of stead—steadfastness." This revelation helps Root endure his ordeal, which is a torture of both physical and psychological dimensions. Finally when Root is beaten unconscious by vigilantes and awakens in jail, concludes Satyanarayana, he has completed his initiation with a symbolic death and rebirth.[53]

Throughout this initiation, Steinbeck implicitly compares the novice's behavior with that of the veteran. Even their dress indicates the differences in their character. Root's "blue turtle-neck sweater" suggests his (at least initial) softness; Dick's "peajacket," on the other hand, reflects his psychologically tough outer shell (95). While Root is openly frightened about the possibility of a raid, the seasoned activist has learned to control his emotions, masking his fear beneath a facade of party slogans. "If someone busts you," Dick tells Root, "it isn't him that's doing it, it's the System. And it isn't you he's busting. He's taking a crack at the Principle" (104). While Dick is a static figure, hardened into his words and actions by party dogma, Root is dynamic and changes as the narrative progresses. Openly fearful throughout most of the story, Root eventually proves himself. By overcoming his fright, he earns his place among veteran organizers. The outcome is, in Gajewski's words, not the victory of communism over capitalism or vice versa, but the "victory of a human being over human nature."[54]

Regardless of Dick's Marxist slogans, Lisca notes a parallel between the two activists and the early Christian martyrs. Even though the two men have been tipped off about the raid, they choose to face a sure beating because of a "Principle" (104). The poster depicting a "man in harsh reds and blacks" (99) becomes a god to whom they are disciples. Root especially resembles Christ when he shouts to his attackers, "You don't know what you're doing" (107), a modern English paraphrase of Christ's words on the cross. "Father, forgive them; they know not what they do" (Mark 23:34). Root begins to sound so Christian, in fact, that Dick takes offense and corrects him with Marxist rhetoric. " 'You lay off that religion stuff, Kid.' He quoted, " 'Religion is the opium of the people' " (108). Gajewski cites Root's religious attitude toward social questions as an "error" in Steinbeck's portrayal of the two communist organizers. Root's attitude does, in fact, seem at times more Christian than Marxist. Lisca discovers in the novice's speeches the "Christian concepts of the brotherhood of man, loving one's enemies, and turning the other cheek, as well as the divine sacrifice."[55] In this way, Root foreshadows sacrificial figures Jim Nolan in *In Dubious Battle* and Jim Casy in *The Grapes of Wrath*.

Steinbeck's subtle artistry in "The Raid" goes easily unnoticed behind the story's political and psychological contexts. For example, he creates suspense with two nearly imperceptible motifs. The first is the slow, steady passage of time. The nervous Root asks Dick for the time on at least four occasions. Since we learn early in the story that the meeting is scheduled for eight o'clock, when "quarter-past nine" (106) arrives and no one has appeared, something is obviously wrong. With each minute that elapses after eight, Root has greater cause for concern. As a result of Steinbeck's careful demarcation of time, we are fully prepared for the vigilantes' dreaded arrival. A second motif, night sounds, adds further suspense. Barking dogs, rustling winds, and the rumble of motor cars can be heard outside the deserted building where Dick and Root await their fainthearted comrades. Six times Steinbeck repeats this motif (98, 100, 103, 104, and 105), which further marks the passage of time and suggests the isolation of the activists. In the final sequence, Steinbeck adds new sounds, an alarm clock and train, and heightens suspense with near silence before the mob arrives (105). This subtle artistry, along with the story's political and psychological contexts, makes "The Raid" more than a mere reflection of contemporary events.

"The Vigilante" (1936)

"The Raid," as mentioned above, is not the only *Long Valley* story based on a contemporary event. Just as Steinbeck used the activities of farm-labor organizers in California's San Joaquin and Imperial valleys to create "The Raid," he based "The Vigilante" on an actual lynching that occurred in San Jose. Other similarities exist between the two stories. Both reveal Steinbeck's interest in the phenomenon of group violence and both portray vigilantes behaving according to Steinbeck's "group man," or phalanx, theory. The major difference between the treatment of vigilantism in the two works is that although in "The Raid" Steinbeck views the mob through the eyes of two of its victims (Root and Dick), in "The Vigilante," he takes us inside the violent group itself by focusing on one of its members (Mike). In Owens' words, "The Vigilante" comprises "Steinbeck's only attempt to delve into the mind of one of the common cells of the mob."[56]

One night Mike joins a group of vigilantes who storm a jail and lynch a black prisoner. As the mob bursts through the jail door, Mike himself becomes a human battering ram. He is one of the first to pull the rope that hangs the impassive prisoner, and he rips a piece of denim from the victim's clothes as a souvenir. When the mob begins to burn the corpse, Mike skulks away. Suddenly overcome by loneliness, he walks from the darkened scene (the street lights have been shot out) toward a tavern displaying a neon sign "BEER". Mike shows his denim souvenir to the bartender, Welch, who offers to buy it and then pours Mike a free beer. Soon Welch closes the bar and the two men walk together into a neighborhood of nice houses and well-trimmed lawns. When Mike reaches his own house, his wife accuses him of being with a woman. He simply tells her to read the morning paper. When he looks in the mirror, however, Mike feels as if he has been with a woman.

That Steinbeck based "The Vigilante" on an actual lynching has been verified by James P. Delgado, U.S. National Park Service historian. According to Delgado, San Jose's "Night of Shame" occurred on Sunday, 26 November 1933, when a mob of several thousand people emptied San Jose's taverns and assembled in front of the Santa Clara County Jail. Their collective aim, as Delgado recounts it, was instant retribution against two prisoners—

Thomas Harold Thurmond and John Maurice Holmes—who had confessed to kidnapping and brutally murdering Brooke Hart, the scion of one of the town's wealthiest families. Earlier in the day on 26 November fishermen had found Hart's horribly mutilated body in lower San Francisco Bay. When this news reached San Jose, the mob went wild. Using an iron pipe as a battering ram, they crashed through the jailhouse door, beat the sheriff unconscious, and dragged Holmes and Thurmond across the street to Saint James Park, where the lynching and corpse burning took place.[57]

Delgado proves beyond doubt that Steinbeck had the November 1933 San Jose hangings in mind when—about six months later— he composed "The Vigilante." Since the author's first wife, Carol Henning Steinbeck, was a native of San Jose and much of her family lived there, Steinbeck was familiar with its people and environs. Residing at the time in nearby Los Gatos, he also would have read about the hangings, which were front-page news in northern California papers for nearly three weeks.[58]

In "The Vigilante," Steinbeck makes only one substantial change from the real hangings: he substitutes a single black prisoner for the two confessed murderers, Holmes and Thurmond. Aside from this, the San Jose lynching and Steinbeck's fictional account are nearly identical. As Delgado points out, the frenzied mob in Steinbeck's story, the battering ram bursting through the jail door, the park nearby where the hanging takes place, the vandalized street lights, and the igniting of the corpse with newspapers recall almost exactly the events of San Jose's "Night of Shame." In addition, the ordeal of Steinbeck's black prisoner resembles that of Thomas Harold Thurmond, who hit his head in the jail cell (like Steinbeck's character) and then passively submitted to the mob.[59]

More similarities between the San Jose lynchings and Steinbeck's fictional account can be found in his warm-up draft for "The Vigilante," entitled "Case History," whose manuscript is owned by the Steinbeck Research Center at San Jose State University. In this abandoned draft, the prisoner (like Holmes and Thurmond) is accused of kidnapping and murder, and the discovery of the victim's body (as happened in San Jose) incites citizens to vigilantism. "Case History" not only confirms that Steinbeck modeled "The Vigilante" after the San Jose lynchings but also reveals his ultimate purpose in the story—to provide an illustration of his "group man," or phalanx, theory, which holds that a group has desires, hungers, and strivings of its own, independent of the units (human or animal) that compose it. Steinbeck views the phalanx as all-powerful, harnessing the energies of its units, who submerge their individual identities in this entity so much larger than themselves.

"The Vigilante," in its final form, explores the "feelings of a man just deprived of a phalanx." As Benson points out, now "no longer part of the whole, [Mike] feels strangely empty, let down, and alone." The structure of "The Vigilante" is, therefore, retrospective, as Mike recounts—in discontinuous fragments—the events of the evening. "Steinbeck builds on the man's feeling of emptiness," says Benson, "suggesting at the conclusion of the story that the life of this particular phalanx has paralleled the course of emotions during the sexual union of a man and a woman."[60]

This sex-and-violence relationship in the story is indicated by Mike's "petulant" wife (141). After Mike participates in the lynching, she accuses him, "You been with a woman" (141). Mike then mutters to himself: "By God, she was right. . . . That's just exactly how I do feel" (141). Mike's postphalanx feelings ("tired and kind of sleepy," but "satisfied" [140]) do indeed seem similar to those of postcoitus, while his "surge of emotion" (133) during the hanging resembles, as Benson suggests, the excitement of sexual union. The "underlying sexuality to the lynching" is also noted by Barbour, who finds a troubling double irony in the story's premise. "If lynching is a substitute for sexuality, then sexuality is essentially an act of personal aggression."[61]

In addition to the sexual implications of Mike's behavior, critics have offered other reasons for his becoming a vigilante. French argues that sheer boredom and a shrewish wife lead Mike to violence. Franklin E. Court says his behavior can be attributed to a "fantasy of race superiority," and Gajewski similarly calls Mike an "average American racist." While interesting, none of these readings of "The Vigilante" take into consideration the early draft, "Case History," or the San Jose lynchings on which the story is based. These two sources confirm that Steinbeck used the vigilante-style hangings in the story primarily to illustrate his "group man" theory. Thus, Mike becomes a vigilante not because he is sexually frustrated, bored, or a racist, but because as a "unit man" he longs to attach himself to a group.

"Breakfast" (1936)

"Breakfast" has been variously called a "warmup" exercise, an "episode," a set of "working notes," a "fragment," and "the slightest of stories in *The Long Valley*." Technically a sketch, "Breakfast" is another short fiction, like "The Vigilante," that Steinbeck derived from a contemporary event. During the summer of 1934, he ventured out among Dust Bowl migrant workers camped in the Salinas area and listened to their stories. According to Benson, on "such a foray along a country road," Steinbeck picked up material for the sketch. While many critics, and even Steinbeck's longtime editor, Pascal Covici, believe this piece to have been part of Steinbeck's notes for *The Grapes of Wrath*, Benson says that "its composition preceded by two years the earliest research and by three years the earliest writing" on *The Grapes of Wrath*. Benson concludes that "Breakfast" probably emerged from Steinbeck's preparation for *In Dubious Battle*."[62]

Though Steinbeck may have composed the sketch well before he researched or wrote *The Grapes of Wrath*, "Breakfast" certainly resembles this novel in theme and context. F. W. Watt has found that the "half articulate joy in simple humanity" that imbues the sketch is the same that fills the "vaster room" of *The Grapes of Wrath*.[63] Steinbeck, in fact, incorporated a revision of "Breakfast" into chapter 22 of the novel. In this revision, he gives the characters names (they are anonymous in the earlier piece) and changes the first-person point of view to third-person.

In both versions, the scene opens on a cold, early morning, with a man (Tom Joad in *Grapes*) walking down a country road before sunrise. He happens upon a young woman nursing a baby as she cooks on a rusty iron stove. Behind her, two stubble-bearded men emerge from a tent, and the elder asks the newcomer, "Had your breakfast?" They invite him to squat down with them around a packing crate, and the nursing woman sets out bacon, gravy, hot biscuits, and coffee. After breakfast, when the elder man rises and faces the east, the brilliant light of dawn reflects in his eyes. The hosts invite their guest to pick cotton with them, but he politely declines and walks on alone down the road.

Steinbeck's use of a first-person narrator in "Breakfast" intensifies the feeling of warmth and beauty engendered by the sketch. By funneling the action through the eyes of a single involved participant, Steinbeck unifies the narrative and brings the reader close to the characters and their ritual communion. (The immediacy of this first-person perspective is lost in *The Grapes of Wrath*, given the novel's third-person point of view.) "Breakfast" is further unified by the slow but steady progress of the dawn, framing the morning repast of the migrant family with degrees of increasing light. Steinbeck suggests this progress with color imagery from the "lavendar" (89) of earliest light to the "reddish gleam" (92) of near sunrise. Further unity comes from the narrator's opening and closing the sketch with nearly the same confession that he doesn't know why the incident fills him with pleasure.

Critics, too, have grappled with the meaning of this brief piece. Owens, among others, concludes that "Breakfast" is a preparatory sketch, "of interest primarily because it later found its way into *The Grapes of Wrath*. James A. Hamby, in contrast, discovers in "Breakfast" Steinbeck's vision of the perfectability of humankind, a vision he articulated in his Nobel Prize acceptance speech; according to Hamby, Steinbeck translates biblical ideals into strictly human actions to show that the people, not God, must be their own salvation. Similarly, Edwin M. Moseley explains the migrant family's generosity with their repast as a ritual communion, suggesting an indomitable faith in what Gajewski calls "universal brotherhood."[64]

"Johnny Bear" (1937)

As evident in "Breakfast," "The Vigilante," and "The Raid," Steinbeck frequently based his short fiction on real places and people. "Johnny Bear" provides another example. In this unusual tale, Steinbeck portrays the coastal town of Castroville, California (sketched in his earlier "The Days of Long Marsh") and its most bizarre denizen—a bearlike imbecile with an uncanny ability to reproduce the human voice. On the first page of "Johnny Bear" the narrator describes the "village of Loma," built (like Castroville) on a "low round hill that rises like an island out of the flat mouth of the Salinas Valley in central California" (145). At the center of Loma's cultural life is a huge, moronic cretin modeled on a real person (or persons) Steinbeck discovered near Castroville. Webster Street, a friend of the author, recalls the occasion.

> One day we were coming back from Palo Alto on the way to Salinas and we stopped for a beer at a bar just outside Castroville. We were sitting there talking, and suddenly we heard the bartender speaking to somebody wearing bib overalls. We listened for a while. The bartender said, "And then what did you do?" and the guy went through all sorts of motions. He didn't talk with his fingers as in sign language, rather he illustrated what he did. He was mute, he could hear but could not speak. I'm certain that John based the story of "Johny Bear" [sic] on that episode. As a matter of fact, on the way back he said, "Did you pay attention to that fella, the guy in the overalls? You know he could do a lot of harm, that guy."[65]

Nelson Valjean explains the origins of the story differently. Valjean recounts how the young Steinbeck (like the narrator in "Johnny Bear") worked on a dredging barge near Castroville. Apparently disliking the meals served by the crew chef (as does the narrator), Steinbeck ate at the "little Bennet Hotel in Castroville." Inside the Bennet he regularly observed an unusual customer—a "dim-witted gorilla of a man whose hairy hands swung from powerful arms and nearly reached his knees." According to Valjean, Steinbeck's former superintendent on the dredger, R. B. Cozzens, is "convinced that this awesome boarder became John's prototype for the titular role in *Johnny Bear*."[66]

Actually, the story has less to do with this anthropoidal half-wit, than with the village of Loma, whose monuments to respectability—the Hawkins sisters—he topples. Johnny Bear frequents the Buffalo Bar, where he begs whiskey from patrons in a most unusual way. When anyone buys him a drink, Johnny Bear mimics voices he has secretly overheard. One evening the narrator, who works on a nearby swamp dredger, hears his own words and those of a woman he has been dating repeated by Johnny Bear. Their replayed conversation embarrasses everyone in the bar, especially the narrator. To earn another whiskey, Johnny Bear then mimics the voice of Emalin Hawkins scolding her sister, Amy, for indiscretion. An uncomfortable silence overtakes the bar, since the Hawkins sisters are the town's aristocrats. A few evenings later, Johnny Bear recites the sisters' words again, this time revealing that Amy has attempted suicide. Everyone in the bar is dumbstruck. But not so much as on a subsequent evening when Johnny discloses that the pregnant Amy Hawkins is dead. Buffalo Bar patrons are ashamed, for Loma's first family has been disgraced.

The story's title, "Johnny Bear," suggests that the plot revolves around the moronic half-wit who acts as "a kind of recording and reproducing device, only you use a glass of whiskey instead of a nickel" (164). Rather, the tale is primarily concerned with the fall from respectability of the Hawkins sisters and its repercussions in the community. Steinbeck, in fact, originally entitled the story "The Sisters." Although Loma's response to the supposed disgrace of the Hawkins women provides the story's central interest, the narrative contains other competing interests which flaw its structure, giving it what F. W. Watt has called a lack of coherence.[67]

The two most prominent competing interests are the swamp dredger subplot and Johnny Bear himself. Valjean, as mentioned above, documents Steinbeck's employment on a dredger "draining lakes and canals near Castroville." Thomas Kiernan reports that the work was "tedious and boring" but afforded the young Steinbeck an opportunity to observe the "illiterate, though colorfully and profanely articulate" men he was working with (who called him, incidentally, "Johnny boy").[68] While his ability to particularize these experiences lends the story an air of reality, Steinbeck's frequent references to the dredger barge and its freak accidents, suspicious cooks, and droning diesel engine seem cumbersome details cluttering the plot.

The other competing element is, of course, Johnny Bear. Steinbeck sometimes uses such "subnormal characters less as objects of interest in themselves than as vehicles for getting at otherwise hidden truths about others," according to French. Yet Johnny Bear remains so consistently in view during the story that Edmund Wilson has mistaken him for the protagonist. This strange cretin eavesdrops on unsuspecting citizens of Loma and then exposes their darkest secrets. Hence, Johnny Bear has been likened by Lisca to an artist who "holds a mirror up to mankind and reveals

Part 1. The Short Fiction: A Critical Analysis

through his mimetic talent the hidden festers of society."⁶⁹ Nonetheless, since this half-wit genius merely duplicates others' words
and actions, he cannot be said to be the story's protagonist—a
role played by the Hawkins sisters.

The secret sins of Emalin and Amy Hawkins constitute an entire
story in themselves. In these two sisters, Steinbeck creates the
prototype of the several Cain-Abel relationships in *East of Eden*
(1952). Caleb and Aron from that novel demonstrate the differences
between these opposite types: the one is cold, stern, calculating,
and even diabolical; the other, sensitive, warm, and compassionate.
Emalin Hawkins resembles the Cain figure, Amy the Abel. Emalin
is unsympathetic, even cruel, when the fragile Amy's midlife
passion for a Chinese share-cropper is aroused. Emalin's overriding
concern for the family's "respectability" most probably costs her
sister's life. Amy's repression leading to her death is symbolized
by the "check-rein" on the Hawkins's horse which is entirely "too
short" for comfort (157). While, to my knowledge, no real-life
models for these sisters have been found, Steinbeck's own high
school mathematics teacher was named, coincidentally, Emma
Hawkins.

But it is not these sisters, so much as what they represent, that
buttresses the village of Loma. We learn of their importance from
the narrator's friend, Alex Hartnell. "The Hawkins women, they're
symbols. They're what we tell our kids when we want to—well,
to describe good people" (154–55). We see this reflected in their
impressive home. According to Owens, "The Hawkins sisters'
aristocratic house, carefully walled in by a seemingly impenetrable
cypress hedge, is the small town's unfallen garden, and the sisters
bear the weight of this burden."⁷⁰ Their garden of pure virtue
must balance the moral murkiness, if not the blatant evil, of the
supposedly less scrupulous members of the community. Loma's
evil tendencies are symbolized by its fog and its "great swamp
like a hideous sin" (158). Fog imagery becomes a motif: "nasty
fog," (148), "evil-smelling fog" (154), and "slow squirming mist"
(155). And just before Johnny Bear reveals the dark secrets of
the Hawkins sisters, the fog clings to their cypress hedge. "Fog
balls were clustered about it and others were slowly moving in"
(164).

The story's surprise suicide ending—which hinges on the notion
that Amy Hawkins's pregnancy is doubly degrading since her lover

52

is a Chinese man—is by today's standards obviously racist. When Steinbeck wrote the story the fear of the "yellow peril" (rise and eventual dominance of the Chinese) was widely shared by Americans, especially Californians.[71] There are other hints of racial prejudice in this story and the next. Mae Romero, the "pretty half-Mexican girl" (148), has a reputation for looseness; though while Loma citizens consider her affairs insignificant, Amy Hawkins' liaison sends shock waves through the community.

"The Murder" (1934)

Such attitudes carry over in "The Murder," in which Jim Moore, befuddled by his Yugoslav wife, can barely resist calling her a "damn foreigner" (175). On his wedding day, Moore ignores his new father-in-law's advice. "Jelka is Slav girl. He's not like American girl. If he is bad, beat him. If he's good too long, beat him too. . . . He's not like a man that don't beat hell out of him" (173). Jelka becomes Moore's dutiful wife, though silent and aloof. Soon Moore seeks the companionship of the "noisy girls" at the Three Star in Monterey (174). One Saturday evening when riding to Monterey, he learns from George, a neighbor, that thieves have killed one of his calves. Moore returns home under a full moon to discover Jelka in bed with her male cousin. After a moment's reflection, Moore cocks his rifle, aims between the cousin's eyes, and pulls the trigger. Once a deputy sheriff dismisses the murder charge, Moore beats his wife bloody with a bull whip. Remarkably, Jelka smiles, fries her husband eggs, and becomes generally more personable.

Robert Murray Davis argues that many critics have gingerly sidestepped "The Murder" because this "enormously disturbing" story seems allied to the "John Wayne mystique that only a dominated woman and a dominant man will be happy together." Does "The Murder" actually illustrate that "some wives are happier when beaten regularly, and must be so treated if a marriage is not to result in adultery and violent retribution," as F. W. Watt has (ironically) proposed? This view may be unpalatable to some critics who fault the story for racial and antifeminist prejudices, and to others who detect a sexual double standard, since "Jim is not faithful, but he demands fidelity from his wife."[72] The most puzzling question about this "enormously disturbing" and radically different story is, finally, what lead Steinbeck to write it?

A likely explanation is that Steinbeck imaginatively re-created a real murder and wife beating. This might account for Jelka's behaving so unlike Elisa Allen, Mary Teller, and other female characters in *The Long Valley* when she readily accepts her husband's sexual double standard and acquiesces to (even desires) physical abuse from him. Robert M. Benton conjectures that the "The Murder" is indeed "an account of an actual event" very likely intended for *The Pastures of Heaven* (1932). Steinbeck once described his proposed material for *Pastures* in this way, "There have been two murders, a suicide, many quarrels and a great deal of unhappiness in the Pastures of Heaven." Of the two murders mentioned, however, he recounts only one in the book.[73] The second murder most likely evolved into the story presently under discussion. Not surprisingly, "The Murder" resembles most *Pastures* stories in setting, structure, and theme.

Roy S. Simmonds explains that "in the manuscript of 'The Murder' Steinbeck initially set the story in the Corral de Tierra [after which he modeled the Pastures] but subsequently, while the work was still in its primary manuscript stage, changed the setting to the Valle del Castillo."[74] Despite Steinbeck's attempts to disguise the *Pastures* landscape, we can see it clearly in his opening paragraph of "The Murder." "At the head of the canyon there stands a tremendous stone castle" (171). This natural sandstone formation, which in "The Murder" rises above the old Moore ranch, in real life stands sentinel over the Corral de Tierra.

The trouble with this stone castle, according to Brian Barbour, is that it has no bearing on the story. After Steinbeck's initial "painstaking" description, says Barbour, it is "never brought back into the story's movement." Owens argues, on the contrary, that this detail of setting is central to the story's outcome, since it symbolizes Jim Moore's "illusions of chivalry." Says Owens, the castle suggests the "chivalric code which dictates that it is barbarous and 'foreign' to beat a wife even if the wife's culture has conditioned her to expect or even desire the beating."[75]

"The Murder" also resembles in its ironic structure and theme the stories in Steinbeck's 1932 volume. In every *Pastures* tale the jinxed Munroe family precipitates a final disaster that destroys the illusions of the story's protagonist. Jim Moore's illusion that he can treat his Yugoslav wife according to American standards is shattered in much this way. As Lisca explains, "One need only substitute a Munroe for the 'George' who unexpectedly turns Jim back home to find his wife with her lover." Jim's discovery of Jelka's infidelity shocks him into reexamining his values and those of his wife. From this perspective, Davis argues that by the story's conclusion, Moore has finally become "a satisfactory husband and a complete human being." And Kiernan sees the story's lesson in similar terms. "People whose ethnic traditions and mores are different from those of the average American should be treated in light of those differences, even if they are so alien as to be incomprehensible."[76]

While the themes of shattered illusions and respect of cultural differences certainly can be found in the story, the "disturbing" elements of racism (or perhaps xenophobia), sexism, and murder remain. Jelka, as a "foreigner" and a woman, embodies the first two elements. Throughout the story Steinbeck depicts her as aloof, inscrutable, and *different*. "She spoke the language of [Jim's] race out of a mind that was foreign to his race" (174). More telling, though, are the images Steinbeck uses to describe her, in Benton's words, as a "domesticated farm animal."[77] "She was so much like an animal that sometimes Jim patted her head and neck under the same impulse that made him stroke a horse" (173). With her "eyes as large and questioning as a doe's eyes" (172), she "whimper[s]" with pleasure when Moore strokes her hair (174) and she "whine[s] softly, like a cold puppy," when her cousin is murdered (183). Thus, Steinbeck depicts Jelka as foreign and bestial, making her somewhat less than human.

As for the murder itself, the final "disturbing" or provocative element in the story, it would be difficult to deny that this scene, as Steinbeck describes it, is breathtaking. With few words, he rivets our attention. "Jim cocked his rifle. The steel click sounded through the house. . . . The front sight wavered a moment and then came to rest. . . . The gun crash tore the air. Jim, still looking down the barrel, saw the whole bed jolt under the blow" (183). Steinbeck ingeniously foreshadows the murder when Jim dips his hand into the water trough and "stir[s] the moon to broken, swirling streams of light" (182). Since Jelka's lover is identified with the moon throughout the story, Jim's deliberate fracturing of the white orb portends the lover's death.

"Saint Katy the Virgin" (1936)

A far cry from the drama of "The Murder" is "Saint Katy the Virgin," a "burlesque hagiography" set outside the long valley *and* the twentieth century. The backdrop for this combination beast fable and saint's life seems to be medieval Europe "in the year 13——" (189). Thus, Fontenrose calls "Saint Katy" a "maverick in the [*Long Valley*] collection," Benton describes it as "the one story that seems most out of place," and French, "conspicuously different in content and tone." Barbour complains further that "Saint Katy's" inclusion demonstrates Steinbeck's "lack of critical judgment," yet this "lack" must be attributed to Steinbeck's editor, Pascal Covici, who urged the author to include the story.[78]

In "Saint Katy the Virgin," a "bad man" named Roark tithes his wicked pig, Katy, to two brothers from the Monastery of M———. When Brother Paul slips a rope through the sow's nose ring, she bites Brother Colin's leg. Brother Paul kicks Katy in the snout and she chases them up a thorn tree. Hoping to exorcise her evil spirits, Brother Paul dangles an iron crucifix before the pig's eyes. Miraculously, she is redeemed. They lead her back to the monastery, where Father Benedict reprimands the brothers, since Katy—now a Christian—cannot be slaughtered. Nevertheless, through good deeds Katy proves herself worthy of canonization as a virgin (even though she has littered), and her bones become holy relics able to "cure female troubles and ringworm" (200).

Readers familiar with what Watt calls Steinbeck's "longstanding interest in things medieval," may not be surprised by the milieu of "Saint Katy the Virgin." Nelson Valjean explains that Steinbeck probably conceived of the story at Stanford University in 1925. When taking a course in European thought and culture, says Valjean, Steinbeck and some of his classmates so enjoyed Professor Edward Maslin Hulme's humorous remarks on canonization that they decided to investigate ancient hagiography on their own. When they read about a "nearsighted priest who rejoicingly baptized a flock of penguins which he mistook for people," the students "made a game of choosing the most unlikely candidates imaginable for sainthood." Steinbeck selected a pig. He apparently wrote a story (perhaps in verse form) about this pig, "who was turned from her sinful ways into channels of righteousness and a worker of miraculous cures."[79]

Valjean suggests that this college pig story may have been the earliest version of "Saint Katy the Virgin." French agrees that "Saint Katy" probably existed in some form prior to 1932 (its traditional date of composition), when, according to Elizabeth Otis, Steinbeck was supposed to have "dashed [it] off chiefly as an entertainment for himself." French argues that the tale "is written in the mannered, facetious style [Steinbeck] abandoned with the coming of the depression," and reflects an "attitude toward conventional religiosity" like that he also expressed in *Cup of Gold* (1929) and *To a God Unknown* (1933). "Saint Katy" also harkens back to such earlier satirical sketches as "Adventures in Arcademy" (1924), in which various animals represent Stanford University faculty and administrators. Yet, although Steinbeck may have composed some version of "Saint Katy" as early as 1925, it was not until eleven years later, in 1936, that Covici-Friede issued the tale privately as a monograph, "signed and limited to 199 copies."[80]

As much as Steinbeck has been criticized for writing about animals, "Saint Katy" is the only *Long Valley* story in which an animal acts as the protagonist. Although Katy, the pig, plays this role, her chief function seems to be to point out failings in human beings and human institutions. Steinbeck especially targets the Church for satire, but Watt claims that his "irreverent handling of the church is perhaps to be taken more as rough fun than serious criticism." In this spirit, Lisca enjoys the "hilarious parodies of medieval arguments concerning the power of exorcism, the nobility of the lion . . . , the power of the crucifix . . . , [and] the definition of virginity." And Stanley Young conjectures that "Voltaire would have loved Katy, but Disney will get her."[81]

Sanford E. Marovitz attempts an allegorical reading of the story based on the premise that Steinbeck may have "begun his sketch by writing ostensibly about medieval Europe while thinking, in fact, about the California coast." Marovitz suggests that the setting "P——" in the story signifies Pacific Grove, the "M——" Monterey, and the year "13——," a transposition of 1931, the year Steinbeck may have composed the final version of the story.[82] If Steinbeck indeed worked on it at this time, he would have been living in Pacific Grove and thus "Saint Katy" might comprise a veiled satire of this town and its people. This reading leaves unknown, however, the identities of Roark and his converted pig.

A final and perhaps more important question remains: Is "Saint Katy the Virgin" a tale only in good fun, or is it, on some level, to be taken seriously? Critics respond to this question variously. Some call it a "hilarious," "rollicking, grand story"; others, a "comedy of a lower kind," full of "bafoonery" and "clowning"; and still others complain that it "might better have been left in private circulation." The *Springfield Weekly Republican* perhaps best articulates this last group's sentiments. "Saint Katy the Virgin" "merely adds itself to the long catalogue of irreverent tales that have aimed satire and ridicule at priest and church since the close of the dark ages."[83]

The Red Pony Stories (1933–1936)

Critics have been almost unanimous in their acclaim for the four thematically linked stories that constitute *The Red Pony*—"The Gift" (1933), "The Great Mountains" (1933), "The Promise" (1937), and "The Leader of the People" (1936). Mizener credits this collection with "an integrity, a responsibility to experience and a consequent unity of surface and symbol" that Steinbeck never again achieved. Barbour calls it "a successful tale" containing some of "Steinbeck's most deeply felt work." And French praises the series as "one of [the author's] works in which form and content are most perfectly integrated."[84]

Considering Steinbeck's widely acknowledged success in crafting *The Red Pony,* one might not suspect that when he began writing these four stories he was bracing himself for his first encounter with the death of a loved one. It was summer 1933, and Olive Hamilton Steinbeck, the author's mother, had recently suffered a massive stroke.[85] He wrote to George Albee: "I don't know whether I told you that mother is now paralysed and will linger perhaps a year. It has been a bad time. . . . I have to fight an atmosphere of blue fog so thick and endless that I can see no opening in it."[86]

Later recalling this experience, Steinbeck was to say that facing death brings about "the first adulthood of any man or woman," and in his *Red Pony* stories he attempts to depict this painful process. In this sense, the four tales constitute a bildungsroman, which chronicles the autobiographical protagonist's path toward maturity. As Arnold L. Goldsmith points out (see his essay in part 3), Jody Tiflin, who begins the stories as a somewhat naive boy, undergoes an initiation into the reality of death, as well as the joy of new life.[87] In "The Gift" Jody endures the premature passing of his frisky pony, Gabilan. In "The Great Mountains" and "The Leader of the People," he contemplates the aging and eventual demise of the Indian, Gitano, and of Jody's own grandfather. And in "The Promise" the boy observes the violent end of the mare, Nellie, as she gives birth to a shiny new colt. The two omnipresent principles in these stories of death and life at first seem antithetical to Jody, as do the symbolic "opposites and enemies" on the Tiflin ranch that represent them, the black cypress and the green tub (269). Yet his initiation affords him the opportunity to see these seemingly opposite principles as one and the same.

Steinbeck maintains the third-person point of view throughout all four stories. Writing from the boy's perspective and occasionally entering his sometimes troubled mind, Steinbeck achieves a unique portrayal of life on a California ranch. Jody and the other characters are sketched economically and believably. Says Arthur Mizener, "We are wholly convinced by Jody's feelings for the life of nature and by its culmination in his love for his red pony and his grief at its death." Billy Buck, the old Indian Gitano, and Jody's pioneer grandfather are equally compelling, as are the many animals in these stories: Gabilan the pony, Nellie the mare, and Smasher and Doubletree Mutt, Jody's rambunctious dogs. No wonder, then, that critics have universally praised this story cycle, which Harry Thornton Moore says "crowns" *The Long Valley* collection.[88] Without doubt, *The Red Pony* is one of Steinbeck's finest achievements in short fiction.

"The Gift" (1933)

Originally entitled "The Red Pony," "The Gift" begins Jody's initiation. The story recounts how Carl Tiflin's gift of a pony to the ten-year-old Jody teaches him some difficult lessons. Jody names the untrained colt Gabilan, after the sunny eastern mountains bordering the Tiflin ranch. With cowhand Billy Buck's guidance, the boy begins in late summer to halter-train Gabilan, hoping to ride him before the winter rains. But this hope is never realized. Left in the corral one day, Gabilan gets soaked in a downpour and Billy Buck neglects to lead him to shelter. The pony becomes dreadfully ill, and the guilt-ridden cowhand is unable to revive him. Near death early one morning, Gabilan staggers out of the Tiflin barn into the fields, where Jody finds him circled by buzzards. Although the boy bludgeons one of the huge black birds, Gabilan cannot be saved.

Jody's attack on the buzzard seems to be his attempt to strike back at death for taking Gabilan. The boy's developing awareness of death becomes an important stride toward his maturity.[89] But even though his pony dies, Jody also experiences the wonders of new life. When he ascends to the brush line of the Tiflin ranch, Jody frequently looks down on the "great black kettle under the cypress tree . . . where the pigs were scalded" and then turns back to see the cold spring that runs into a "green mossy tub" (206). The brush line is his place of retreat and contemplation, and his several trips there during the story reveal his growth and change. When he ascends the first time (before receiving Gabilan) he senses "an uncertainty in the air, a feeling of change and of loss and of the gain of new and unfamiliar things" (206). These premonitions foreshadow coming events. Once he has acquired the red pony, Jody finds new enthusiasm for life. This enthusiasm quickly fades, however, when the pony falls ill. Just before Gabilan's death, Jody again ascends to the brush line and sits on the "mossy tub" in view of the "dark cypress tree." To his eyes, the "place was familiar, but curiously changed" (235). Actually, the landscape itself has not altered as much as the boy who perceives it. Jody himself has changed as a result of his pony's brief days on the Tiflin ranch.

Besides the black cypress and green tub, Steinbeck employs other images in the story that evoke the cycle of death and life. According to Goldsmith, these include the change of seasons, "the buzzards flying overhead, the life and death of Jody's pony Gabilan, and the death of the buzzard Jody kills."[90] The turning of the seasons, for example, parallels Gabilan's brief life and premature death. The story begins in the bright sunshine of late summer (when Gabilan arrives at the Tiflin ranch), continues through the stubble fields and lengthening shadows of fall, and concludes in the dark and rainy winter (when the pony dies). On the day of Gabilan's death, young grass (a "new green crop of volunteer" [231]) has already surfaced, indicating the coming of spring and suggesting the perpetuity of life (237).

Just as spring grass betokens new life, buzzards are obvious symbols of death. Early in the story Steinbeck introduces these dark and unwelcome visitors when "two big black buzzards [sail] low to the ground," indicating an "animal had died in the vicinity" (206). That Jody knows the meaning of these predators (he "hate[s] them" [206]) becomes clear in the conclusion when he spots "a high circle of black buzzards" hovering over his dying pony (237). Although the boy understands that the birds signal the demise of his pony, he cannot fathom how these winged predators of death have a legitimate place in nature. When he grabs one before it can fly away, its "red fearless eyes" gaze at him, "impersonal and unafraid and detached" (238). Death, as Jody sees it in the bird's red eyes, preys on its victims with blank indifference.

"The Great Mountains" (1933)

The theme of death continues in the next story, "The Great Mountains," as Jody contemplates the approaching demise of the venerable Indian, Gitano, and of the Tiflin's decrepit horse, Easter. Jody again retreats to the brush line where the "mossy tub" brimming with cold spring water helps him assimilate these further experiences (240). An additional element in this second *Red Pony* story is Jody's fascination with the great, brooding mountains separating the Tiflin ranch from the Pacific Ocean. Jody's fascination constitutes, in Owens' words, the "blossoming of [his] questing impulse, his desire to transcend the known and secure world" for the dark and mysterious "Great Ones," the rugged Santa Lucia Mountains.[91]

Gitano appears one summer day, announcing that he has come home to die. According to the Indian, the Tiflin acreage was once the site of his family rancho, making it a fitting place for him to spend his last days. Carl Tiflin disagrees, ordering the old Indian to leave by the next morning. Jody visits Gitano that evening in the bunkhouse and marvels at his gleaming rapier with a golden basket hilt. By morning the old man has disappeared into the "Great Mountains"; he is riding Easter, whom Carl Tiflin (tacitly comparing him to Gitano) has said is worthless and ought to be shot. When Jody lifts his eyes toward the mountains and thinks he sees a crawling speck, the thought of Gitano, his sword, and the "Great Ones" saddens him.

The death theme in the story is suggested by the "Great Mountains," by the ancient horse, Easter, and by the old Indian, Gitano. The "Great Ones" loom as the most powerful symbol of death and its mystery. As we saw in Pepé Torres' attempt to flee his pursuers in "Flight," Steinbeck frequently uses the Santa Lucias as a region of death.[92] To Jody these western mountains seem forboding, "impersonal," and "aloof" (242). Thus when comparing the dark and brooding "Great Ones" to the bright and "jolly" Gabilan range to the east, Jody shivers "a little at the contrast" (242). Like Easter and Gitano, these mountains evoke the unfathomable mystery of death, a mystery Jody is confronted with again in this story as he was in "The Gift."

The thirty-year-old horse, Easter, comes to be identified with Gitano. Both are, in the Indian's words, "too old to work" and both "just [eat] and pretty soon [die]" (249). Both make similar separate entrances "over the brow of the hill" on the Tiflin ranch. And both are so thin that bones jut out under their skin, and they hobble or walk in hard jerks (243, 248). Carl Tiflin underscores these similarities. When he says, "It's a shame not to shoot Easter. . . . It'd save him a lot of pains and rheumatism," Carl looks "secretly at Gitano, to see whether he noticed the parallel" (249). Not surprisingly, an affinity develops between the old Indian and Easter. When Gitano makes "a curious sharp sound with his lips," Easter ambles over and allows him to rub "the lean neck under [his] mane" (250).

While Easter's name suggests resurrection and life everlasting, Gitano at first seems to represent only death. Thus, he is received on the Tiflin ranch as an unwelcome visitor. Carl Tiflin tells Gitano, "Don't come to die with strangers" (246). But the natural cycle of life and death moves the Indian to return to his place of birth, even though the Tiflins refuse to accommodate him. While the elder Tiflins see only trouble in Gitano, Jody recognizes his abiding dignity and marvels at his gleaming rapier. Richard F. Peterson argues that this rapier, with its golden hilt, links the old Indian with the tradition of the quest for the holy grail. Peterson sees Gitano as a "maimed king" who inspires a younger quester (Jody) to restore his wasted kingdom (the Tiflin ranch?).[93] Thus, like Easter, Gitano himself suggests renewal, if not resurrection and perpetual life.

At the story's end, Jody ascends again to the brush line to contemplate the meaning of Gitano's brief but momentous visit. As we learn earlier in the story, even during the dry summer season, a "stretch of fine green grass" grows where "the spring-pipe fill[s] the round tub and the tub spill[s] over" (240). Jody retreats to this perpetually green spot to contemplate the lessons of life and death he has learned. Whether he knows it or not, Jody's "sympathies have been broadened" by this experience.[94]

"The Promise" (1937)

While both "The Gift" and "The Great Mountains" deal with the cycle of life and death, in "The Promise," Steinbeck presents this central theme even more graphically. To replace Gabilan (who has died in the first story), Carl Tiflin offers a newborn colt to his son if he will work off the cost of impregnating their mare, Nellie. One spring afternoon Jody walks the mare to Jess Taylor's ranch to be bred by the wild and powerful black stallion, Sundog. After the mare's conception, Jody waits nearly a year for her to foal. On the dark night when Nellie's pregnancy reaches full term, she struggles painfully in labor. Realizing her foal is turned the wrong way, Billy Buck tries to right the colt inside of Nellie. When this fails, he quickly grabs for a horseshoe hammer and lets it fall on her forehead until she dies. With his pocket knife, the ranch hand saws the tough belly and delivers a slick black colt. Billy lays the wet bundle at Jody's feet and explains: "There's your colt. I promised. And there it is. I had to do it—had to" (278–79).

A healthy colt has been born at the cost of the mare's life. And once again, Steinbeck suggests the interrelatedness of these two principles—death and life—with the black cypress and the green tub. As in the two earlier stories, the blackness of the cypress (traditionally a funereal tree) and the killing that occurs under its boughs represent death. Once, while standing under the black cypress and contemplating the birth of his promised colt, Jody becomes disturbed. "It seem[s] to him an unlucky thing to be thinking of his colt in the very slaughter place. . . . To counteract any evil result of that bad conjunction he walk[s] quickly . . . to the brush line" until he reaches the "green grass" and "trilling water" of the old tub (269). This "thin stream of spring water [running] into an old green tub" stands for life itself. Its surroundings perpetually cool and green, even in the dry, brown days of summer, the mossy tub again becomes a place of refuge for Jody. During times of change and crisis, the "cool green grass and singing water [soothe] him" (268).

With the black cypress and the green tub forming the dialectic of his life, Jody continues his strides toward maturity begun in the earlier *Red Pony* stories. Although to Jody the fact of death has by now become unequivocal, the nature of procreation remains somewhat a mystery. In "The Promise," however, he witnesses not only the birth of Nellie's colt, but also Nellie's breeding with Sundog. From these he learns that just as the onset of death can be turbulent (recall Gabilan's last hours), so too the creation of new life. Jody's looking on as Nellie couples with the stallion introduces the boy to the mysteries of sexual union. During Nellie's conception and long gestation, Jody even participates vicariously as an imaginary sire and expectant father. For example, when Nellie nears her time of delivery, Jody grows nervous, worried, even "frantic" (274). And like a stereotypical father-to-be, when he daydreams about his newborn colt, he feels "warm and proud" (274). Thus, although his knowledge of sexuality remains imperfect owing to his youth, Jody at least begins to recognize sex as a foundation of life.[95]

Reinforcing this sexual theme, Steinbeck depicts the seasonal habits (especially breeding habits) of various birds and animals. When the story opens and spring is in the air, a "green odor" lingers on the hillsides spurring frenzied energy in horses, lambs, and "young clumsy calves" (257). Nellie becomes "crazy as a coot" (262). On fences, "blackbirds," "meadowlarks" and "wild doves" sing with rejuvenated vigor (262). Some of this jubilation in both birds and animals seems to imply sexual arousal, such as when Nellie, in heat, backs up against a gate, "rubbing her buttocks on the heavy post" (259, 261). Later, ripening "wild oats" (265) suggest Nellie's fertilization and pregnancy. As Jody leads Nellie to be bred with Sundog, the boy passes these wild oats along the road, "whose heads were just clearing their scabbards" (262). The phallic implication of their "heads" is echoed by the aroused Sundog's "stiff, erected nostrils" (263). Once Nellie is impregnated, Steinbeck again employs the "wild oat" image—this time to suggest the onerousness of gestation and birth. Like Nellie, "the wild oats were ripening. Every head bent sharply under its load of grain" (265).

Further suggesting the life cycle, Steinbeck evokes the vivid colors of the seasons, from the spring day when Nellie is bred to the winter night when she dies bearing her colt. The story opens in the "green and gold" of spring, with its cast of "silver" leaves, "blue" snakes, "yellow" grasshoppers, and "gold-" stomached horned toads (256–57). As the narrative progresses through the year, Steinbeck rarely misses an opportunity to brighten the story with seasonal colors. With the coming of summer, he evokes the "yellowing hillsides" (264). In the "warm bright autumn" he notes that "the poison oak turn[s] red" (270). Finally, when winter approaches he says that the hills blacken under the steady rain (273) and the nights become "black and thick" (275), so black that on the tragic night of Nellie's death, "no light . . . penetrate[s] into the cup of the ranch" (277). This cycle of the seasons fills nearly an entire year, though the narrative cuts off abruptly in midwinter (the February night when Nellie dies), rather than returning to the spring where it began.

Like the changing of the seasons, "The Promise" is ultimately a story of transition, a chronicle of Jody's uncertain strides toward maturity in light of his exposure to the relationship between death and procreation. Jody discovers not only this relationship, but also the sexual union of male and female. The implications of the latter are perhaps more difficult for him to comprehend than those of the former. Though arguably more experienced at the story's end than at its beginning, Jody remains both a child and an adult; his behavior varies from uncannily mature to surprisingly puerile. To help himself assimilate the profound facts of death and procreation, he retreats, as always, to the ridge line on the Tiflin ranch, to contemplate the "opposites and enemies" that symbolize them—the black cypress and the green tub (269).

"The Leader of the People" (1936)

"The Leader of the People" marks a departure from the three previous stories and was not included in the original *Red Pony* volume (1937). While sharing the same setting and, with one important exception, many of the same characters with these other tales, in "The Leader of the People" Jody's initiation into the mysteries of life and death becomes secondary to Steinbeck's emerging interest in group behavior. Steinbeck embodies this interest in the story's dominant character, Jody's nostalgic grandfather, a veteran wagon train leader of the westward movement who reminisces about long phalanxes of humanity crossing the prairie. The old man's memories of "westering" with the "great crawling beast" become the central focus of the story, as he passes along the lore of his unique generation to an appreciative grandson. Some critics question whether the grandfather's tales of "westering" constitute simply another lesson on Jody's path toward maturity or whether these tales instead comprise, in Donald Houghton's words, "an unfortunate, confusing, and unnecessary digression which tears at the emotional and thematic unity of the story."[96]

Steinbeck composed "The Leader of the People" in 1934 when, inspired by his biologist friend, Ed Ricketts, he began speculating about group behavior. Evidence of this speculation can be found in several works composed from 1934 through the early 1940s, such as the short stories "The Raid" (1934) and "The Vigilante" (1936) and the longer works *In Dubious Battle* (1936), *The Grapes of Wrath* (1939), *The Sea of Cortez* (1941), and *The Moon Is Down* (1942). Each of these, to some degree, reflects Steinbeck's notion of a group as an entity with desires, hungers, and strivings of its own that actually controls the behavior of the units (individual humans or animals) that constitute it. As noted above, Steinbeck called such an aggregation of units a "phalanx." Like Mike in "The Vigilante," Jody's grandfather is one of Steinbeck's archetypal "unit-men," since he lives fully only when he is part of a group ("a whole bunch of people made into one big crawling beast" [302]) or when he reminisces about these experiences.[97]

Not all of the grandfather's "westering" stories, however, serve merely to illustrate Steinbeck's theory of the "group man." Robert Morsberger argues that these stories, in fact, constitute "the crucial experience" in the grandfather's generation, and hence are the "basis of the generation gap" between Jody and the old man.[98] In this sense, the grandfather resembles a bard in the tradition of Homer and Beowulf, transmitting oral history to a new generation. When he tells his grandson about hunting Indians (291), eating buffalo meat (293), and defending the circle of covered wagons (295), the old pioneer passes on the lore of his generation to a willing listener from a younger generation.

At the end of the story, however, when the dejected old man mentions "the big crawling beast," he seems to become a mouthpiece for Steinbeck's theory of the "group man." As Philip J. West points out, the grandfather's final speech marks a stylistic change in the story from the heroic to the elegiac.[99] The old pioneer, who begins as a poet and seer, concludes as a petty and pitiful figurehead who did not so much lead the people as merely front their column. In his own words: "If I hadn't been there, someone else would have been the head. The thing had to have a head" (302). Thus his heroic stature diminishes as he paints a much-altered picture of his role in "westering."

The grandfather's last speech also departs from the hunting motif established in his earlier tales (of soldiers, buffalo, and Indians), this hunting motif being linked to the prominent symbol in the story—Jody's mice hunt. Jody's hunt and the mice themselves take on various meanings as the story progresses. The story opens with Jody's joyous anticipation of slaughtering the "plump, sleek, arrogant mice" who have been living comfortably for many months in a haystack. To Jody the mice are big game, and he imagines himself in pursuit of them as a heroic hunter like his grandfather; next, the old man (perhaps jokingly) says Jody's hunt is typical of "the people of this generation" who have stooped to hunting tiny vermin; and finally, since the mice are "smug in their security, overbearing and fat" in their haystack, they further suggest degeneration and, in John V. Hagopian's words, the "tame and settled mode of life" of the present generation.[100] This symbolic use of the furry creatures anticipates Steinbeck's later treatment of them in *Of Mice and Men* (1937).

Even though "The Leader of the People" departs significantly from the thematic patterns of the three earlier *Red Pony* stories, we can nonetheless see some evidence of the cycle of life and death established in them. The grandfather, for example, represents an ambiguous combination of these two principles. Dressed almost entirely in black ("black broadcloth suit," "black tie," and "black slouch hat") and reaching the Tiflin ranch when the "lowering sun" casts dark flickering shadows (290), the old man obviously suggests death. Yet conversely, as James C. Work points out, the venerable pioneer also represents a primitive, life-renewing force introduced into the somewhat isolated and stagnant existence of the Tiflin ranch.[101]

The grandfather is old in body yet, like his grandson, young in spirit; both, as Howard D. Pearce indicates, are romantic dreamers compared to the more matter-of-fact, if not pedestrian, Carl Tiflin.[102] Pearce also notes the recurring images of blackness and whiteness in the story, which further suggest patterns of death and life. A "flock of white pigeons" perch in the black cypress tree, for example, until Jody throws a stone and starts the white birds in flight (283). This is the only mention of the black cypress in the story, while the green tub, which represents life and renewal elsewhere in *The Red Pony*, is absent. It is perhaps noteworthy, finally, that "The Leader of the People"—the atypical tale in the series—has become the *Red Pony* story most hotly debated by critics and one of Steinbeck's most frequently anthologized works.

"From Salinas to the World": Stories of the 1940s and 1950s*

Although Steinbeck's best-known short fiction appears in *The Long Valley*, this collection comprises only about one-third of his canon in the genre. The *Pastures of Heaven* (1932) contains at least nine complete tales, and Steinbeck published another dozen or more uncollected stories during the 1940s and 1950s. Since *Pastures*, as a short story cycle, displays slight generic differences from other texts analyzed in part 1, it is discussed in the final section. In the present section, we examine the uncollected stories.

During the 1940s and 1950s Steinbeck wrote and sold short pieces to such popular magazines as *Colliers, Harper's, Playboy, Reader's Digest, Punch,* and the *Atlantic.* These later stories—including two O. Henry Award–winners—were never gathered in a single volume, though some appear in Kiyoshi Nakayama's *Uncollected Stories of John Steinbeck* (Japan, 1986). Steinbeck's work from this period differs from his *Long Valley* tales in several ways: while nearly every story of the 1930s, as we have seen, reveals the author's identification with that region in California known as "Steinbeck Country," settings in the later works become more national and international in scope. Steinbeck takes us abroad to England, northern Africa, Mexico, France, and then home again to the America of his youth (California) and of his later years (New York).

The frequently urban settings of these later stories radically change the atmosphere of Steinbeck's fiction: as a close observer of nature in *The Long Valley,* he draws crisp images of the floral and animal life around the Salinas Valley; in his uncollected tales

* This chapter originally appeared as "Uncollected Stories of the 1940s and 50s" in R. S. Hughes, *Beyond the Red Pony: A Reader's Companion to Steinbeck's Complete Short Stories* (Metuchen, N.J.: Scarecrow Press, 1987), 105–25. Reprinted by permission of the publisher. The chapter title, "From Salinas to the World," is used by permission of Shigeharu Yano.

of the 1940s and 1950s, however, he often turns indoors to domestic scenes, sometimes modeling characters after members of his own immediate family. Noticeably absent are such "strong women" as Elisa Allen in "The Chrysanthemums" (1937) and such animal-like and grotesque creatures as the titular character in "Johnny Bear" (1937). Beginning in the late 1940s, stories became increasingly autobiographical. In tales like "His Father" (1949), Steinbeck paints thinly veiled portraits of himself: an urban, middle-class family man (or divorced father) preoccupied with the concerns of his children.

Besides Steinbeck's tendency to use himself and his family as characters, another striking feature of these later stories is their diversity in style: loose and episodic ("The Summer Before" [1955]), tight, spare, and objective ("How Mr. Hogan Robbed a Bank" [1956]), allegorical ("The Short-Short Story of Mankind" [1955]), as well as the elevated, Poesque style of "Affair at 7, Rue de M——" (1955). Steinbeck also introduces several new themes including divorce, nuclear holocaust, and a child's discovery of sexual differences. At the same time, he continues to develop familiar themes of the 1930s, such as respectability, as in his first story published during the 1940s, "How Edith McGillcuddy Met R. L. Stevenson."

"How Edith McGillcuddy Met R. L. Stevenson" (1941)

Although the story was published in August 1941, Steinbeck composed the O. Henry Memorial Award–winning "How Edith McGillcuddy Met R. L. Stevenson" seven years earlier in 1934.[1] With its careful descriptions of flowers, birds, and animals of the Salinas Valley, "Edith McGillcuddy" reminds one of "The White Quail" (1935) and "The Chrysanthemums" (1937), both written during the same period. The narrative, based on a true incident told to Steinbeck by Mrs. Edith Wagner, begins one Sunday morning in Salinas during the summer of 1879. Twelve-year-old Edith ambles innocently toward Sunday school when she is enticed by the barefooted Suzy Nugger to ride a funeral train to Monterey. Once at the cemetery, Edith wanders to the seashore and stumbles upon a frowzy little girl named Lizzie, who leads her to an unusual couple: a woman who smokes cigarettes and a long-haired man. Lizzie disappears, leaving Edith behind to enjoy tea with her congenial hosts. When the whistle of the returning funeral train blows, Edith scurries away, and the tale ends. "That was how Edith McGillcuddy met Robert Louis Stevenson."[2]

While the ostensible point of Edith's journey is her chance meeting with the Scottish writer,[3] Steinbeck focuses greater attention on her position in the moral and social hierarchy of frontier Salinas. According to Steinbeck, in 1879 the "dirty little California cow-town" of Salinas consisted of three moral elements: the "vicious," the "wavering," and the "good." Although the McGillcuddys are a pious family who belong to the "good" element, Edith occasionally drifts toward the "vicious" "in the manner of the company she [keeps]" (559). Steinbeck's three-part division of the community is particularly evident on the funeral train. Passengers riding in the front cars belong to the "good" people of Salinas: "ladies and gentlemen in black formal clothes [sitting] stiffly" (562), along with the officiating priest. These are the town's stern and righteous citizens. Cars further back carry Salinas's "wavering" populace—"less formal" riders crowding together with their "lunch baskets and paper bags and cans of milk" cluttered between the seats (563). Upon seeing this middle group, Edith sighs with relief that she and Suzy are "not the only ones who were combining a funeral and a free train ride" (563). The "vicious" layer—frequenters of the town's twenty saloons, as well as Suzy Nugger and her ilk—ride in the last car, where several boys are fighting, snatching the caps of passengers, and throwing them from the speeding train. Thus, Steinbeck seats passengers according to their social position in the community. The nearer to the front of the train, the closer they are to the priest and the "good" element—and hence to "respectability."

But even as Steinbeck divides the train's passengers into a social hierarchy, he begins to blur these distinctions with colorful floral and animal imagery. As the train puffs away from the station, its bell tolling mournfully, wind rushes by, blowing flowers and ruffling women's dresses and the priest's surplice. In the stir created by the departing train, sparrows and blackbirds take to wing, ladies push back their veils to gobble sandwiches, and children throw "orange peels and apple cores at one another" (564). The birds, veiled women, ruffled priest, and frolicking children all embraced by the flower-perfumed breeze emphasize the oneness of all things. Even the locomotive becomes a part of this indivisible whole, personified as an iron horse with head of billowing black smoke, and belly puffing clouds of vapor. Steinbeck seems to suggest that, moral and social hierarchy notwithstanding, all passengers ride on the same train to the same destination.

Even though the various layers of Salinas life commingle on the funeral train, none of its passengers can shift from one element to another as does Edith. Once she leaves home neatly dressed for Sunday school, Edith's deteriorating appearance reflects her fall from the best level of Salinas society to the worst: when she climbs aboard the train with Suzy, Edith's "stiff and perfect" pink hair ribbon—signifying the "good" element—is ruined (560); she scuffs her brightly polished shoes; her face becomes "streaked with red" (563) from an all-day sucker Suzy gives her. And finally, Edith tears the knee out of one of her stockings (563). By the time Edith's journey is complete, she resembles a waif like her low-life companions, Suzy and Lizzie.

In this soiled and disheveled condition, Edith meets Robert Louis Stevenson—the "long-haired young man" whose eyes are "shining with fever" (570). Stevenson's sickly appearance, according to Roy S. Simmonds, can be attributed to "almost a month of hardship spent crossing the Atlantic and the North American continent" to be reunited with his beloved, Fanny Osborne.[4] Edith's brief encounter with Stevenson and his companion—while no doubt the origin of Steinbeck's interest in the tale—fills only a small part of the narrative. Steinbeck devotes the larger portion to the theme of dubious "respectability," showing how the daughter of a "good" Salinas family, in order to meet the renowned author, must be lured from her righteous (if somewhat hesitant) path toward Sunday school by the "wavering" and "vicious" elements of this burgeoning frontier town. "How Edith McGillcuddy Met R. L. Stevenson" is perhaps the most poetically sensitive story Steinbeck published during the 1940s and 1950s. While a masterpiece in subtlety and tone, the story also demonstrates some of Steinbeck's most effective—because nearly imperceptible—social criticism.

Wartime Stories (1943)

One bibliographical challenge in the study of Steinbeck's short fiction of this period involves the author's *New York Herald Tribune* dispatches from the European theater during World War II. As we can observe from the selection of these in *Once There Was a War* (1958), Steinbeck the journalist is often indistinguishable from Steinbeck the fiction writer. Is "Craps," for example, an impressionistic account of an actual event?[5] Is it fictionalized, and therefore a short story? Or is it a little of both? Some pieces in *Once There Was a War,* like "Bob Hope" (88–91) and "Lilli Marlene" (62–65), cannot be mistaken for fiction, but others like "Craps" certainly can.

In the introduction to his 1958 volume, Steinbeck says, "The events set down here did happen" (xi). Yet in the same breath he confesses that some of the pieces are "fairy tales. . . . They are as real as the wicked witch and the good fairy, as true and tested and edited as any other myth" (xx–xxi). Moreover, Steinbeck closes the introduction as if he were launching into a fictional narrative. "There was a war, long ago—once upon a time" (xxi). Most critics agree that at least some of the dispatches in *Once There Was a War* are fictional. French remarks that "some of the reports . . . have an embryonic fictional form." Similarly, Lisca says, "occasionally, the communiqués are in the form of short stories."[6]

Steinbeck often attributes his war "stories" to someone other than himself. He begins "Craps," for example, by calling it "one of Mulligan's lies" (112). Similarly, in "The Cottage That Wasn't There" (68), he introduces an army sergeant to narrate the tale. Steinbeck very seldom takes responsibility for what he says in *Once There Was a War.* "I never admitted having seen anything myself. In describing a scene I invariably put it in the mouth of someone else" (xvi). Consequently, the reader is hard-pressed to find a single "I" in the entire volume. On those infrequent occasions when Steinbeck refers to himself, he does so obliquely by saying, "this writer" (102).

By doing this, Steinbeck distances himself from his subjects, who are predominantly quick-witted enlisted men like Private Big Train Mulligan (84, 102), Eddie the crapshooter (112), and Sligo the clever deserter (130). In other words, Steinbeck covers the "human interest" stories—"the hopes, fears, and activities of 'G.I. Joes' under the various conditions of war."[7] Occasionally he focuses on the few lieutenants and captains among the men; but for the most part his heart belongs to the little guys who fight for their country and their lives, without much say in how the battle lines are drawn. The protagonists in *Once There Was a War,* then, are like the Joads in *The Grapes of Wrath* (1939): common people caught up in forces beyond their control, yet usually with the will and cleverness enough to endure.

One dispatch in which Steinbeck obviously colors facts with fancy is "The Story of an Elf" (190–94), first reprinted in 1944 as "The Elf in Algiers."[8] The story takes place in the Alletti Hotel in Algiers amidst a gathering of thirsty war correspondents and a British consul. Suddenly in a puff of blue smoke, a small elf appears. The leprechaun introduces himself as "Charlie Lytle," a self-appointed provider of happiness for weary troops and journalists. At the request of one reporter, the elf causes three cases of Haig and Haig scotch to materialize out of nowhere. The delighted men call it a miracle. But one of them, Jack Belden, is unconvinced. He asks for a bottle of "La Blatt's Pale India Ale," and instantly Charlie Lytle produces it. That night the euphoric correspondents find that they even enjoy an air raid.

"The Story of an Elf" is obviously one of the "fairy tales" Steinbeck refers to in his introduction to *Once There Was a War* (xx). That the piece is fabricated from his own imagination is evidenced by Steinbeck's long-standing interest in leprechauns. When a student at Stanford, Steinbeck often told stories to his friends about ghosts and elves. One such story, recalls Stanford classmate Frank Fenton, involved a "blue leprechaun who flung a ham on the floor." Steinbeck, says Fenton, "insisted that leprechauns and elves were very real."[9] The similarities between this early elf story and the later one appearing in *Once There Was a War* are too obvious to mention. Steinbeck had apparently managed to keep alive his fascination with leprechauns even through the war.

One example of a dispatch that Steinbeck puts "in the mouth of someone else" (xvi) is "The Cottage That Wasn't There" (68–71). The narrative opens in London near Hyde Park's lake Serpentine, where a sergeant lying in the grass begins to narrate what he calls a "ghost story" (68–69). The sergeant explains that one night when walking along a country road, he saw a light shining in the window of a cottage. Inside the scene was pleasant: a small fireplace, a white cat, and a woman, about fifty, sewing. The sergeant was puzzled that the cottage had no blackout curtains, yet he decided not to question its inhabitants. Even more puzzling, however, was the soldier's later recollection that there is no cottage on that country road, only the bombed-out remains of one. This worries him because, as he tells us, he doesn't "believe stuff like that" (71). In "The Cottage That Wasn't There" Steinbeck cannot be accused of telling half-truths or lies, because evidently he records the sergeant's tale exactly as he heard it. Nevertheless, the resulting narrative has all the earmarks of a short story, including an O. Henry surprise ending. True facts seldom arrange themselves in such tight dramatic form. Yet, similar surprise endings occur in other stories Steinbeck borrows from talkative G.I.s.

Such a tale is "Craps" (112–16). That Steinbeck repeats this story secondhand has already been established. "This is one of Mulligan's lies" (112), he confesses. Mulligan is "Private Big Train Mulligan" (84, 102), the subject of two earlier dispatches in *Once There Was a War*. "Craps" features a wizard crapshooter named Eddie who never loses on Sunday. Several crap games spring up when Eddie's troop ship sails on Tuesday, but he resists them until Sunday when stakes become higher and he knows he can win. He walks into the hottest game on deck and begins to win big. Suspense builds as he rolls for the largest pot of the day. Snake eyes! Eddie loses. In disbelief, he gasps, "I win on Sunday, always win on Sunday" (116). Then a sergeant explains that before Eddie's fateful roll, the ship had crossed the international date line and, by doing so, Sunday was lost. This unexpected conclusion suggests that, rather than merely a factual dispatch, "Craps" is a consciously crafted narrative.

Given the example of "Craps" and the other wartime stories discussed above, how are we to evaluate Steinbeck's insistant remark, "The events set down here did happen" (xi)? We can certainly believe Steinbeck's claim that someone (such as a puzzled sergeant or a Private Big Train Mulligan) told him these stories. Yet does this mean that the events depicted actually took place? Steinbeck's cautionary words provide the most reliable answer: these pieces are "as real as the wicked witch and the good fairy, as true and tested and edited as any other myth" (xxi).

"The Time the Wolves Ate the Vice-Principal" (1947)

Four years after filing his sometimes fanciful dispatches from the war, Steinbeck published a shockingly different kind of story in the obscure *'47, Magazine of the Year.* "The Time the Wolves Ate the Vice-Principal" (March 1947) is a rejected interchapter from *Cannery Row* (1945), which Steinbeck's publishers concluded bore "little relationship to the rest of the book."[10] In addition to its gruesome violence, the tale's Salinas backdrop makes it unfit for Steinbeck's novel set among the sardine canneries of Monterey.

Written in the objective, spare style of "Flight" (1938), "The Time the Wolves Ate the Vice-Principal" describes the grisly slaughter of Mr. Hartley, an ailing high school administrator.[11] Early one morning a pack of wolves gathers on the lawn of the Salinas courthouse. One great gray wolf leads them through the streets to an old Airedale, which they instantly devour. Next they come upon Mr. Loman, who is opening his music store. Fortunately, Loman spots them and quickly slams the door. Finally, the wolves pick up the scent of Mr. Hartley. Although Hartley sees them coming a block away, his flight is in vain. The wolves catch him on Mrs. Harris's porch and rip him to pieces. The sleeping Mrs. Harris doesn't even wake up.

"The Time the Wolves Ate the Vice-Principal" provides yet another example of Steinbeck's "phalanx" theory, showing how several stray animals, given a leader, can be transformed into a ravenous "gray mass." They sniff aimlessly on the courthouse lawn until the great gray wolf appears and then "a kind of purpose" comes on them (26). The story also demonstrates Steinbeck's ability to shape even the sparest materials into a naturalistic drama. Clearly, in this tale only the fittest survive. Of the wolves' intended victims, two are aged and infirm, and cannot defend themselves. The Airedale is "dignified," but "so old he did not smell [the wolves] coming" (26). The convalescing vice-principal, Mr. Hartley, runs too slowly to escape them. Only the "fit" character—the sharp-eyed and quick Mr. Logan—survives.

Beyond these phalanx and Darwinian themes, in "Wolves" Steinbeck attacks "respectable" society's insensitivity and moral indifference. That Mrs. Harris slumbers through the vice-principal's slaughter is an example of this dangerous complacency. According to French, Steinbeck believed that such lax attitudes helped to facilitate World War II, a war he had just witnessed on several fronts before he wrote this gruesome tale.[12] Given its compactness and unity of effect, "The Time the Wolves Ate the Vice-Principal" is a satisfying tale. Its coldly objective description of Mr. Hartley's slaughter reminds one of Steinbeck's unsentimental account of propagating and expiring tidepool animals in *The Sea of Cortez* (1941).

The Josh Billings Story and Other Intercalary Chapters in Cannery Row (1945)

Although "The Time the Wolves Ate the Vice-Principal" is the only *Cannery Row* interchapter (although omitted) to have been published separately, several other of these interpolated tales can be read independently of the novel. Nine such interchapters appear to be entirely self-contained.[13] The most self-contained of all is a tale whose plot and characters seem very remote from the main narrative, and whose date of composition precedes by several years that of *Cannery Row*. On 12 February 1939 Steinbeck wrote to Elizabeth Otis: "The Josh Billings story I just haven't written. The leg has been too bad."[14] The "Josh Billings story" Steinbeck refers to is the offbeat piece published six years later in *Cannery Row*. Appearing as chapter 12 in the novel, this sketch chronicles the meandering journey of the famous humorist's intestines, haphazardly discarded by an embalmer after Billings's death and only at the last minute rescued from becoming mackerel bait.

Although critics have postulated thematic similarities between the Josh Billings tale and surrounding chapters in *Cannery Row,* this interchapter is an odd addition to the novel. Calling the Billings piece one of the few interchapters "whose function is obscure," Lisca conjectures that the tale is perhaps "only intended to illustrate the great difference between the public's slight regard for a living literary figure and its disproportionate concern for the disposition of his dead body."[15] Similarly, French admits that the Billings "episode does not at first seem related to the preceding chapter [11] about the Palace Flophouse boys' difficulties in fixing a truck that they borrowed for a frog hunt." Both of these chapters burlesque people's "suspicions of innovations that will ultimately change their culture," says French, innovations like the Model T Ford (appearing in chap. 11) and the embalming of a corpse before interment (alluded to in chap. 12).[16] If these justifications for inclusion of the Billings piece seem farfetched, it may be because Steinbeck did not compose the odd narrative specifically for *Cannery Row*. Moreover, Billings died in 1885, some fifty years before the action in the novel takes place.

Another interchapter like the Josh Billings tale that stands out from the main plot is chapter 24, the story of an aspiring but broke writer/cartoonist and his imaginative wife. The Tom and Mary Talbot story is unique for two reasons: first, at about 1,200 words, it is twice as long as the average interchapter in *Cannery Row*. And, second, it lacks the waterfront setting of most of the novel's episodes. It may be assumed that, because of its context, the piece transpires somewhere near Cannery Row; however, nothing in the sketch suggests this. The backdrop might just as likely be Salinas, where fantasy-prone Mary Teller in "The White Quail" talks to her flowers in much the same way that Mary Talbot visits with her neighborhood cats.

Outside of the Josh Billings tale and perhaps the Tom and Mary Talbot narrative, the balance of the *Cannery Row* interchapters seem to have been composed specifically for the novel. Of these, a few generalities can be made: most are approximately six hundred words in length and present a cameo of a single character or a pair of characters. Only one interchapter departs from this pattern: chapter 2, in which Steinbeck establishes an atmosphere—or better, a perspective—through which the reader may view the entire novel. But after chapter 2, the remaining interchapters focus on such characters as the old Chinese man with the flapping shoe sole (chap. 4); Mr. and Mrs. Malloy, who live in a rusting boiler pipe (chap. 8); the uncoordinated and unloved Frankie (chap. 10); the skater atop Holman's flagpole, and the curiosity he arouses (chap. 19); Henri the painter (chap. 22); Joey and Willard's disagreement and fight (chap. 24); Frankie's theft of a clock (chap. 28); and the lonely gopher in search of a mate (chap. 31).

"The Miracle of Tepayac" (1948)

Published on Christmas day, 1948, in *Collier's,* "The Miracle of Tepayac" marks a radical departure from the religiously unorthodox *Cannery Row.* Drawing on the 1531 legend of Our Lady of Guadalupe, Steinbeck retells the story of Juan Diego, an Indian widower who wanders in the mountains near Cuautitlan, Mexico. One morning upon reaching the summit of Tepayac, Juan Diego experiences a vision of the Queen of Heaven, who orders him to have the bishop of Mexico erect a temple in her honor on Tepayac. When Juan Diego visits Mexico City, however, the bishop tells him to reflect upon the vision and come back later. Then the Indian hikes once more up Tepayac, where the Holy Mother encourages him to seek out the bishop again. But, as before, the bishop sends him away, this time to bring from the Virgin a "sign beyond words."[17] Finally she does provide Juan Diego such a sign: beautiful roses of Castile, which Juan Diego gathers into his cloak. When the Indian delivers them to the bishop, the roses have imprinted the image of the Virgin on the cactus-fiber cloak. Falling to his knees, the bishop agrees to build a temple to Our Lady of Guadalupe on Mount Tepayac, and the happy Juan Diego cares for the shrine until his death.

The stark contrasts between the lofty heights of Tepayac, where Juan Diego receives his vision, and the world below of Mexico City, where the bishop resides, show Steinbeck in his familiar role of advocate for the common man. During Juan Diego's shuttles between these two locales, the mount of Tepayac becomes a kind of "church invisible" where Juan Diego's soul is filled with the spiritual presence of the Virgin. The bishop's chamber, on the other hand, is to the Indian merely the "church visible," where the prelate carries on the administrative functions of worship, but without direct communication with the Holy Mother. Because the Lady selects the humble Juan Diego to deliver her sign, the roles of priest and parishioner are reversed: the common man's vision takes precedence over the prelate's ecclesiastical authority.

The story of Our Lady of Guadalupe has been retold many times since its legendary occurrence on Saturday, 9 December 1531. Willa Cather, for example, recounts it in her novel, *Death Comes for the Archbishop* (1927). Steinbeck's version of the tale is interesting for its attributing grief to Juan Diego over the loss of his wife, Maria Lucia. Steinbeck seems to diverge from the legend when he says that at the time the Virgin appeared to Juan Diego on Tepayac he was "lost in sorrow" (22). According to the legend, Maria Lucia had died in 1529, two years before her husband saw his vision. Rather than "wandering over the hills, spending his strength the way a grieving man does" (22) as Steinbeck characterizes the Indian, Juan Diego was merely hiking to mass over the mountain as he and Maria Lucia had done every Saturday morning for many years.[18] This slight departure from established sources has autobiographical implications: having recently lost his second wife through divorce in October 1948, and his friend Ed Ricketts to a train accident a few months earlier, Steinbeck himself may have felt the pain he attributes to Juan Diego in "The Miracle."

That Steinbeck needed to write to take his mind off his suffering, and perhaps even to make money after a financially upsetting divorce, is apparent in "Miracle." While he adds a few personal touches to the legend, it lacks the vigor, earthiness, and rich imagery of his best short fiction. Later in his life, Steinbeck's creative abilities would revive and he would write one of the finest short stories of his career. Presently, however, he seemed to be impaired by the tragic events of the year.

"His Father" (1949)

While we must read between the lines in "The Miracle of Tepayac" to find evidence of Steinbeck's troubled personal life during the late 1940s, in the autobiographical "His Father," he deals directly with one of his gravest concerns: separation from his two sons. With the breakup of Steinbeck's marriage to Gwyndolyn Conger, his two boys were to live with their mother in New York. According to the divorce settlement, Steinbeck (then residing in Pacific Grove, California) would have them for two months during each summer. The first of these annual visits was to take place in the summer of 1949. But even before then, Steinbeck became eager to see his sons. Traveling on impulse to New York sometime in April, he became concerned after seeing that his children had as their only playground a busy urban street.[19] Upon returning to California, Steinbeck wrote a brief short story based on this reunion with his boys, which appeared the following September in *Reader's Digest*.[20]

"His Father," filling only two-and-a-half pages of the magazine, concerns a young boy taunted by insensitive children about his missing father. Once the children learn that the boy's parents are divorced, they glare at him with accusing eyes. Distraught and angry, he nonetheless endures their abuse until one day his father unexpectedly appears. To his playmates, the happy boy exclaims, *"He's here! You want to see him?"* (21).

The fictional father who surprises his son with an unannounced visit is obviously modeled after Steinbeck himself. "His Father" is autobiographical in other ways as well. The protagonist, "going on seven years old," resembles Steinbeck's first son, Thom, who was five when the story appeared. The urban setting with "taxis and kids and tricycles and baby buggies" suggests the neighborhood in New York where the two boys lived with their mother. And the atmosphere of suffering that imbues this cityscape is evidently a reflection of young Thom Steinbeck's (and perhaps the author's) despondency (19).

For such a brief story, "His Father" is built upon a rather intricate chronology. Most essential background information is narrated through flashbacks, especially the young protagonist's painful encounters with his neighbors. These flashbacks set the stage in the last scene for the father's unexpected visit. Thus, the story develops and maintains psychological tension, which is not relieved until the closing lines. Besides its noteworthy focus on a topical subject—the children of divorce—"His Father" marks the first time Steinbeck uses himself and his family as models for characters in his fiction.

"The Great Roque War" and "The Pacific Grove Butterfly Festival" in Sweet Thursday (1954)

Like *The Grapes of Wrath* and *Cannery Row, Sweet Thursday* is another Steinbeck novel in which intercalary chapters appear. In this 1954 volume, however, only chapter 8, "The Great Roque War" and chapter 38, "Hooptedoodle (2), or The Pacific Grove

Butterfly Festival" are autonomous stories. Coincidentally, both of these concern the town of Pacific Grove, California.

In "The Great Roque War" Steinbeck focuses on the obsession of Pacific Grove residents over a complicated version of croquet. Originally intended for leisure and recreation, the roque courts quickly become a literal battle ground because of fierce competition between "the Greens" and its opposition, "the Blues." The bitter rivalry begins to penetrate all aspects of life, including politics. Finally, Deems, the man who donated the courts to the town, hires a bulldozer to turn them into a "ragged hole in the ground."[21] This proves to be the only way to check the roque epidemic.

Pacific Grove citizens look equally bad in "Hooptedoodle (2)," which concerns their annual monarch butterfly festival. Through some quirk of nature "great clouds of orangy Monarch butterflies" (259) return at the same time every year to Pacific Grove. Once their migration begins to attract tourists, the town fathers—equating tourism with dollars—decide to cash in on this natural wonder. They create the "Great Butterfly Festival," which brings the city profits until one fateful year when the monarchs do not return. Sin is blamed, as the community goes into convulsions over their lost revenue and credibility.

Both of these *Sweet Thursday* interchapters are ironic and mildly humorous; yet neither furthers the main plot concerning the romance of Doc and Suzy. Though we might grant that these two interchapters add a certain tone or atmosphere, both are essentially isolated from the rest of the novel in terms of plot and character. They also indicate a gradual shift in the subject matter of Steinbeck's short fiction from serious domestic issues in "His Father" to the humorous, even bizarre, episode discussed next in "The Affair at 7, Rue de M——."

"Affair at 7, Rue de M——" (1955)

Readers familiar with *The Short Reign of Pippin IV* (1957) will recognize the Paris setting of Steinbeck's second O. Henry Award-winning story from this period, "The Affair at 7, Rue de M——." Its subject matter, style, and tone, however, are worlds apart from anything Steinbeck had previously written. At this phase in his career, Steinbeck seems to have experienced a crisis in style, fearing that his eminently successful techniques of the 1930s were becoming a kind of "straitjacket," threatening to destroy him as a writer.[22] Hence, he tried to set out in a new direction. "A whole revolution is going on in me," he told Elia Kazan. "It's hard to throw over 30 years work but necessary if the work has pooped out. It isn't that it was bad but that I've used it up."[23]

Steinbeck's grappling for creative alternatives to his earlier style is evident in the exaggerated Poesque atmosphere of "Affair at 7, Rue de M———," which blends Gothic elements with the detached tone of a detective story. The plot is simple, yet extraordinary. To an old, distinguished address in Paris, an American writer brings his wife, daughter, and two little sons. John, the younger son, enjoys chewing bubble gum until one day he discovers his gum is chewing itself! John's father extracts the moist blob from the boy's mouth and places it on a desk, but the gum—still pulsating—slides back toward the boy. The father hurls it out the window, but the gum returns. Then he beats it with an African war club and drops it into the Seine. That night the gum returns. Finally, he covers the undulating blob with a bell jar. After one week, the once menacing gum finally becomes languid, no longer a threat to young John.

Right from the story's title, "Affair at 7, Rue de M———," Steinbeck seems to parody Edgar Allan Poe. We might recall "The Murders in the Rue Morgue" (1841), for example, which is also set in Paris and whose tragic events are even referred to in the tale as an "affair." And Steinbeck's cool and rational first-person narrator (modeled after Steinbeck himself) resembles Poe's meerschaum-puffing raconteur in "Rue Morgue." It is perhaps no coincidence, then, that Steinbeck's narrator lights his own pipe at the close of "Affair at 7, Rue de M———."

Other Poesque touches include the "African war club . . . studded with brass" with which young John's father beats the renegade gum into a thin pulp,[24] and an ornate, elevated style in which Steinbeck's customary Anglo-Saxon diction gives way to Romance and Latinate parlance like *arrondissement* and *aficionado* (258, 259). For example, the eight-year-old John says to his father, "I came to your work room to await your first disengagement, wishing to acquaint you with my difficulty" (261). One would be hard-pressed to find such a stilted expression in Steinbeck's earlier work, especially spoken by a child. Obviously, Steinbeck wrote "Affair" with French readers (whose fancy for Poe is well known) in mind. The story appeared first in French—as *"L'Affaire de l'avenue de M——"* (*Figaro* 1 [28 August 1954], 436—and not until nearly one year later in English, in *Harper's Bazaar.* With its oddly humorous subject and elevated diction, "Affair at 7, Rue de M——" is an uncharacteristic Steinbeck story that demonstrates the author's versatility and willingness to experiment.

"The Summer Before" (1955)

Published in the British magazine *Punch* and (unlike "Affair") never reprinted in America, "The Summer Before" (May 1955) provides a warm glimpse of Steinbeck's early days in Salinas. The story includes a humorous sketch of the author's childhood pony, Jill, and cameo appearances by his sister, Mary, and his young friends, Glen Graves and Max Wagner. With its Salinas backdrop, child characters, and loose, episodic construction, "The Summer Before" resembles *The Red Pony,* except that in "Summer" Steinbeck adopts the first-person point of view. The main plot involves Willie Morton, a Salinas boy who lives with his protective mother. One summer day Willie's friends invite him to a swimming party on the Salinas River, but his mother screams in opposition. Willie ultimately defies her and joins his friends on the river bank. When they strip off their clothes to swim, however, Willie refuses to disrobe. Later, his friends return from the water to discover Willie missing. Soon they spot him under water caught by his overalls' strap on a sunken tree. When a nearby Japanese farmer rescues him, Willie's strap breaks and his pants fall down. To everyone's amazement, Willie is a girl!

Steinbeck plants several clues in the narrative about Willie's gender. The other boys know Willie is somewhat "strange just by the way he [stands] off and [looks]" at them.[25] In addition, Willie's mother carefully ensures that Willie uses the toilet alone and avoids swimming with the neighborhood boys (649, 651). Despite these hints, the story's ending still surprises. And no one is more surprised than Willie's friends—several boys intrigued by their inadvertent discovery about Willie. Yet, in "The Summer Before," Steinbeck seems little inclined to explore the implications of their new sexual knowledge, and instead uses the narrative as an occasion to string together several loose strands of his childhood memories of Salinas. The first third of the narrative, in fact, contains several reminiscences unrelated to the story's central action. Owing to these autobiographical indulgences, the story lacks structural unity. Nonetheless, Steinbeck's charming vignettes about his pony and childhood friends offer readers a rare look at the author's early years through his own eyes.

"The Short-Short Story of Mankind" (1955)

While "The Summer Before" demonstrates that Steinbeck was able to recall events nearly fifty years in his past, in "The Short-Short Story of Mankind" (or "We're Holding Our Own")[26] he turns to his present day (the 1950s) for material, focusing on a crucial issue of the day: nuclear war. His method of dealing with this topical subject, however, is to envision the origins of war in prehistoric times. Steinbeck chronicles a series of quarrels that break out among different tribes, beginning in the Stone Age. In this brief allegory, he shows how innovative people whose inventions stand to benefit mankind are slain by their jealous and ignorant contemporaries—"Nobody can put a knife in the status quo and get away with it" (328). Stone Age Elmer, for example, invents a rock and brush house and is slain for his efforts. Ironically, Elmer's own people later embrace his invention and worship him as a deity. Then Max designs a tent of animal skin and suffers the same fate as did Elmer. Violence among tribes and against individuals continues until modern times. Then missiles render geographic boundaries irrelevant, and nations begin to merge. Concludes the narrator, we have no other choice: join together or face extinction.

When "The Short-Short Story of Mankind" first appeared in November 1955, the threat of nuclear war, and hence of human extinction, loomed ominously on the horizon.[27] Steinbeck apparently wrote the story to conjecture about the possibilities for survival of the human race, noting our tendency to resist change, and to destroy those who perpetrate it. These twin tendencies do not bode well for mankind; for how can a people progress if they systematically eliminate those who would lead them out of the darkness? The irony of this is not lost on Steinbeck, who sees the same kind of behavior mirrored in modern times. "Now we've got the United Nations and the elders are right in there fighting it the way they fought coming out of caves" (329). Today, as in the past, the old and conventional thwart the young and inventive. Steinbeck concludes that we must change our ways, for "it'd be kind of silly if we killed ourselves off after all this time" (329).

The charge by some critics that Steinbeck's later works suffer from excessive moralizing seems warranted with regard to "The Short-Short Story of Mankind." Only one-fourth of the piece contains dialogue, while the bulk comprises an obvious allegory in which Steinbeck tells (rather than shows) the reader what is wrong with the human race. Considering the complexities involved, his prescription to cure our collective ills seems simplistic. Moreover, the story's alternating humorous and pessimistic tone blurs whatever statement Steinbeck had intended to make.

"How Mr. Hogan Robbed a Bank" (1956)

Just four months after "The Short-Short Story of Mankind" appeared, Steinbeck's most artistically successful story of the 1940s and 1950s was published in the *Atlantic Monthly.* The setting and central characters of "How Mr. Hogan Robbed a Bank" are familiar to readers of *Winter of Our Discontent* (1961), yet the story's theme is markedly different from that of the novel. While Ethan Allen Hawley in *Winter* fully understands the moral implications of succumbing to the temptations of pride, greed, and betrayal of friends and associates, Mr. Hogan's bank robbery affords him not the slightest pang of guilt. Steinbeck gives no indication of Hogan's motives, and refuses to attribute any larger meaning to his actions.[28]

Since Mr. Hogan—a grocery clerk, husband, and father—realizes that most bank robberies fail from excessive "hanky-panky," he keeps his theft simple. For one year he observes activity at the bank around the corner from the grocery store where he works. Early on the day of the heist, a Saturday morning before Labor Day, Hogan walks to the grocery store, cuts out a Mickey Mouse mask from a cereal box, and grabs a silver revolver. Entering the bank just after it opens, he steals more than eight thousand dollars and flees. That evening he hides the cash in a case holding his Knight's Templar uniform, except for two five-dollar bills: one he gives to his son for receiving honorable mention in an "I Love America" essay contest, and the other to his daughter for being a good sport. "What a fine family!" Mr. Hogan concludes. "Fine!"[29]

French calls "Mr. Hogan" "truly vintage Steinbeck," a story in which he finally "achieves the nonteleological viewpoint he [had] long sought."[30] All indications suggest, however, that when he wrote the story Steinbeck had none of these aspirations in mind. As frequently happened in his career, some works that he expected to be "major" became critical failures, while others that he wrote merely for his own relaxation were highly acclaimed. Examples of this latter type include "The Gift" and *Cannery Row*. To these two works, "Mr. Hogan" may be added. Steinbeck expressed wonderment at the circumstances of its composition. "I am constantly amazed and to a certain extent frightened by the vagrant tendency of my mind and writing direction. It seems so often to take its own direction—can be resisted but goes into a pout if it is resisted. An example of this was 'Mr. Hogan.' I had no intention of writing him. He just started and came out."[31]

Consequently, "Mr. Hogan" appeared as a lighthearted, "frivolous satire and fantasy,"[32] a "smart-alec work . . . rare among Steinbeck's" works.[33] Unlike the typical crime or detective story, it offers few surprises and generates little, if any, suspense. Nothing about Hogan's bank heist is nerve-racking, breathtaking, or even mildly exciting. Steinbeck describes the robbery in such matter-of-fact terms that grand theft begins to resemble any mundane routine like making tea. Yet while routines often become mindless, Mr. Hogan's caper is a thoroughly conceived and highly conscious act. Steinbeck underscores this contrast between Hogan's way of doing things and that of his peers (who do not "notice things" as he does) and satirizes the "dangers of getting into a rut"—of becoming so stultified by habit as to lose the capacity to observe new and changing phenomena.[34] This is obviously the plight of Hogan's friends and neighbors. The only real surprise about his bank robbery is, then, that Hogan can so easily outwit those around him whose lives are bound up in leaden routines. Steinbeck implies that the superior person is not so much the individual who behaves according to traditional values (e.g., the American work ethic) as the one who is fully conscious and able to see through society's shams and false bottoms. These are Mr. Hogan's strengths, and, to paraphrase Steinbeck, they stand him in good stead.

"Case of the Hotel Ghost—Or . . . What Are You Smoking in That Pipe, Mr. S.?" (or "Reunion at the Quiet Hotel") (1957)

Though perhaps his finest story of the 1940s and 1950s, "How Mr. Hogan Robbed a Bank" was not to conclude Steinbeck's career in short fiction. "Case of the Hotel Ghost . . ." appeared on 30 June 1957 in the *Louisville Courier-Journal;* an abbreviated version of the story (retitled "Reunion at the Quiet Hotel") was published seven months later on 25 January 1958 in the London newspaper the *Evening Standard.* Both versions seem to be based on John and Elaine Steinbeck's experiences in Italy and England during a European tour begun in March 1952.[35]

The *Courier-Journal* text of the story begins with a facetious comparison of Italian and English ghosts. Steinbeck mentions first a haunted house in Florence whose apparitions frightened even the German occupation forces during the war. British ghosts, Steinbeck then implies, are milder than their Italian counterparts. He reluctantly admits having met the English variety once in London. The last paragraph of this droll introduction in the *Courier-Journal* text becomes the first paragraph of the *Evening Standard* story. From this point on, the two narratives vary only slightly from one another.

"Case of the Hotel Ghost—Or . . . What Are You Smoking in That Pipe, Mr. S.?" involves the Steinbecks' brief stay at a quiet London hotel where the author was quartered during the war. After Steinbeck's old cronies—Albert the desk clerk, Max the lift operator, and George the room attendant—greet him with indifferent politeness ("It's just the English manner," Steinbeck tells his wife),[36] the couple retire to their room and dine on "thick, mushy soup completely without flavour" and "veal chops breaded with old washcloths" (9). The next evening they decide to go out to an Armenian restaurant in Soho. Upon their return, the hotel has vanished. No trace of the building remains except a deep hole with rubble piled around it. Rather than try to explain the hotel's collapse, they merely inform the authorities that their passports have been stolen.

The crumbling hotel can be seen as a symbol for the narrator's abortive attempt to rekindle his memories of the war. That he can no longer find inspiration or solace in the past is perhaps an autobiographical statement. When the story appeared, Steinbeck was beginning to fear that he might never write well again. By 1960 Steinbeck reportedly had told Elizabeth Otis: "My time is over. . . . I should bow out."[37] "Case of the Hotel Ghost" may very well foreshadow the diminution of his powers, the collapsed building representing the last flickers of his creative light. The story, while engaging, lacks the vigor of Steinbeck's earlier work, its flaccid style echoing the theme of decay. One of the best examples of this earlier work, considered by some critics to rival *The Long Valley* as Steinbeck's major achievement in short fiction, is *The Pastures of Heaven.* This impressive short story cycle is discussed next.

A Steinbeck Short Story Cycle:
The Pastures of Heaven

During his career, Steinbeck composed several works that can be considered short story cycles. Forrest L. Ingram defines a story cycle as "a set of stories linked to each other in such a way as to maintain a balance between the individuality of each of the stories and the necessities of the larger unit." Ingram adds to this definition that the reader's experience of each story is "modified by his experience of the others."[1] Within the whole spectrum of the story cycle genre are, at one extreme, groups of tales so highly unified as to approximate the novel, and at the other, collections of loosely linked stories. Steinbeck's *Tortilla Flat* (1935) provides an example of the novellike story cycle, while his *Red Pony* (1937) illustrates the looser variety.

In between these two extremes is *The Pastures of Heaven* (1932), which Steinbeck conceived of and designed as a short story cycle. As he told Ted Miller in early 1930, "I have thought of a series of short stories which I have wanted to write for a long time . . . tied together Decameron fashion.[2] Later, in a letter to Mavis McIntosh, Steinbeck explained more fully his material for the volume.

> There is, about twelve miles from Monterey, a valley in the hills called Corral de Tierra. Because I am using its people I have named it Las Pasturas del Cielo. The valley was for years known as the happy valley because of the unique harmony which existed among its twenty families. About ten years ago a new family moved in on one of the ranches. They were ordinary people, ill-educated but honest and as kindly as any. In fact, in their whole history I cannot find that they have committed a really malicious act nor an act which was not dictated by honorable expediency or out-and-out altruism. But about the Morans ["Munroes" in *Pastures*] there was a flavor of evil. Everyone they came in contact with was injured. Every place they went dissension sprang up. There have been two murders, a suicide,

many quarrels and a great deal of unhappiness in the Pastures of Heaven, and all of these things can be traced directly to the influence of the [Munroes].[3]

In *The Pastures of Heaven*, Steinbeck recounts the Munroes' ill-fated dealings with nine of the twenty families mentioned in the letter. One additional story (chap. 2) outlines the history of the "cursed" Battle farm and of the similarly "cursed" Munroe family who settle on it. Each story, as Steinbeck explains, is "complete in itself, having its rise, climax and ending," yet all of the tales are linked "by the common locality and by the contact with the [Munroes]."[4]

Throughout his adult life, Bert Munroe has been cursed by a series of business failures. Upon moving to the Battle farm, his fortunes seem to improve; thus, he half-seriously jests that his curse and that of the farm "got to fighting and killed each other off."[5] "That's a good one," responds his new neighbor, T. B. Allen, "but here's a better one. Maybe your curse and the farm's curse has mated and gone into a gopher hole like a pair of rattlesnakes. Maybe there'll be a lot of baby curses crawling around the Pastures the first thing you know" (20). F. W. Watt argues that this, in fact, does happen; "for the valley Eden has more than its share of serpents; each episode tells of a 'fall.' "[6]

As Steinbeck's most obvious framing device in *The Pastures of Heaven*, the Munroe family appears in every tale. Yet, though the "Munroes provide the physical connecting link between the stories," according to French, *Pastures* "is not so much about them . . . as about their effect on others." The Munroes become the catalyst, but not the true cause, of the downfall of several of their unsuspecting neighbors. Says Joseph Fontenrose, "The apparent tranquility of each resident was founded on an unhealthy adjustment, either an evasion of reality or an unrealizable dream." What the Munroes provide these residents is "a moment of truth" when they must see themselves as they really are. Thus, the unfortunate end of the protagonists in the stories would eventually have occurred even without the Munroes' intervention. For this reason, Ingram argues that "the dynamics of the cycle must be studied as much through *their* [the protagonists'] actions and attitudes as through the attitudes and actions of the Monroes." Most of these protagonists are alike in one respect: they suffer from illusions that, in some cases, are the product of or lead to mental illness. Their various illusions become another important internal link between the stories, just as the psychological abnormalities among Anderson's characters connect the stories in *Winesburg, Ohio.*[7]

The Pastures of Heaven is also unified by its "consistently ironic tone," according to French, and an ironic title, prologue, and epilogue. The title's irony stems from the word *heaven,* which suggests a celestial realm where the righteous dwell in perfect harmony. Ironically, Steinbeck's earthly "heaven" hosts nearly every conceivable human imperfection; consequently, discord spreads among its inhabitants. "Even in a potential or apparent paradise," as Anita Yancy says, "human nature is flawed and is the instrument of its own destruction." As if to underscore its terrestrial nature, Steinbeck modeled his Pastures of *Heaven* on the real-life Corral de Tierra, which means "fence of *earth.*"[8] The book's title, therefore, foreshadows its stories, which illustrate the impossibility of a paradise in this world.

The prologue (chap. 1) and epilogue (chap. 12) frame *The Pastures of Heaven,* developing and reiterating the irony suggested by its title. In this frame, characters seeing the lush valley for the first time marvel at its beauty and imagine living there in peace, prosperity, and happiness. In the prologue, a Spanish corporal pursuing runaway Indian slaves in 1776 first discovers the serene valley and whispers, "Holy Mother! . . . Here are the green pastures of Heaven to which our Lord leadeth us" (2). This "bearded, savage" soldier, who whips "brown backs to tatters" and fornicates rapaciously, dreams with "sentimental wistfulness" of "a little time of peace" before his death (2–3). But an Indian woman infects him with the pox and, "when his face beg[ins] to fall away," he dies "locked in an old barn" far from the Pastures (3). The irony of the prologue is entirely self-contained, in that the Spanish corporal's dream of peaceful retirement in the valley is juxtaposed with the nightmare of his gruesome and lonely death.[9]

The epilogue reiterates the ironic premise established in the prologue. When a sightseeing bus stops along a ridge overlooking the pastures, several awestruck passengers peer down in wonder. Brilliant squares of green orchards, yellow fields, and violet earth shimmer in the "golden gauze" air of the last sunlight (239–40).

A "successful man" imagines himself subdividing the whole valley for tremendous profit (240). A newlywed couple gazes longingly upon its gentle slopes until the wife's reproving eyes remind her new husband, "It would be nice—but I can't, of course" (241). A "young priest" envisions a little church where "no poverty, no smells, no trouble" would daunt him (241). An "old man" dreams of retiring in the peaceful valley and piecing together the many fragments of his life (241). Even the "bus driver" fancies himself with a nice "little place down there" (241).

Of the misfortune and tragedy that have occurred in the Pastures, these sightseers know nothing. They have heard of neither the Munroes nor the evils that have befallen their neighbors. From this stems the epilogue's principal irony. "By the time the epilogue is reached," says Watt, "the reader . . . has seen how much external appearances of beauty, innocence and peace belie the fully human experience that is the lot of those who live in 'the sweet valley in the hills.' "[10] While the reader recognizes these "external appearances" for what they are, the characters in the epilogue do not. Only through their naive eyes can the dream of the heavenly pastures live on. Their reaffirmation of this dream, despite the earthly (or even hellish) lives of Pastures residents, completes the ironic frame of the volume.

The first story (chap. 2) to appear within this frame concerns the history of the cursed Battle farm. Steinbeck tells us that Pastures residents consider the farm evil because of "one horrible event" and "one impenetrable mystery" (5). George Battle migrates west to the Pastures in 1863, buys land in the center of the valley, and marries a religious fanatic and epileptic, Myrtle Cameron. Myrtle bears them a son before being committed to the Lippman Sanitarium for twice attempting to burn the house. It is to John Battle, who inherits his mother's epilepsy and "mad knowledge of God" (7), that the "horrible event" occurs. John devotes his life to flushing out devils on the Battle's thorny and tangled acres. One evening he dives for a rattlesnake (believing it embodies the devil) and is struck three times in the throat. When John is finally found, the sight of his buzzard-eaten corpse makes Pastures residents "dread" the Battle farm ever after (8).

The Mustrovics take over the vacant, unkempt farm ten years later. The old man and woman, who live in the kitchen of the boarded-up house, are "rarely seen" by the people of the valley,

Part 1. The Short Fiction: A Critical Analysis

but their son works "every daylight hour," making the land "grow beautiful again" (10). Two years after the Mustrovics arrive, the "impenetrable mystery" occurs. One day when neighbors notice that the farm looks deserted again, they discover that the Mustrovics have vanished. Their breakfast of porridge and fried eggs sits on the table uneaten. Once again weeds spring up on the Battle farm, and more than one Pastures resident says, "I wouldn't own it if you gave it to me" (11).

Five years later the Munroes buy the forsaken parcel, refurbish the house from floor to ceiling, and transform the weed-choked land into one of the garden spots of the valley. Far from endearing themselves to the community, however, by "removing the accursed farm and substituting a harmless and fertile farm" (19), the Munroes arouse the suspicions of Pastures residents. Through kindness and sensitivity, Bert Monroe and family eventually win acceptance from their new neighbors. The curse that for several generations has plagued the Battle farm is, in time, forgotten.

Besides explaining this curse in chapter 2, Steinbeck also sketches cameo portraits of the Munroes, and foreshadows how each will intrude on the lives of his or her neighbors. Mrs. Munroe—a plump, conventional housekeeper—decides just once where to place her new furniture, and from that moment on each piece is "fixed forever, only to be moved for cleaning" (13). Her fixity of mind crops up again in chapter 6, when she puts an end to the jolly, carefree life of the Junius Maltbys. On visiting the Pastures school one day, Mrs. Munroe insists on giving raggedly clad Robbie Maltby new shirts and overalls. Although the teacher tries repeatedly to dissuade her, Mrs. Munroe's mind is set. Her intransigence causes Robbie's embarrassment and precipitates the Maltbys' departure from the Pastures.

Mae Munroe, destined to become the carbon copy of her mother, thinks constantly of marriage. Her "smooth cheeks," "ripe lips," and "voluptuous" figure (hinting of "future plumpness") excite the fancy of both Pat Humbert (chap. 10) and Bill Whiteside (chap. 11); Humbert discovers only after redecorating his house "Vermont style" to lure her that Mae has become engaged to Whiteside. From then on the dejected Humbert avoids his redecorated house, sleeping instead in the barn. Mae's effect on the Whitesides seems equally devastating. She convinces fiancé Bill Whiteside to leave his family farm for a Ford partnership in

94

Monterey—shattering his father's and grandfather's dream of building a Whiteside dynasty in the Pastures.

Seventeen-year-old Jimmie Munroe is a former high school Casanova, whose sinful past gives him an advantage over "the younger girls of the valley" (16). During a school dance, Jimmie hustles the beautiful but naive Alice Wicks (chap. 3) outside under the willow trees. Alice's chastity just barely survives when her mother screams at Jimmie, "You keep away from this girl or you'll get into trouble" (37). On learning of the incident, Alice's father, Shark Wicks, bolts to the Munroe farm with a rifle. Although he decides not to shoot Jimmie, Shark is detained and (because of his reputed, though nonexistent, wealth) is required to post a bond well above his means. Embarrassed by this revelation, Wicks chooses to leave the Pastures.

At seven, Manny is the Munroes' youngest child. A Steinbeck "subnormal" character, Manny's brain development has been arrested by an adenoid condition. He sometimes sits for hours "staring into space" or beats "his forehead on the floor until the blood [runs] into his eyes" (16). Manny appears later in chapter 4 with another subnormal character, the artistically gifted "little frog," Tularecito. When Bert Munroe finds deep holes dug in his orchard, he suspects Manny. Not Manny, but Tularecito has done the digging—in search of gnomes. When Bert begins to fill in one of the holes, Tularecito clobbers him with a shovel. Tularecito is apprehended and committed to an asylum for the criminally insane, while the subnormal Manny remains comfortably and securely at home with the Munroes.

Bert Munroe causes more harm in the Pastures of Heaven than the rest of his family combined. Having previously suffered several business failures, when Bert buys the Battle farm, his "shoulders straighten," his "face los[es] its haunted look" and he becomes happy for the first time in years. "The doom [is] gone. He kn[ows] he [is] safe from the curse" (18). With his misfortunes behind him, Bert becomes more confident, even jokes with his neighbors and feels no hesitancy in asking them favors. A kindly and respectable man, he is soon elected to the school board.

In chapter 5, following a neighborly impulse, Bert sets out uninvited to welcome the Van Deventers, a new family in the valley. His friendly gesture precipitates (or at least precedes) the shotgun death of the deranged Hilda Van Deventer, at the hands of her equally ill mother. In chapter 11, acting on similar good intentions, Bert offers to help John Whiteside burn off some brush. When sparks fly, the pride of the Whiteside tradition—their distinguished home—is destroyed by fire. And in chapter 9, Bert offhandedly invites himself to witness a San Quentin hanging with his neighbor Raymond Banks. After Banks secures a special invitation for him from the warden at San Quentin, the fainthearted Munroe backs out. He tells Banks about an old man who hacked a red rooster to a gruesome death. Munroe, fearing the execution will be equally gory, not only spoils the San Quentin trip for himself, but for Banks as well.

Bert's sometimes perverted sense of humor also causes trouble in the valley. In chapter 7, he fibs to Allen Hueneker's wife that her homely husband has run off with Maria Lopez, one of two sisters who offer their bodies as "encouragement" to loyal customers of their Mexican restaurant. As a result of Bert's practical joke, the sheriff closes down the Lopez sisters' eatery, and the two women become prostitutes in San Francisco. And in chapter 8, during several school board meetings, the jovial Bert cannot resist telling stories about his wayward and drunken hired hand. Molly Morgan, the new school teacher, fears that Munroe speaks of her own missing father. To avoid being confronted with the disturbing truth about her alcoholic parent, Molly resigns her teaching post and leaves the Pastures. Thus, the intrusive behavior of Bert Munroe and other members of his family precipitates these catastrophes, or, at least, stark realizations, among Pastures residents.

Shark Wicks (Chapter 3)

Jimmie Munroe, as mentioned above, appears in the tale concerning Edward "Shark" Wicks. In this story, Steinbeck continues to develop Jimmie's character based on his cameo portrait as a teenage Casanova in chapter 2. In the Shark Wicks story we learn that Jimmie has "kissed at least a hundred girls, and on three occasions, he [has] had sinful adventures in the willows by the Salinas River" (31–32). Not surprisingly, it is under the "willows" (37) that Jimmie coaxes Alice Wicks, soon after they meet at the high school dance. In this way, Steinbeck carefully foreshadows

Jimmie's behavior and thereby links the Shark Wicks story with the chapter preceding it.

Jimmie's attempted seduction of Alice Wicks has a more profound effect on Alice's father than on the young woman herself. Shark Wicks maintains two grand illusions, both of which are shattered by Jimmie's encounter with his daughter. Shark's first illusion, and his "greatest pleasure," derives from his "being considered a wealthy man" (24). Although he has never in his life possessed more than five hundred dollars, Wicks trumps up an imaginary fortune exceeding one hundred thousand. Through shrewd investments and devious dealings, Shark manages to increase this paper fortune and thereby to develop a reputation in the Pastures as, ironically, "nobody's fool" (34).

Shark's second illusion concerns his beautiful but stupid daughter, whom he believes must be guarded like a "Dresden vase" (32) against possible damage. Shark's obsession with Alice becomes extreme when she reaches fourteen. Every month at the appropriate time he "wolfishly" asks his wife, "Is she all right?" (29). He begins to regard "the possible defloration of his daughter as both loss and disfigurement" (28), which would render her valueless, since he views her as a fine possession to be "hoarded" and "gloated over," rather than loved (29). As the narrator tells us, "no man ever guarded his prize bitch when she was in heat more closely than Shark watched his daughter" (29). Steinbeck carefully designs a two-tiered plot developing both of Shark's illusions, then cleverly involves two Munroes in destroying the illusions. First, Jimmie Munroe, in Shark's mind at least, defiles his untouchably pure daughter (Wicks does not realize that Alice's seduction progressed no further than a few kisses). Second, Bert Munroe, by requiring Shark to post a bond after he threatens Jimmie with a rifle, explodes the myth of Wicks's reputed fortune. While Shark's two illusions seem to be shattered by the Munroes, Fontenrose contends that T. B. Allen, the Pastures storekeeper, actually causes Wicks's downfall, "by telling him unwisely about Alice's encounter with Jimmie at the dance and unnecessarily calling his attention to the gun case in his store."[11]

Several critics argue persuasively that the Munroes (and perhaps T. B. Allen) actually do Shark a favor by shattering his illusions. Louis Owens says that Shark is "much better off after he has been exposed, for at the end of the story he has . . . an opportunity to make real money by real applications of his talents to win real self-esteem." Similarly, French contends that the Munroes have "done good by destroying an illusion that has limited the effectiveness of a man and kept his wife uncomfortable and unhappy." And Fontenrose suggests that with his illusions gone, Wicks finally realizes "the futility of keeping a ledger of fictitious transactions and [leaves] the Pastures to make real investments." Indeed, Shark is probably capable of building an actual fortune given his skill in "sagacious investing" and his record of offering "startlingly good" financial advice to his admirers (24).[12]

But before he could undergo this transformation, Wicks would first have to overcome his stinginess, a trait reflected in his Pastures farm. Yancy points out that in *The Pastures of Heaven,* farms and houses often function as metaphors of character.[13] In Shark Wicks's case, his habit of irrigating his orchard, while seeing "no reason for wasting good water around the house" reflects his miserliness. Similarly, the "old sacks, . . . papers, bits of broken glass and tangles of baling wire" (25) strewn about suggest his obsessive focus on his ledger fortune, while neglecting his family. Consequently, the Wicks home becomes "the only unbeautiful thing on the farm" (25). Shark's character is also reflected in his own appearance—his "blunt, brown face and small cold eyes" suggesting a calculating money grubber who is "never so happy as when he [can] force a few cents more out of his peaches than his neighbors [do]" (21). In this way, Shark builds a reputation as a tricky man who drives hard deals.

While throughout the story Shark remains an odd combination of tightwad and speculator, his wife blossoms into a dynamic, well-rounded character. Katherine Wicks, like Elisa Allen in "The Chrysanthemums," provides an example of what Marilyn H. Mitchell calls a Steinbeck "strong woman" (see part 3), taking on strengths normally associated with men, but lacking in their own husbands.[14] When Shark is publicly disgraced by the Munroes and returns home a broken, defeated man, his "loss of vitality" awakens in Katherine a new strength (44); she experiences a surge of energy, as a "strong instinct" prompts her to stroke his forehead. "Suddenly the genius in Katherine became power and the power gushed in her body and flooded her. In a moment she knew what she was and what she could do. She was exultantly happy and very beautiful. . . . She had known she could do this. As she sat there the knowledge of her power had been born in her, and she knew that all her life was directed at this one moment. In this moment she was a goddess, a singer of destiny" (45).

As Shark's flagging spirits revive, Katherine's power seems to ebb from her body and flow into him. Their old attitudes reassert themselves—Shark becomes sure again, while Katherine feels frightened by her sudden loss of power. Yet her metamorphosis adds still another dimension to this perhaps most technically excellent story in the *Pastures*. With its complex two-tiered plot and thematic appropriateness for the volume, Steinbeck no doubt placed the Shark Wicks story early in the book for good reason: it is an accomplished tale that could easily stand on its own and, at the same time, it well illustrates the major themes that link the individual stories in the cycle.

Tularecito (Chapter 4)

Just as the Shark Wicks story reaches its climax at the Munroe farm, so too does the tale of the strange "little frog," Tularecito. Both Wicks and Tularecito are apprehended for threatened or actual assaults on a Munroe—Shark, carrying a rifle, pursues Jimmie; Tularecito, swinging a shovel, smashes Bert. While in the former story the Munroes' actions lead logically to Shark's disgrace, in the latter, the Munroes are only coincidentally involved in Tularecito's demise. As Howard Levant says, "[Tularecito] could have dug in anyone's orchard. The fact that he digs in Bert's orchard is too overtly accidental to have much convincing fictional significance."[15] The Munroes have even less to do with Tularecito's eventual commitment to a mental institution, than does his imaginative teacher, Miss Morgan, who inspires him to search underground for gnomes.

Despite the Munroes' slender connection to the plot, the Tularecito story is noteworthy for the "little frog" himself, whose body resembles his name: "short chubby arms, and long loose-jointed legs," with a large head sitting "without interval of neck between deformedly broad shoulders" (48). Forerunner of "Johnny Bear" (1937) and Lennie Small in *Of Mice and Men* (1937), Tularecito is one of the first "subnormal" characters in Steinbeck's fiction.[16] Like Manny Munroe, who makes his only significant appearance in this story, Tularecito's brain ceases to develop during his childhood. Though his body grows strong as a man's, he remains a child mentally. Thus, Tularecito "is one of those whom God has not quite finished" (53).

While "subnormal" Manny Munroe spends his time "staring into space" and beating "his forehead on the floor" (16), Tularecito is energetic and multitalented. He gardens with the same gifted "planting hands" (49) that Elisa Allen displays in "The Chrysanthemums" (1937), he milks cows swiftly and gently, breaks mad horses without riding them, and, most important, he draws and carves lifelike animals of every imaginable description. Fond of his own artwork, Tularecito cannot abide anyone carelessly handling or destroying these animals, and this gets him into trouble at school. One day when several children begin to erase his animal drawings from the chalk board, Tularecito attacks. The "ensuing battle wreck[s] the schoolroom" and prompts the teacher, Miss Martin, to resign (51).

The replacement teacher, Miss Morgan, who better understands the "little frog," lays off "a border around the tip of the blackboards for him to fill with animals" and she buys him "a huge drawing pad and soft pencil" (54). While the class works on assignments, Tularecito sketches his creatures. Miss Morgan not only accommodates this special student's needs but also stimulates him by reading stories about "elves and brownies, fairies, pixies, and changelings" (56). But what most deeply touches him are her readings about the lives and habits of gnomes. He drops his art pencil and listens intently. After school when he asks Miss Morgan where he can find the gnomes, she playfully advises him to search for them at night.

Thus in the evening Tularecito takes a shovel to "dig for the little people who live in the earth" (59). Experiencing the extreme loneliness of one who is different, he aims to rejoin his own kind. "I must go home to them," he explains (60). The narrator tells us that, fittingly, there is something "troglodytic" in this strange child's face, suggesting a primitive, cave-dwelling race. Tularecito actually looks like a gnome, according to Fontenrose, and therefore "identifies himself with the little people."[17] He even hears them calling to him "deep in the cool earth" (60). Thus, he begins searching for gnomes and coincidentally ends up in Bert Munroe's orchard.

Louis Owens argues that society is ultimately "responsible for Tularecito's tragedy because it has not the greatness of vision or heart to recognize and accept Tularecito's difference." Tularecito's difference from his neighbors is principally organic. His mental inadequacy and ugly froglike body, however, are more than compensated for by his special gifts. Thinking of the protagonist's artistic talent, Timmerman asks, "How far does [the artist] pursue his instincts and gifts before others call him insane and lock him away?"[18] The "little frog" proves that one can be both an artist and an idiot—both sophisticated and primitive. But such a creature does not rest well with Pastures residents, whose narrow sympathies will not admit someone so unlike themselves. Thus, Tularecito is indeed called insane and locked away.

Helen Van Deventer (Chapter 5)

The Helen Van Deventer story provides a still further example of characters with a mental deficiency or illness. "By juxtaposing the Tularecito and Van Deventer tales," says Richard F. Peterson, "Steinbeck illustrates his belief in two different types of abnormal individuals." Tularecito is "mentally deficient," while Hilda and Helen Van Deventer are "mentally unbalanced," even "demented." Although Peterson believes Tularecito to be less dangerous than either of the Van Deventers, he contends that in Steinbeck's world, society confines those like the "little frog," who are "primitive but uniquely gifted," while it "permits madness to flourish if it can disguise itself with a mask of respectability." Fontenrose underscores the irony in this. "Tularecito, retarded mentally but quite sane, [is] committed to a hospital for the insane; Hilda, intelligent, but quite mad, [is] never committed."[19] A further irony stems from the behavior of the psychotic Helen Van Deventer, who murders her own daughter with a shotgun, and is not even suspected of her crime.

In his letter (quoted above) to Mavis McIntosh about *The Pastures of Heaven,* Steinbeck mentions that there "have been two murders" in the formerly peaceful valley.[20] Of these two murders, the Hilda Van Deventer killing is the only one to appear in the book. Hilda, born mentally ill six months after the accidental death of her sportsman father, grows up an intractable child. She lies repeatedly to her mother, explodes in uncontrollable rage, and maliciously destroys anything within her grasp. When Dr. Phillips, the family physician, recommends committing Hilda to a hospital for the insane, Helen refuses. Not until Hilda begins escaping from the confines of their San Francisco home does Helen decide to move to Christmas Canyon in the Pastures. Bert Munroe stops by to welcome his new neighbors and hears Hilda screaming at her barred window. When the fourteen-year-old proposes marriage to him, Bert senses something is wrong and inquires at the front door, but to no avail. Hilda soon flees, her mother pursuing her with a shotgun. The coroner rules Hilda's death a suicide.

Helen's motivation for killing her daughter stems from an insatiable hunger for tragedy. Helen's morbid need to endure pain began early in life. As a teenager, she "mourned six months," looking "like a widow," when her Persian kitten was poisoned (64). Her father then died, and the mourning continued "uninterrupted." When she married Hubert Van Deventer, he shot himself only three months after their wedding. Helen mourns her husband up to thirteen years after his death. As Dr. Phillips tells her: "You love the hair shirt. . . . Your pain is a pleasure. You won't give up any little shred of tragedy" (70).

Flashbacks in the story reveal how Helen habitually relives her husband's tragedy. On moving from their Russian Hill home in San Francisco to the Pastures, Helen builds a special trophy room as a memorial to her husband and holds frequent vigils there, conjuring his image. "She almost [sees] him before her. In her mind she [goes] over the shape of his hands, the narrowness of his hips and the length and straightness of his legs" (76–77). With this ritual, Helen dwells on Hubert's death, resigning "herself to a feeling of hopeless gloom" (78).

A revolution occurs in Helen, however, when she moves to Christmas Canyon. She is "filled with a new sense of peace" and protection from "the tragedies which had beset her for so long" (78). This "new, delicious peacefulness," this "sudden joy" and "anticipation" (79) helps her to forget her husband. "She [does not] want to think of Hubert any more," since the thought of him almost kills her new sense of peace (80). Hence, in his memorial room when she attempts her "old habit" of conjuring Hubert's image, she finds he is "gone, completely gone" (82). She "thr[ows] open the wide windows to the night," leans out toward her garden and muses: "It's just infested with life. . . . It's just bursting with life" (83). Owens characterizes Helen's change as a rebirth, "from the repression of the old life into the freedom of the new."[21]

But does Christmas Canyon represent for Helen peacefulness and rebirth, or does it rather imply a further bearing of her cross?[22] With the memory of her deceased husband suddenly expunged from her life, Helen's momentary exuberance fades into a feeling of emptiness. Helen's perverted need to endure tragedy and to mourn reasserts itself. As Dr. Phillips says, she loves "the hair shirt" and "won't give up any little shred of tragedy" (70). At the moment Helen experiences this reversion of feeling, Hilda flees from their new Pastures home. Helen begins to realize how she can fill the void left by Hubert. She "unlock[s] the gun case and [takes] down a shotgun" (83). Flashbacks prepare us for Helen's pursuit of Hilda. Earlier she has remembered Hubert's admonition about hunting with a shotgun. "I don't want you ever to shoot at a still target—ever (80).

That Bert Munroe's visit immediately precedes the murder is coincidental. Dr. Phillips has warned Helen that her daughter "may run off with the first man she sees" (69). Bert happens to be that "first man." His wife even chides him for being "just curious" to see the Van Deventer's new home. Thus, Fontenrose views Bert's motive as "curiosity" and his "impulse to neighborliness . . . like his impulse to philanthropy, stereotyped and thoughtless."[23] Nonetheless, Bert Munroe does not precipitate the shattering of Helen's illusions; the Pastures of Heaven itself does, showing her that she can enjoy life and discard the gloomy garments of her mourning. Unfortunately, she reverts to her old, unhealthy behavior. Like other Pastures residents, she *almost* finds paradise.

Junius Maltby (Chapter 6)

Although ostensibly different, the stories of Helen Van Deventer and Junius Maltby have several similarities. Both Van Deventer and Maltby move from San Francisco to the Pastures to improve their health or quality of life. Both characters' spouses die, leaving them a child of their same sex to rear single-handedly. Both are idle, though for different reasons—Helen is wealthy, Junius poor. But perhaps their most important similarity is that while the Pastures proves beneficial to both newcomers, they eventually revert to the old, unhealthy patterns of living they exhibited before coming to the little valley. Helen rekindles her morbid love of tragedy; the weak-lunged Junius resumes his potentially fatal existence in the damp climate of San Francisco.[24]

The Maltby story begins when a serious lung condition brings Junius to the Pastures from a stultifying clerkship in the city. He boards with the widow Mrs. Quaker, who soon marries him and dies in childbirth with their son, Robert Louis ("Robbie"), named after Junius's favorite writer, Robert Louis Stevenson. Although Junius's health improves, he becomes an irresponsible farmer and an unconventional father. Weeds, instead of crops, spread over his fine bottom land, and Robbie grows up in bare feet and torn overalls. The liberally educated Junius, however, teaches his son the wonders of great books and nature. Thus, even though poorly dressed, Robbie wins the affections of his schoolmates with his active imagination and knowledge of the many outdoor games Junius has taught him. Regardless of their impoverished appearance, Junius and Robbie Maltby become the most "gloriously happy" (95) residents of the valley.

But theirs is a fleeting happiness, thanks to the "people of the valley" (90). A "dark cloud," says Peterson, "hover[s] over Junius' paradisiacal life," one he is "completely unaware of."[25] The men of the valley resent "his good bottom land, all overgrown with weeds, his untrimmed fruit trees and his fallen fences." The women loath his "unclean house with its littered dooryard and dirty windows." And everyone hates his "idleness and his complete lack of pride." Thus, the "people of the valley" begin to think of the Maltbys as "outcast[s]" from "decent society" (95). The difference between Junius and his neighbors is clear to them: While they "built small fortunes, bought Fords and radios, put in electricity . . . , Junius degenerated and became a ragged savage" (94–95).

What especially galls the women of the valley is how Robbie Maltby grows up. They call "horrible" the way he dresses in rags and lives in "squalor" (95). But the women are reluctant to interfere, that is, until Robbie begins attending the Pastures school.

Says Mrs. Banks, "We couldn't do anything now if we wanted to. . . . But just as soon as the child is six, the county'll have something to say, let me tell you" (96). Thus, the plot to "give the poor little fellow a few things he never had" is hatched (95). As the narrator tells us, the whole valley lies in wait for the moment when Robbie enters school. Once he does, "the people of the valley" have their way. There is no indication that Mrs. Monroe acts in collusion with her neighbors; more likely, she gives Robbie clean new clothes one day at school purely out of charity. But whether she acts in concert with others, or alone, she carries out the wishes of Pastures residents.

The basic conflict in values in the story involves the middle-class notions of "progress" and "respectability" held by "the people of the valley" as opposed to the Edenic, nonconformist, and happy-go-lucky life-style lived by the Maltbys. In this conflict, Benson sees the typical oppositions in Steinbeck's fiction: imagination versus reality, creativity versus pragmatism. Steinbeck establishes in this story nothing less than "the dimensions of good and evil in his fiction," says Peterson, the "good" embodied in "the simple happy lives of the Maltbys" and their "qualities of self-reliance and adaptability and their simple and heroic faith in the visionary power of words; the "evil" in "middle-class respectability," the "real enemy to individual thought and behavior." "The end result," concludes Peterson, "is the triumph of middle-class respectability and mediocrity over the values evident in the lifestyle of Junius and his son."[26]

Unfortunately, Junius does not have the courage of his convictions, believing he has done something "monstrous" to his son. The key to the destruction of the Maltbys' happy world lies in the lines by Stevenson that Robbie uses in a writing exercise. "There is nothing so monstrous but we can believe it of ourselves." That Junius so readily accepts his neighbors' values, which directly contradict his own, is disappointing. He may be, indeed, a "weak man, unable to cope with even the simple society of the Pastures," in Astro's words.[27] Upon leaving the valley, he tells Miss Morgan: "I didn't know I was doing an injury to the boy, here. . . . I didn't know what people were saying about us." The school teacher replies, "You don't believe everything silly people tell you, do you?" But Junius can only respond that he must not bring up his boy like a "little animal" (113–14).

A phrase uttered by the Maltbys' dour hired hand, Jakob, best describes the story's outcome: "eviction from the Garden of Eden" (107). Steinbeck must have realized the sadness of this conclusion; in the privately printed monograph version of the story, entitled *Nothing So Monstrous* (1936), he added an epilogue bringing Junius and Robbie back to the Pastures. They "occup[y] a cave in the outlying wilderness," where farmers come in the evenings to hear Junius tell them tales about Herodotus, Delphi, and Solomon. The Maltbys have returned to paradise. Steinbeck closes the epilogue with these words: "I don't know that this is true. I only hope to God it is."[28]

The Lopez Sisters (Chapter 7)

The theme of the "eviction from the Garden of Eden" also seems to apply to the story of Maria and Rosa Lopez. Yet, although the Lopez sisters, like Maltby, leave the Pastures for San Francisco, their acreage, unlike Maltby's, consists of a barren, rocky hillside where "practically nothing would grow" (115). In two important ways, however, Maltby and the Lopez sisters are alike. Neither is a respected member of the community, and neither realizes his or her poor standing with Pastures residents until too late. The "ladies of the valley" (122), who fear and resent the protagonists in each story, spread rumors and hatch plots that help to bring them down.[29]

Since Rosa and Maria live on "forty acres of rocky hillside," whose "starved soil" supports little more than "tumble-weed" and "flowering sage" (114), the two sisters must earn their living by means other than farming. When their father dies, leaving them this unfertile land and no money, the plump, jolly sisters decide to open a restaurant specializing in enchiladas and other "SPAN-ISH COOKINGS" (116). Though the sisters claim to be "the best makers of tortillas in the valley," their customers, at first, are few. Then Rosa devises a unique promotional scheme. One day when a customer eats three enchiladas, she gives herself to him. When Maria also adopts this practice, business begins to pick up. As they become more prosperous, Rosa and Maria never let their "sins" accumulate. Following each sin, the devout Catholics kneel before a porcelain Virgin (conveniently placed between their bedrooms) and pray for forgiveness.

While the porcelain Virgin may forgive their sins, the "ladies of the valley" do not. "Inevitably . . . the whisper went about that the Lopez sisters were bad women" (122). "It is impossible to say how these ladies knew . . . nevertheless they knew" (122). Unwittingly, Bert Munroe fulfills their unspoken desire to expose these "bad women." One day when Maria is driving her horse-drawn wagon into Monterey, she gives a lift to the homely, apelike Allen Hueneker. When Bert Munroe sees the two riding together he decides—for a good joke—to tell Hueneker's jealous wife that Allen has run off with Maria. The next day the sheriff calls on the Lopez sisters with a complaint that they are operating a "bad house." They must either close their restaurant or face arrest. No longer able to support themselves in the Pastures, Rosa and Maria opt to become prostitutes in San Francisco.

The Lopez sisters' demise comes as no surprise, having been foreshadowed by the "whispers" circulating about them in the valley (122), and by the repeated suggestion that their good fortunes will not last. Early in the story, for instance, one good-humored customer tells Rosa: "You're living too high. This rich living is going to bust your gut wide open if you don't cut it out" (119). The two sisters consequently feel a "foreboding" about this "happy time" in their lives. "What a shame it cannot last," they say to themselves; and "in fear that it would not last, Maria [keeps] large vases of flowers in front of her Virgin" (121). Thus, although Rosa and Maria delude themselves about the true nature of their "profession" (Owens calls their restaurant a "three tortilla whorehouse"[30]), some inkling of reality must seep through.

Generally, though, "the Lopez sisters view themselves as perfectly honest women in a business world," doing nothing immoral. They deceive themselves that serving up their sexual favors to customers with hearty appetites is somehow different from selling their bodies outright. When Bert Munroe's practical joke precipitates their exposure as "bad women," the Lopez sisters finally become what the community has thought them all along—prostitutes. Says Owens, "Like all of the illusions festering in the valley, the illusion nurtured by Maria and Rosa could not stand very much reality." The Munroes provide them with a "moment of truth," in which they can see themselves as they actually are, though the sisters never seem to admit that they have been prostitutes all along.[31]

Steinbeck views Rosa and Maria's commercial venture humorously, much in line with his view of prostitution elsewhere in his fiction. Typically, Steinbeck inverts traditional morality so that prostitution becomes a legitimate and socially beneficial institution, while those who oppose it seem insensitive, inhumane, and even ignorant. The Lopez sisters provide another example of what Robert E. Morseberger calls Steinbeck's "happy hookers," since he treats "the oldest profession with amused tolerance if not downright sentimentality." Mimi Reisel Gladstein believes that while hookers have a "positive place" in Steinbeck's fiction, he paints a "hopelessly romantic" picture of them, adhering to the "myth of the whore with a heart of gold." Yet "to that description" of prostitutes, says Gladstein, Steinbeck "adds a spine of steel."[32] Steinbeck also takes the sisters' religion lightly; while they are devout Catholics, their many prayers of forgiveness offered to a porcelain Virgin seem to be little more than rationalizations for their behavior.

"Although the sisters ply a scandalous trade," says French, Bert Munroe "destroys their happiness not as an agent of outraged morality or even decency, but simply because he thinks of 'a good joke.' " Munroe's joke forces an abrupt conclusion that leaves unanswered the questions of commercial ethics, morality, and religion raised in the story. This conclusion may seem contrived because the Lopez sisters story was originally part of an unpublished Webster F. Street play, "The Green Lady," the kernel of Steinbeck's *To a God Unknown* (1933). Apparently deciding against using the episode in the novel, Steinbeck saved it instead for *Pastures*.[33] Besides the tale's abrupt ending, other signs suggest that it was not written specifically for the short story cycle. The brief narrative is only about half as long as most others in the volume, and its setting, as mentioned above, reflects not the Edenic atmosphere of the Pastures but rather the drought-plagued terrain of *To a God Unknown*. The Lopez sisters, then, are not really evicted from an earthly paradise; they abandon their "forty acres of rocky hillside" (115) for what promises to be the more fertile soil of San Francisco.

"Molly Morgan" (Chapter 8)

That Bert Munroe's perverted sense of humor precipitates the ousting from the valley of two virtual prostitutes seems a venal offense, if not a community service; that his penchant for jocularity frightens away the Pastures' new and promising school teacher, however, constitutes a disservice to both the teacher and the people of the valley who have come to love and depend on her. Though Steinbeck, at least in jest, views the professions of both the Lopez sisters and Molly Morgan as salutary, only Molly is respected for her efforts. Despite this difference, the female protagonists in each story cling firmly to (for them) necessary illusions. Just as the Lopez sisters delude themselves that "encouraging" their customers with sexual favors differs from outright prostitution, so too does Molly Morgan delude herself that her alcoholic father is a glamorous adventurer who will someday return for her.

Molly has good reason to deceive herself about her father, and her past. George Morgan was a periodic drunk who left home for six months at a time. Molly's youth passed uncomfortably with her two brothers and affection-starved mother in an "old, squalid, unpainted house" (135). But once in a long while a "great event" occurred—Molly's father came home. His surprise visits were like holidays. He thrilled the children with stories of exotic lands, and in his suitcase he bore gifts for everyone. After a few weeks of such celebration, George Morgan always left and took his childrens' hearts with him. Then, at the end of one visit, he left and never came home again. After two years, Molly's mother gave him up for dead. But Molly has continued to believe that he is alive. "Somewhere in the world he lived beautifully, and sometime he would come back" (143).

Molly arrives in the Pastures of Heaven to interview for a teaching position with school board clerk Richard Whiteside. She tells Whiteside a carefully censored version of her life, while simultaneously recollecting to herself and to the reader, in five italicized flashbacks, the darker side of her past. Together these five flashbacks form a composite picture of Molly's youth of privation and loneliness—her father's final disappearance, her mother's decline and death, and Molly's lonely struggle at the

Teacher's College in San Jose. These reminiscences add to the complexity of Steinbeck's "well-made" plot.[34]

The plot turns on Molly's illusions about her father. George Morgan provides an example of a character type Steinbeck would use elsewhere in his fiction, says Fontenrose, "the ne'er-do-well as chivalric figure." The name Morgan, harks back to Steinbeck's first novel, *Cup of Gold* (1929), in which adventurer Henry Morgan sets out to capture the riches and glamour of the world.[35] While the strong and ambitious Henry Morgan succeeds in his worldly exploits (only later to question the value of his conquests), George Morgan shuffles through life as a weak and irresponsible drunk whom his daughter happens to idolize. Molly's penchant for romanticizing shadowy figures like her father can be seen when she delights in the legend of the local outlaw, Vasquez. She even hikes to an abandoned hut where the robber once made his hideout and implicitly compares her father with the romantic bandit. Bill Whiteside disturbs Molly's fantasies with a more realistic view of both Vasquez and her father, calling the former a "thief" and killer (149) and the latter an "irresponsible cuss" (146).

Bill Whiteside—with his cold realism—is the kind of person Molly must avoid in order to maintain her illusions about her father. While Molly deftly keeps away from the younger Whiteside, she has little control over her encounters with Bert Munroe, a member of the school board whose meetings Molly is expected to attend. During several of these meetings, Munroe humorously describes the wayward behavior of his drunken hired hand. Molly, who cannot help thinking this man is her own missing father, resigns her teaching post rather than risk confronting the disturbing truth. French says that in this story Munroe's "crude humor becomes a cruel weapon" as he "destroys the happiness . . . of an innocent, sensitive girl who is an unqualified asset to the community that loves her."[36]

Indeed, it is difficult to see anything good for the protagonist or the "people of the valley" resulting from Munroe's actions. "Molly's fear that this man might be her father indicates well enough that she knew her father's real character," says Fontenrose, "but she wanted to keep the illusion of a gay and charming adventurer, the romantic figure which he had represented himself to be." Thus, Bert Munroe's blunder may prompt just one of many retreats from reality in store for Molly during her life. Her behavior suggests a disturbing allegiance to the past; she protects "her childhood memory of her father as a modern Galahad," in Peterson's words, "even at the cost of losing a pleasant home and a rewarding teaching position."[37]

Raymond Banks (Chapter 9)

That each protagonist responds differently to his or her Munroe-induced "moment of truth" is nowhere more evident than in the stories of Molly Morgan and Raymond Banks.[38] While Molly Morgan flees the uncomfortable "truth" provided her by Bert Munroe, Raymond Banks grudgingly, and perhaps only partially, faces it. The other principal difference between these characters involves their imaginations. Molly identifies with and has fantasies about her absentee father; Raymond Banks has a "meagre imagination" (161), in contrast, and is unable to empathize with the prisoners hung at San Quentin before his own eyes. He continually thirsts for "profound emotion," since he can experience feelings only vicariously through the emotional responses of others.

Raymond Banks is a broad, "beef-red" poultry farmer, whose nose and ears are "painfully burned and chapped" and whose eyes are "black as soot" (156–57). Banks runs the cleanest, most orderly acreage in the Pastures. His farm buildings are whitewashed "immaculate and new" and betray none "of the filth so often associated with poultry farms." His thousands of "clean" and magnificently "white" fowl complement the dark green, well-tended fields of alfalfa and kale they feed on (155). A jolly man who enjoys children, Banks plays Santa Claus at school Christmas parties. Though he is universally admired for his good nature and his model farm, one thing troubles the people of the valley about Banks: his occasional trips to San Quentin to witness executions.

Bert Munroe becomes curious about Banks's sojourns to San Quentin and one day begs an invitation to accompany him. After Banks makes the arrangements, the fainthearted Munroe backs out. Munroe then compounds his blunder by recounting a morbidly gruesome scene from his boyhood, which probably decreases Banks's appetite for chicken, as well as for executions. The incident involves an old man who clumsily hacks a red rooster to a slow, grisly death. Bert has never been able to forget this bloody slaughter

111

and he fears the San Quentin hanging will be just as ghastly. Munroe tells this morbid chicken story, as Fontenrose aptly points out, "to a man who kill[s] chickens every day and [thinks] chicken the best food in the world."[39] Munroe concludes by insulting Bank. "If you have any imagination, you'd see for yourself, and you wouldn't go up to see some poor devil get killed" (174).

Although Banks may lack imagination, he is not a violent man, nor does he contemplate death with curiosity or morbidity. "While Raymond likes hangings," as Lisca points out, "he is not a cruel man nor a pervert." In fact, the narrator tells us, "No strain of cruelty nor any gloating over suffering took him to the gallows" (161). Bert Munroe's interest in the execution, on the other hand, stems from morbid curiosity. He seems to relish in every detail of the bloody rooster story he tells Banks and he takes perverse pleasure in recounting a hanging in which the rope "pulled [the victim's] head right off" (173). Munroe only lacks a strong enough stomach to act on his morbid curiosity. "It is obvious that Steinbeck intends to show that Raymond has the healthy attitude," says Lisca, "and that it is Bert Munroe who has the sick one."[40]

How culpable is Munroe for interfering with Banks's affairs? Critics have differed markedly on this question. "By asking Banks for an invitation, then turning it down, and then finding fault with Banks," says Fontenrose, "Munroe deliberately act[s] in such a way as to affect Banks's behavior." French contends further that "Munroe wantonly and quite deliberately sets out to destroy another man's illusions in order to protect his own." Owens argues, to the contrary, that "rather than wantonly destroying Banks's illusions, Munroe has, by his very human reaction [to the thought of execution], interjected into Banks's sterile world a greater awareness of the enormity of death." And, finally, Levant sees an underlying purpose in Munroe's actions. "By nagging Banks for an invitation to an execution," Bert fulfills the function of making "Banks aware of the community's secret opinion of him."[41]

Banks's "meagre imagination" (161) and his inability to experience "profound emotion" except vicariously through others point up serious voids in his character. The worst effect of his obtuseness is that he lacks empathy for prisoners executed in his presence. "Raymond didn't think of the condemned any more than he thought of the chicken when he pressed the blade into its brain" (161). The principal irony of the story, however, is that while

Bert Munroe self-righteously ridicules Banks for observing hangings, Munroe himself is the more perverse and morbid. To repeat French's words, Munroe "destroys another man's illusions in order to protect his own."[42]

Pat Humbert (Chapter 10)

Pat Humbert, the next Pastures resident whose life is touched by the Munroes, also nurtures an illusion. But Humbert differs from Raymond Banks, in that while Banks is a gregarious, sociable, and popular man, Humbert is shy, retiring, and lonely. Though he desperately seeks the company of others, sadly Pat Humbert "never bec[omes] a part of any group he join[s]" (187).[43] Thus, ten years after Humbert's parents die, leaving him alone on their farm, he embraces the illusion that he will soon overcome his "appalling loneliness' by marrying Mae Munroe (185). Though she has not knowingly encouraged him (nor has Humbert told her or anyone of his intentions), Pat is crushed when he discovers Mae Munroe is engaged to someone else.

When his nagging, critical parents pass away, Pat Humbert is a homely, backward man of thirty. Since the elder Humberts' incessant demands have kept him at home every night of his life, Pat becomes bewildered by his new freedom. By day, he works furiously in his fields. By night, he seeks to quelch the awful pain of loneliness in gatherings of people—joining the "Masons and the Odd Fellows" and getting "himself elected to the school board" (186–87). Pat lives in the kitchen of the Humbert farmhouse and never enters the stuffy parlor and sitting room, which seem to be haunted by his deceased parents. He closes off these rooms and fails to maintain the rest of the house, as well.

After ten years, the Humbert farmhouse "[lies] moldering with neglect" (188). A white Basksia rose has risen in the front yard and engulfed the entire structure with a huge mound of roses. Seeing this beautiful display, Mae Munroe one day tells her mother she would like to see the inside of Humbert's place, since it reminds her of a Vermont home. Pat—now forty and more than twice May's age—overhears this conversation and is inspired to redecorate his farmhouse, Vermont style. He breaks into the two closed-off rooms, destroys their furnishings, and rips out their partition, making one large room. Then he orders new furniture and, when the new pieces arrive, goes to the Munroes to invite Mae over. Only then does Pat learn that Mae has become engaged to Bill Whiteside. Humbert's dreams shattered, the dejected and still-lonely man slinks home and sleeps in the barn.

Since Pat Humbert appears in three previous tales, we know about his loneliness before coming to his own story. In the tale of Junius Maltby, Pat is introduced as a member of the school board, putting himself up for election because he was "a lonely man who had no initiative in meeting people and who took every possible means to be thrown into their contact" (108). Pat's clothes are "as uncompromising, as unhappy as the bronze suit on the seated statue of Lincoln" (108). Steinbeck develops this analogy in Humbert's own story, sketching him "very much like Lincoln as a young man. His figure [is] as unfitted for clothes as Lincoln's was. His nostrils and ears [are] large and full of hair" (186). Socially inept, Pat has "no conversation" and he knows he adds "little to the gatherings he frequent[s]" (186). Appropriately, Levant calls Humbert an "isolated man" who having been in youth "cut off from life by a fostered sense of duty to care for his sickly, despotic parents," finds it difficult as an adult to begin a new life. And Fontenrose suggests that since Humbert has never had the opportunity to be young, he becomes "the product of his past and of his hateful parents."[44]

Pat's problem is that, at the core of his being, he has no identity apart from his former role as helper and errand boy for his selfish parents. As in Steinbeck's "The Harness" (1938), in which Peter Randall remains a psychological slave to his wife even after she dies, Pat Humbert continues to be hamstrung by his deceased parents. As we have seen, Emma Randall's domination of her husband is symbolized by the harness she once made him wear; Pat Humbert's parents haunt him through the stuffy parlor and sitting room he associates with them. Thus he fears these two rooms and can only begin a new life once he demolishes them and in the process, "brush[es] the cobwebs from his eyes" (193). He transforms the two smaller rooms (representing his parents) into one larger room (signifying the new Pat). But he cannot sustain his new life, built on the unrealistic dream of installing Mae Munroe in this redecorated room, once he discovers that she intends to marry another.

How culpable are the Munroes in Pat Humbert's reversion to his lonely self? Fontenrose argues that Mae Munroe does "not encourage Pat Humbert to remodel his inner rooms in Vermont style and to think of marrying her: she [does] not even know that he had overheard her admiring remarks about his house. And she cannot be blamed for consenting to marry Bill Whiteside." "The tragedy," says Fontenrose, "lies in Pat's character and past." Timmerman also sees Humbert as a victim of the past, since his parents have emotionally crippled him and then left him alone in adult life while he is still emotionally a child, unable to account for the adult reality that Mae might marry someone else. As Fontenrose aptly concludes, "So Pat end[s] as he began; the Munroes cannot be said to have disrupted his condition, but only to have disturbed it."[45]

The Whitesides (Chapter 11)

Just as the Munroes are not responsible for Pat Humbert's reversion to his former haunted and lonely self, so too they cannot be blamed entirely for the fall of the Whiteside "dynasty," which actually collapses under its own weight. Humbert, as we have seen, proves to be more a victim of his own past than of the Munroe's machinations; similarly, the Whitesides bring to the Pastures their own ancestral "curse," which predestines their demise. On the surface, however, the marriage plans of Mae Munroe and Bill Whiteside appear to shatter the dreams of protagonists in both stories—Pat Humbert's, of installing Mae in his lonely life, and John Whiteside's, of having his son rear the next generation of Whiteside children in their ancestral Pastures home.

Mae is not the only Munroe who facilitates the destruction of the Whiteside tradition. In this final story, once again several Munroes unwittingly team up against one of their neighbors. When Bert Munroe (with an assist from Jimmie) convinces John Whiteside to burn off some brush on his land, sparks fly in a whirlwind and Whiteside's grand and beautiful home—the most important symbol of the family heritage—burns to the ground. Lisca notes the irony of the house being "inadvertently destroy[ed] by the father of the young girl who is taking Bill [Whiteside] away."[46]

But the Whitesides' own curse, which followed them to the Pastures many years before, is primarily responsible for this catastrophe.

In 1850, Richard Whiteside journeyed west to escape this curse. For the last three generations, the Whitesides had produced only one male heir. During the third generation (when Richard was born) their New England home had burned. Richard comes to the Pastures of Heaven to found a new Whiteside "dynasty," building a durable redwood and slate home on the spot where a whirlwind gives him a sign. Then the family history repeats itself. Richard marries Alicia, who bears one child, John. John marries Willa, who gives birth to one son, Bill. And Bill weds Mae Munroe and, breaking with family tradition (Mae convinces him to move to Monterey), leaves the Pastures home, which is soon destroyed by fire.

Each succeeding Whiteside generation grows less attached to the family heritage established by patriarch Richard Whiteside. John Whiteside becomes "ambitionless" and feels "his interest in the land lapsing" (224, 226). John's son, Bill, says Astro, "is even less interested." Bill's rejection of that heritage, says Fontenrose, is "foreshadowed in his failure to listen when, in Bill's boyhood, his father read to him from Herodotus, Thucydides, and Xenophon," the knowledge of whose works is an important part of the Whiteside heritage. Instead, Bill emerges as a money-minded speculator, whose character is illustrated by his trading a heifer, given to him by his father, for a litter of pigs. Bill then sells the pigs for a handsome profit. Thus, Bill's eventual departure from the Whiteside farm for a Ford agency in Monterey is no surprise. As Fontenrose says, "Bill's values [are] Munroe values: he had no feelings of respect for the Whiteside tradition."[47]

As the most important symbol of that tradition, the Whiteside's durable and stately home becomes the focal point of the story. Steinbeck refers to the house as a symbol of the family in four different ways. First, the white color signifies the *White*side heritage. Second, the "eastern slate" roof (206), more durable than the wood shingles typically used in the West, suggests the Whiteside's permanence. Third, the sitting room lined with gilded volumes of the ancients represents the family's tradition of liberal (Harvard) education. And fourth, the "great meerschaum pipe" (207), given to Richard Whiteside by his father-in-law, marks the passage from one Whiteside generation to the next, as the pipe turns in color from creamy white to rich brown to "almost a black in which there were red lights" (220). This change from white to red and black foreshadows the destruction of the Whiteside home, a charred ruin that, according to French, represents "the valley's greatest tragedy," since "John Whiteside has made both the greatest contribution to the community and has dreamed its greatest dreams."[48]

The fire that destroys the Whiteside home has been interpreted in various ways. French says it indicates "the tragic theme of the destruction of the dream of founding a dynasty, suggesting in fifty pages the heart of the matter in such literary monuments as Thomas Mann's *Buddenbrooks* and Faulkner's *Absalom, Absalom!*" "The fire is a testimony to the delusion upon which the would-be dynasty was founded," says Owens. The tragedy is due to Richard Whiteside's "mistaken belief that he could control the future by trapping his descendants in his personal 'uncertain and magical' dream. Commitment to place is desirable in Steinbeck's fiction," continues Owens, "but the desire to entrap others in one's personal and private vision is not." Richard Whiteside's dream having faded by the third generation, his grandson Bill's values are no longer those of the father and grandfather. Thus, "when the Whiteside house [catches] fire," as Fontenrose aptly concludes, "John let[s] it burn, realizing that the only Whiteside son [has] failed him." John realizes "that the Whiteside dream [is] dead; and he [goes] forth to end his days in Bill's house in Monterey."[49]

Conclusion

When the boy John Steinbeck began spinning yarns of ghosts and leprechauns for his childhood friends, he quickly gained a reputation as a "natural" story teller. By high school, he was spending his evenings penning stories in the attic bedroom of the Steinbeck's Salinas home. And by the time he enrolled at Stanford University, he had firmly set his sights on becoming a writer. For the rest of his life Steinbeck pursued his vocation and succeeded, in some ways, well beyond his own expectations.

Steinbeck launched his career with the short story and returned to the form often. He wrote more than fifty stories, yet many of these remain uncollected and unpublished. Although as a youth he was influenced by James Branch Cabell, Donn Byrne, and Jack London, and later by D. H. Lawrence, Sherwood Anderson, and Ernest Hemingway, Steinbeck developed his own distinctive kind of short story. Critics and anthologists frequently disagree on how to categorize his work. Some label it realistic or naturalistic, others regional writing, and still others proletarian or social protest fiction. In truth, while one or more of Steinbeck's stories merit discussion in each of these categories, his whole canon of short fiction is so diverse that it defies these classifications.

His best-known stories evince a unique spirit of place—the "Steinbeck Country," a ruggedly beautiful stretch of central California coastline and inland valleys. Steinbeck peoples this landscape with simple, earthy characters, whose behavior often reveals inner complexities. The men are farmers, ranchers, and blue-collar workers. The women typically assume conventional female roles, though Steinbeck sometimes creates "strong women" who transcend the stereotypes of mother, wife, and homemaker.

The dreams and illusions embraced by these characters provide a recurrent theme in Steinbeck's short fiction. As we have seen, Steinbeck frequently illustrates the human capacity for self-deception, and the complex and disturbing problems that inevitably result. Loneliness, isolation, sexual repression, and the dubious quest for respectability frustrate his protagonists and sometimes prompt them to violence.

Steinbeck writes with a clear and deceptively simple style. Some critics have faulted him for the very accessibility of his prose, assuming incorrectly that it indicates a lack of richness and subtlety. More than twenty years after his death, not surprisingly, Steinbeck remains a curious figure—a Nobel Prize–winning author whose works are read and loved by people around the world, and yet whose critical reputation (after soaring in the late 1930s) generally belies his achievement.

One measure of Steinbeck's success in short fiction is the numerous prizes and honors his stories have won: the O. Henry Memorial Award four times—in 1934 ("The Murder"), 1938 ("The Promise"), 1942 ("How Edith McGillcuddy Met R. L. Stevenson"), and 1956 ("Affair at 7, Rue de M——")—and frequent appearances in Edward J. O'Brien's *Best Short Stories* annuals, as well as in other "best" collections. Fittingly, Steinbeck's most sympathetic critics call him a gifted story writer who produced several masterpieces, including "The Chrysanthemums," "Flight," and *The Red Pony.* Thus, although his canon may be uneven, to recall André Gide's appraisal of Steinbeck, he wrote: "nothing more perfect, more accomplished, than certain of [his] short stories."

Notes

Steinbeck the Short Story Writer

1. Mary Rohrberger, in *The American Short Story: 1900–1945: A Critical History,* ed. Philip Stevick (Boston: Twayne Publishers, 1984), 178; Mordecai Marcus, "The Lost Dream of Sex and Childbirth in 'The Chrysanthemums,'" *Modern Fiction Studies* 11 (Spring 1965): 54; Joseph Warren Beach, *American Fiction: 1920–1940* (New York: MacMillan, 1941), 309; Clifton Fadiman, review of *The Long Valley, New Yorker,* 24 September 1938, 72.

2. See *O. Henry Memorial Award: Prize Stories of 1934,* ed. Harry Hansen (Garden City, N.Y.: Doubleday, 1934), 179–92 (reprints "The Murder"); 1938 volume includes "The Promise"; 1942, "How Edith McGillcuddy Met R. L. Stevenson"; 1956, "Affair at 7, Rue de M——." See also *The Best Short Stories, 1938,* ed. Edward J. O'Brien (Boston: Houghton Mifflin, 1938), includes "The Chrysanthemums"; in O'Brien's

volumes for the years 1934, 1935, 1937, and 1938, ten Steinbeck stories are listed in the "Index of Distinctive Stories" and four of these tales appear on the "Roll of Honor." See also *50 Best American Short Stories: 1915–1939,* ed. O'Brien (Boston: Houghton Mifflin, 1939), and *Fifty Best American Stories: 1915–1965,* ed. Martha Foley (Boston: Houghton Mifflin, 1965); both reprint "The Chrysanthemums."

3. Letter to Mavis McIntosh, January 1933, in *Steinbeck: A Life in Letters,* ed. Elaine Steinbeck and Robert Wallsten (New York: Viking, 1975), 67.

4. Arthur Voss, *The American Short Story: A Critical Survey* (Norman: University of Oklahoma Press, 1973), 268.

5. See Brian Barbour, "Steinbeck as a Short Story Writer," in *A Study Guide to Steinbeck's "The Long Valley,"* ed. Tetsumaro Hayashi (Ann Arbor, Mich.: Pierian Press, 1976), 113–14.

6. Thomas A. Gullason, "The Short Story: An Underrated Art," in *Short Story Theories,* ed. Charles E. May (Athens: Ohio University Press, 1976), 14; Walter Allen, *The Short Story in English* (Oxford: Oxford University Press, 1981), 141, 165; James B. Carothers, *William Faulkner's Short Stories* (Ann Arbor, Mich.: UMI Research Press, 1985), 1; Bryllion N. Fagin, "O. Henryism," in *What is the Short Story?,* rev. ed., ed. Eugene Current-García and Walter R. Patrick (Glenview, Ill.: Scott, Foresman and Co., 1974), 67.

7. See R. S. Hughes, *Beyond The Red Pony: A Reader's Companion to Steinbeck's Complete Short Stories* (Metuchen, N.J.: Scarecrow Press, 1987), 1–2; *Uncollected Stories of John Steinbeck,* ed. Kiyoshi Nakayama (Tokyo: Na'n-un-do Co., 1986). Available in America through the Steinbeck House, Salinas, CA 93901.

8. Nelson Valjean, *John Steinbeck, The Errant Knight: An Intimate Biography of His California Years* (San Francisco: Chronicle Books, 1975), 33, 43.

9. Jackson J. Benson, *The True Adventures of John Steinbeck, Writer* (New York: Viking, 1984), 42, 54.

10. Benson, *True Adventures,* 90; Valjean, *Errant Knight,* 97; A. Grove Day, lecture at the University of Hawaii, Honolulu, 4 March 1985.

11. Benson, *True Adventures,* 90, 95.

12. Hughes, *Beyond The Red Pony,* 92; John Steinbeck, "Autobiography: Making of a New Yorker," *New York Times Magazine,* 1 February 1953, 27.

13. Hughes, *Beyond The Red Pony,* 92; Benson, *True Adventures,* 1.

14. Robert J. Demott, *Steinbeck's Reading: A Catalogue of Books Owned and Borrowed* (New York: Garland Publishing, 1984), xxiii.

15. Thomas Kiernan, *The Intricate Music: A Biography of John Steinbeck* (Boston: Little, Brown, 1979), 90–91.

16. Benson, *True Adventures,* 59–60. See also Edith Ronald Mirrielees, *The Story Writer* (Boston: Little, Brown, 1939), 246.

17. Harry Thornton Moore, *The Novels of John Steinbeck: A First Critical Study,* 2d ed. (Port Washington, N.Y.: Kennikat Press, 1968), 92; DeMott, *Steinbeck's Reading,* xxiv; see also 21, 137.

18. "Fingers of Cloud: A Satire on College Protervity," *Stanford Spectator* 2 (February 1924): 18.

19. Joseph Fontenrose, *John Steinbeck: An Introduction and Interpretation* (New York: Barnes and Noble, 1963), 9.

20. Moore, *Novels of John Steinbeck,* 92; letter to A. Grove Day, 5 December 1929, in *Life in Letters,* 17; see also DeMott, *Steinbeck's Reading,* 20, 137.

21. Benson, *True Adventures,* 34; Fred Lewis Pattee, *The Development of the American Short Story: An Historical Survey* (New York: Harper and Brothers, 1923), 351; DeMott, *Steinbeck's Reading,* 69–70, 159.

22. Malcolm Cowley, introduction to *Winesberg, Ohio,* by Sherwood Anderson (1960; reprint, New York: Viking, 1984), 165; DeMott, *Steinbeck's Reading,* 6–7, 132.

23. Sherwood Anderson, *Winesberg, Ohio,* 165.

24. Moore, *Novels of John Steinbeck,* 92; DeMott, in *Steinbeck's Reading,* argues, to the contrary, that Steinbeck's appreciation for Anderson endured for some time longer, 132. See Peter Lisca, "Steinbeck and Ernest Hemingway," in *Steinbeck's Literary Dimension: A Guide to Comparative Studies,* ed. Tetsumaro Hayashi (Metuchen, N.J.: Scarecrow Press, 1973). 47; Benson, *True Adventures,* 155, 547, 915; DeMott, *Steinbeck's Reading,* 52–53; 151–52.

25. Lisca, "Steinbeck and Hemingway," 52; Benson, *True Adventures,* 150–51; Edmund Wilson, *Classics and Commercials: A Literary Chronicle of the Forties* (New York: Farrar, Straus, 1950), 37.

26. Mimi Reisel Gladstein, *The Indestructible Woman in Faulkner, Hemingway, and Steinbeck* (Ann Arbor, Mich.: UMI Research Press, 1986), 90; Lisca, "Steinbeck and Hemingway," 51.

27. Jackson J. Benson, "An Overview of the Stories," in *The Short Stories of Ernest Hemingway: Critical Essays,* ed. Jackson J. Benson (Durham, N.C.: Duke University Press, 1975), 292–302. Hemingway portrays women more sympathetically in "Up in Michigan" (1923) and "Hills Like White Elephants" (1927), in which one female character is the victim of male sexual aggression and the other of her insensitive boyfriend's repeated attempts to convince her to have an abortion.

28. Richard F. Peterson, "Steinbeck and D. H. Lawrence," in *Steinbeck's Literary Dimension,* ed. Hayashi, 67, 74. See also Reloy Garcia, *Steinbeck and D. H. Lawrence: Fictive Voices and the Ethical Imperative,* Steinbeck Monograph Series, no. 2 (Muncie, Ind.: John Steinbeck Society

of America, Ball State University, 1972); DeMott, *Steinbeck's Reading,* 67–68, 158–59; Clifton Fadiman, review of *The Long Valley, New Yorker,* 24 September 1938, 72; Edmund Wilson, "The Californians: Storm and Steinbeck," *New Republic* 103 (9 December 1940): 786; Peter Lisca, *The Wide World of John Steinbeck* (New Brunswick, N.J.: Rutgers University Press, 1958), 95.

29. Peterson, "Steinbeck and D. H. Lawrence," 78–80; Lisca, *Wide World,* 96.

30. Moore, *Novels of John Steinbeck,* 92–93; DeMott in *Steinbeck's Reading* discusses Cather's influence (24) and lists Steinbeck's reading of each of the other authors mentioned.

31. See Ray B. West, Jr., *The Short Story in America: 1900–1950* (Freeport, N.Y.: Books for Libraries Press, 1968), 45–46; Rohrberger's essay on Steinbeck in *The American Short Story, 1900–1945,* 178–79; and Voss, *The American Short Story,* 268–73.

32. Stanley Young, "The Short Stories of John Steinbeck," review of *The Long Valley, New York Times Book Review,* 25 September 1938, 7; Wilson, *Classics and Commercials,* 35–45.

33. Brian Barbour, "Steinbeck as a Story Writer," 114–26.

Scenes from "Steinbeck Country": The Long Valley

1. Louis Owens, *John Steinbeck's Re-Vision of America* (Athens: University of Georgia Press, 1985), 106–7.

2. Letter to Elizabeth Otis, 2 May 1938, in *Letters to Elizabeth: A Selection of Letters from John Steinbeck to Elizabeth Otis,* ed. Florian J. Shasky and Susan F. Riggs (San Francisco: Book Club of California, 1978), 6; Kiernan, *Intricate Music,* 225–26.

3. Roy S. Simmonds, "The Original Manuscripts of Steinbeck's 'The Chrysanthemums,'" *Steinbeck Quarterly* 7 (Summer–Fall 1974): 104.

4. Letter to George Albee, 25 February 1934, in *A Life in Letters,* 91.

5. Ibid.; Barbour, "Steinbeck as a Story Writer," 122; Benson, *True Adventures,* 276; Owens, *Steinbeck's Re-Vision,* 113; Simmonds, "Original Manuscripts," 104; Marcus, "The Lost Dream," 54.

6. *The Long Valley* (New York: Viking Press, 1938), 9. All subsequent references to this work appear in the text.

7. Simmonds, "Original Manuscripts," 102; Benson, *True Adventures,* 276; Richard Astro, *John Steinbeck and Edward F. Ricketts: The Shaping of a Novelist* (Minneapolis: University of Minnesota Press, 1973), 116; Benton, "Steinbeck's *The Long Valley,*" in *A Study Guide to Stein-*

beck: A Handbook to His Major Works, ed. Tetsumaro Hayashi (Metuchen, N.J.: Scarecrow Press, 1974), 71; Elizabeth E. McMahan, " 'The Chrysanthemums': Study of a Woman's Sexuality," *Modern Fiction Studies* 14 (Winter 1968–69): 458; Barbour, "Steinbeck as a Story Writer," 122; William V. Miller, "Sexual and Spiritual Ambiguity in 'The Chrysanthemums,' " in *A Study Guide to Steinbeck's "The Long Valley,"* ed. Tetsumaro Hayashi (Ann Arbor, Mich.: Pierian Press, 1976), 1–10; Warren French, *John Steinbeck,* 2d rev. ed. (Boston: Twayne Publishers, 1975), 83; Marcus, "Lost Dream," 58; Charles A. Sweet, Jr., "Ms. Elisa Allen and Steinbeck's 'The Chrysanthemums,' " *Modern Fiction Studies* 20 (1974): 210–14; John H. Timmerman, *John Steinbeck's Fiction: The Aesthetics of the Road Taken* (Norman: University of Oklahoma Press, 1986), 67; Owens, *Steinbeck's Re-Vision,* 110–11.

8. Beach, *American Fiction,* 311–14; Marilyn H. Mitchell, "Steinbeck's Strong Women: Feminine Identity in the Short Stories," in *Steinbeck's Women: Essays in Criticism,* ed. Tetsumaro Hayashi, Steinbeck Monograph Series, no. 9 (Muncie, Ind.: John Steinbeck Society of America, Ball State University, 1979), 27, 33.

9. Benson, *True Adventures,* 145, 275–76.

10. Ibid., 276.

11. Barbour, "Steinbeck as a Story Writer," 122.

12. Ernest W. Sullivan II. "The Cur in 'The Chrysanthemums,' " *Studies in Short Fiction* 16 (1979): 215.

13. Benton, "Steinbeck's *Long Valley,*" 72.

14. Stanley Renner, "Sexual Idealism and Violence in 'The White Quail,' " *Steinbeck Quarterly* 17 (1984), 78–79.

15. For a description of the copybook see Martha Heasley Cox, "The Steinbeck Collection in the Steinbeck Research Center, San Jose State University," *Steinbeck Quarterly* 11 (1978): 96–99.

16. Kiernan, *Intricate Music,* 194.

17. Mitchell, "Steinbeck's Strong Women," 26–28.

18. Ibid., 28–30.

19. Ibid., 28; French, *John Steinbeck,* 2d rev. ed., 84–85; Astro, *Steinbeck and Ricketts,* 117; Arthur L. Simpson, " 'The White Quail': A Portrait of an Artist," in *A Study Guide to Steinbeck's "The Long Valley,"* ed. Hayashi, 11–16; Fontenrose, *John Steinbeck,* 62; Owens, *Steinbeck's Re-Vision,* 113.

20. Owens, *Steinbeck's Re-Vision,* 116; Timmerman, *Steinbeck's Fiction,* 69.

21. Joseph Fontenrose, "Steinbeck's 'The Harness,' " *Steinbeck Quarterly* 5 (1972): 96, reprinted in *A Study Guide to Steinbeck's "The Long Valley,"* ed. Hayashi, 47–52.

22. Fontenrose, "Harness," 96; Owens, *Steinbeck's Re-Vision,* 116.

Part 1. The Short Fiction: A Critical Analysis

23. Fontenrose, "Harness," 97.
24. French, *John Steinbeck,* 2d rev. ed., 84; Owens, *Steinbeck's Re-Vision,* 117; Benson, *True Adventures,* 285.
25. For a summary of criticism up to 1970, see John Ditsky, "Steinbeck's 'Flight': The Ambiguity of Manhood," in *A Study Guide to Steinbeck's "The Long Valley,"* ed. Hayashi, 17–24, and Horst Groene, "The Themes of Manliness and Human Dignity in Steinbeck's Story 'Flight,' " *Die Neueren Sprachen* 72 (1973): 278–84; Wilson, *Classics and Commercials,* 37; Lisca, *Wide World,* 99–100.
26. Dan Vogel, "Steinbeck's 'Flight': The Myth of Manhood," *College English* 23 (1961): 226; Paul McCarthy, *John Steinbeck* (New York: Ungar, 1980), 29; John Antico, "A Reading of Steinbeck's 'Flight,' " *Modern Fiction Studies* 11 (1965): 45.
27. Warren French, *John Steinbeck* (New York: Twayne Publishers, 1961), 142; Walter K. Gordon, "Steinbeck's 'Flight': Journey to or from Maturity?" *Studies in Short Fiction* 3 (1966): 454; Chester F. Chapin, "Pepé Torres: A Steinbeck 'Natural,' " *College English* 23 (1962): 676.
28. Vogel, "Myth of Manhood," 225–26; Antico, "Reading," 48; Owens, *Steinbeck's Re-Vision,* 32; William M. Jones, "Steinbeck's 'Flight,' " *Explicator* 18 (November 1959): Item 11.
29. Kenneth G. Johnston, "Teaching the Short Story: An Approach to Steinbeck's 'Flight,' " *Kansas English* 58 (1973): 4.
30. M. R. Satyanarayana, "And Then the Child Becomes a Man: Three Initiation Stories of John Steinbeck," *Indian Journal of American Studies* 1 (1971): 87; Vogel, "Myth of Manhood," 225.
31. Antico, "Reading," 51; Chapin, "Natural," 676; Norman Friedman, "What Makes a Short Story Short?" *Modern Fiction Studies* 4 (1958): 113.
32. Groene, "Manliness and Human Dignity," 280–84.
33. Vogel, "Reading," 225–26; Owens, *Steinbeck's Re-Vision,* 29.
34. Hilton Anderson, "Steinbeck's 'Flight,' " *Explicator* 28 (October 1969): item 12; Edward J. Piacentino, "Patterns of Animal Imagery in Steinbeck's 'Flight,' " *Studies in Short Fiction* 17 (Fall 1980): 443.
35. Antoni Gajewski, "Nowelistyka Johna Steinbecka w latach miedzwojennych," dissertation, Institute of English Philology at Adam Michiewicz University, Poznon, Poland, 1970, 75.
36. Astro, *Steinbeck and Ricketts,* 114; Lisca, 98; French, *John Steinbeck,* 2d rev. ed., 69.
37. F. W. Watt, *Steinbeck* (Edinburgh: Oliver and Boyd, 1962), 46.
38. Maureen Girard, "Steinbeck's 'Frightful' Story: The Conception and Evolution of 'The Snake,' " *San Jose Studies* 8 (1982): 34; Benson, *True Adventures,* 319.
39. Benson, *True Adventures,* 290.

40. *Log From The Sea of Cortez,* xxiii.

41. Webster Street recounts these events, with several inconsistencies, in two different forums: 1) "John Steinbeck: A Reminiscence," in *Steinbeck: The Man and His Work,* ed. Richard Astro and Tetsumaro Hayahi (Corvallis: Oregon State University Press, 1971), 39–40; 2) Martha Heasley Cox, "Remembering John Steinbeck: An Interview with Webster F. Street," *San Jose Studies* 1, no. 3 (1975): 108–27. See also Girard, "Frightful Story," 33–40.

42. A. Grove Day, lecture at the University of Hawaii at Manoa, 4 March 1985, and letter to R. S. Hughes, 7 September 1987.

43. As quoted by Girard, "Frightful Story," 43.

44. McCarthy, *Steinbeck,* 29.

45. Charles E. May, "Myth and Mystery in Steinbeck's 'The Snake': A Jungian View," *Criticism* 15 (1973): 324, 327, 330.

46. *Log from the Sea of Cortez,* 32; May, "Myth and Mystery," 332.

47. May, "Myth and Mystery," 330–31.

48. Benson, *True Adventures,* 227; Owens, *Steinbeck's Re-Vision,* 35, 57.

49. Fontenrose, *John Steinbeck,* 63; French, *John Steinbeck,* 2d rev. ed., 84; Reloy Garcia, "Steinbeck's 'The Snake': An Explication," *Steinbeck Quarterly* 5 (1972): 85–90; Lisca, *Wide World,* 96; Bernard Mandelbaum, "John Steinbeck's 'The Snake': The Structure of a Dream," *English Record* 16 (1966): 24–26.

50. Fontenrose, *John Steinbeck,* 66; Benson, *True Adventures,* 292–93.

51. Peter Lisca, " 'The Raid' and *In Dubious Battle,*" *Steinbeck Quarterly* 5 (Summer–Fall 1972): 90–94; also in *A Study Guide to Steinbeck's "The Long Valley,"* ed. Hayashi, 41–46; Benson, *True Adventures,* 292, 297–98.

52. Benson, *True Adventures,* 293–299, 310.

53. M. R. Satyanarayana, "Initiation Stories," 87–89.

54. Gajewski, "Nowelistyka Johna Steinbecka," 39.

55. Ibid., 42; Lisca, " 'The Raid' and *In Dubious Battle,*" 92.

56. James P. Delgado, "The Facts behind John Steinbeck's 'The Lonesome Vigilante,' " *Steinbeck Quarterly* 16 (1983): 72; Owens, *Steinbeck's Re-Vision,* 127.

57. Delgado, "The Facts," 70–79; see also John Raess, "Steinbeck used San Jose hangings for short story with lynching theme," *Spartan Daily* (San Jose State University), 26 April 1978, 1, 8.

58. Delgado, "The Facts," 72–73; Benson, *True Adventures,* 289.

59. Delgado, "The Facts," 72.

60. Benson, *True Adventures,* 289–90.

61. Barbour, "Steinbeck as a Story Writer," 115.

Part 1. The Short Fiction: A Critical Analysis

62. Benson, *True Adventures,* 291, 298; Watt, *Steinbeck,* 47; Robert M. Benton, "Steinbeck's *The Long Valley,*" 75; Owens, *Steinbeck's Re-Vision,* 106; French, *John Steinbeck,* 81.

63. Watt, *Steinbeck,* 47.

64. Owens, *Steinbeck's Re-Vision,* 106; James A. Hamby, "Steinbeck's Biblical Vision: 'Breakfast' and the Nobel Prize Acceptance Speech," *Western Review* [Western New Mexico University] 10 (Spring 1973): 57–59; Edwin M. Moseley, *Pseudonyms of Christ in the Modern Novel* (Pittsburg: University of Pittsburgh Press, 1962), 182; Gajewski, "Nowelistyka Johna Steinbecka," 98.

65. Street, "John Steinbeck: A Reminiscence," 40.

66. Valjean, *Errant Knight,* 45.

67. Lisca, *Wide World,* 96; Benson, *True Adventures,* 285; Watt, *Steinbeck,* 44.

68. Valjean, *Errant Knight,* 45; Kiernan, *Intricate Music,* 42–43.

69. French, *John Steinbeck,* 85; Wilson, *Classics and Commercials,* 42; Lisca, *Wide World,* 96.

70. Owens, *Steinbeck's Re-Vision,* 118.

71. Warren French, " 'Johnny Bear': Steinbeck's 'Yellow Peril' Story," *Steinbeck Quarterly* 5 (Summer–Fall 1972): 103, 106; also in *A Study Guide to Steinbeck's "The Long Valley,"* ed. Hayashi, 57–64.

72. Robert Murray Davis, "Steinbeck's 'The Murder,' " *Studies in Short Fiction* 14 (1977): 63; Watt, *Steinbeck,* 44; French, *John Steinbeck,* 86; Gajewski, "Nowelistyka Johna Steinbecka," 45.

73. Benton, "Steinbeck's *Long Valley,*" 78; letter to Mavis McIntosh, 8 May 1931, *A Life in Letters,* 43; see Lisca, *Wide World,* 94.

74. Roy S. Simmonds, "Steinbeck's 'The Murder': A Critical and Bibliographical Study," *Steinbeck Quarterly* 9 (1976): 45.

75. Barbour, "Steinbeck as a Story Writer," 120; Louis D. Owens, " 'The Murder': Illusions of Chivalry," *Steinbeck Quarterly* 17 (1984): 11; reprinted substantially intact in Owen's *Steinbeck's Re-Vision,* 121–26.

76. Lisca, *Wide World,* 94; Davis, "Steinbeck's 'The Murder,' " 63; Kiernan, *Intricate Music,* 186.

77. Benton, "Steinbeck's *Long Valley,*" 79.

78. Davis, "Steinbeck's 'The Murder,' " 11; Barbour, "Steinbeck as a Story Writer," 119; Fontenrose, *John Steinbeck,* 60; Benton, "Steinbeck's *Long Valley,*" 79; French, *John Steinbeck,* 80; Sanford E. Marovitz, "The Cryptic Raillery of 'Saint Katy the Virgin,' " *Steinbeck Quarterly* 5 (Summer–Fall 1972): 108; also in *A Study Guide to Steinbeck's "The Long Valley,"* ed. Hayashi, 73–80.

79. Watt, *Steinbeck,* 45; Valjean, *Errant Knight,* 92.

80. Valjean, *Errant Knight,* 92; French, *John Steinbeck,* 87; Marovitz, "Cryptic Raillery," 107–8.

81. Edmund Wilson, *Classics and Commercials,* 42, discusses Saint Katy as an animal character; Watt, *Steinbeck,* 45; Lisca, *Wide World,* 94; Young, "Short Stories," 7.

82. Marovitz, "Cryptic Raillery," 110.

83. Lisca, *Wide World,* 94; Young, "Short Stories," 7; Gajewski, "Nowelistyka Johna Steinbecka," 96; Davis, "Steinbeck's 'Murder', " 11; review of *The Long Valley, Springfield Weekly Republican* (Springfield, Mass.), 6 October 1938, 8.

84. Arthur Mizener, "Does a Moral Vision of the Thirties Deserve a Nobel Prize?" *New York Times Book Review,* 9 December 1962, 4; Barbour, "Steinbeck as a Story Writer," 122; French, *John Steinbeck,* 2d rev. ed., 63.

85. Benson, *True Adventures,* 261.

86. Letter to George Albee, *A Life in Letters,* 73.

87. "My Short Novels" in *Steinbeck and His Critics: A Record of Twenty-Five Years,* ed. E. W. Tedlock and C. V. Wicker (Albuquerque: University of New Mexico, 1957), 38; Arnold L. Goldsmith, "Thematic Rhythm in *The Red Pony,*" *College English* 26 (1965): 392.

88. Mizener, "Moral Vision," 4; Harry Thornton Moore, *The Novels of John Steinbeck: A First Critical Study,* 2d ed. (Port Washington, N.Y.: Kennikat Press, 1968), 53.

89. Howard Levant, "John Steinbeck's *The Red Pony:* A Study in Narrative Technique," *Journal of Narrative Technique* 1 (May 1971): 77–85.

90. Goldsmith, "Thematic Rhythm," 391–94.

91. Ibid., 392; Owens, *Steinbeck's Re-Vision,* 51.

92. Owens, *Steinbeck's Re-Vision,* 11, 34.

93. Richard F. Peterson, "The Grail Legend and Steinbeck's 'The Great Mountains,' " *Steinbeck Quarterly* 6 (1973): 9.

94. French, *John Steinbeck,* 90.

95. Goldsmith, in "Thematic Rhythm," 391, estimates that Jody is twelve; Lewis Owens, in *Steinbeck's Re-Vision,* 54, suggests that Jody has not yet reached the teen years.

96. Donald E. Houghton, " 'Westering' in 'The Leader of the People'," *Western American Literature* 4 (Summer 1969): 122–24.

97. See Astro, *Steinbeck and Ricketts,* 64–65.

98. Robert E. Morsberger, "In Defense of 'Westering' " in *Western American Literature* 5 (Summer 1970): 146.

99. Philip J. West, "Steinbeck's 'The Leader of the People': A Crisis in Style," *Western American Literature* 5 (1970): 125–26.

100. John V. Hagopian and Martin Dolch, *Insight I: Analyses of American Literature* (Frankfurt: Hirschgroben, 1962), 232.

Part 1. The Short Fiction: A Critical Analysis

101. James C. Work, "Coordinate Forces in 'The Leader of the People,'" *Western American Literature* 16 (1982): 279–89.

102. Howard D. Pearce, "Steinbeck's 'The Leader of the People': Dialectic and Symbol," *Papers on Language and Literature* 8 (Fall 1972): 418.

"From Salinas to the World":
Stories of the 1940s and 1950s

1. On page 1 of the manuscript copybook owned by the Steinbeck Research Center at San Jose State University, Steinbeck lists "Edith McGillcuddy" among a group of "stories completed summer of 1934." Since Edith Wagner initially expressed interest in publishing her own version of the story, Steinbeck withdrew his manuscript from his literary agents and did not attempt to publish it until several years later—with Mrs. Wagner's blessing. See Robert H. Woodward, "John Steinbeck, Edith McGillcuddy, and *Tortilla Flat,*" *San Jose Studies* 3 (1977): 70–73; and Robert S. Hughes, Jr., "Steinbeck's Short Stories: A Critical Study," dissertation, Indiana University, 1981, 175, 290–91.

2. "How Edith McGillcuddy Met R. L. S.," in *The Portable Steinbeck,* rev. ed., ed. Lewis Gannet (New York: Viking Press, 1943), 572. All further references to this work appear in the text. The story was originally published in *Harper's Magazine,* August 1941, 252–58.

3. See Roy S. Simmonds, "John Steinbeck, R. L. Stevenson, and Edith McGillcuddy," *San Jose Studies* 1 (November 1975): 29–39.

4. Ibid., 29.

5. *Once There Was a War* (New York: Viking Press, 1958), 112–16. All further references to this work appear in the text. See also Hayashi, *A New Steinbeck Bibliography, 1929–1971* (Metuchen, N.J.: Scarecrow Press, 1973), 15, for a listing of Steinbeck's 1943 war dispatches in the *New York Herald Tribune.*

6. French, *John Steinbeck,* 2nd rev. ed., 28; Peter Lisca, *The Wide World of John Steinbeck* (New Brunswick, N.J.: Rutgers University Press, 1958), 185.

7. Lisca, *Wide World,* 185.

8. In *Pause and Wonder,* ed. Marjorie Fischer and Rolfe Humphries (New York: Julian Messner, 1944), 401–3.

9. Valjean, *Errant Knight,* 82–83.

10. Lisca, *Wide World,* 212; see also Hughes, "Steinbeck's Short Stories," dissertation, 310–16.

11. "The Time the Wolves Ate the Vice-Principal," *'47, Magazine of the Year* 1, no. 1 (March 1947): 26–27. All further references to this work appear in the text.

12. French, *John Steinbeck,* 2nd rev. ed., 119–20.

13. Lisca, *Wide World,* 208.

14. Letter to Elizabeth Otis, *Letters to Elizabeth,* 14.

15. Lisca, *Wide World,* 211–12.

16. French, *John Steinbeck,* 2nd rev. ed., 117.

17. "The Miracle of Tepayac," *Collier's,* 25 December 1948, 23.

18. See Donald Demarest and Coley Talor, eds., *The Dark Virgin: The Book of Our Lady of Guadalupe* (New York: Academy Guild Press, 1956), 115–17.

19. Letters to Bo Beskow, 19 November 1948 and 9 May 1949, *A Life in Letters,* 341, 352.

20. "His Father," *Reader's Digest,* September 1949, 19–21. All further references to this work appear in the text.

21. *Sweet Thursday* (New York: Viking Press, 1954), 55–56. All further references to this work appear in the text.

22. Letter to Elizabeth Otis, 17 September 1954, *A Life in Letters,* 497.

23. Letter to Mr. and Mrs. Elia Kazan, 14 September 1954, in *A Life in Letters,* 496.

24. "The Affair at 7, Rue de M———," *Harper's Bazaar,* April 1955, 112, 202, 213; reprinted in *Prize Stories of 1956: The O. Henry Awards,* ed. Paul Engle and Hansford Martin (New York: Doubleday, 1956), 262. All further references to this work appear in the text.

25. "The Summer Before," *Punch,* 25 May 1955, 649. All further references to this work appear in the text.

26. Original title: "We're Holding Our Own," *Lilliput* 37 (November 1955): 18–19; this appears later as "The Short-Short Story of Mankind," *Playboy,* April 1958. The text cited here is from *The Permanent Playboy,* ed. Ray Russell (New York: Crown Publishers, 1959), 325–29.

27. Lawrence William Jones, "An Uncited Post-War Steinbeck Story: 'The Short-Short Story of Mankind,' " *Steinbeck Quarterly* 3 (1970): 30–31.

28. Warren French, "Steinbeck's Winter Tale," *Modern Fiction Studies* 11 (1965):66. French also explains the relationship between the story "Mr. Hogan" and the novel Steinbeck generated from it, *The Winter of Our Discontent.*

29. "How Mr. Hogan Robbed a Bank," *Atlantic Monthly,* March 1956, 61. All further references to this work appear in the text.

30. French, *John Steinbeck,* 170.

31. Letter to Elizabeth Otis, 7 March 1956, *Letters to Elizabeth,* 65.

32. French, "Steinbeck's Winter Tale," 68.

33. French, *John Steinbeck*, 2nd rev. ed., 160.

34. French, *John Steinbeck*, 170.

35. Kiernan, *Intricate Music*, 299, 304, 310.

36. "Reunion at the Quiet Hotel," *Evening Standard* [London], 25 January 1958, 9. All further references to this work appear in the text. Roy S. Simmonds kindly acquainted me with the earlier *Courier-Journal* text.

37. Kiernan, *Intricate Music*, 310; letter to Elizabeth Otis, June 1960, *A Life in Letters*, 668.

A Steinbeck Short Story Cycle: The Pastures of Heaven

1. Forrest L. Ingram, *Representative Short Story Cycles of the Twentieth Century: Studies in a Literary Genre* (The Hague: Mouton Press, 1971), 13–15.

2. As quoted in Benson, *True Adventures*, 209.

3. Letter to Mavis McIntosh, 8 May 1931, in *A Life in Letters*, 42–43.

4. Ibid.

5. *The Pastures of Heaven* (New York: Penguin Books, 1982), 20. All further references to this work appear in the text.

6. Watt, *Steinbeck*, 36.

7. French, *John Steinbeck*, 40; Joseph Fontenrose, *Steinbeck's Unhappy Valley* (Berkeley, Calif.: Albany Press, 1981), 9, 15; Ingram, *Story Cycles*, 41–42.

8. French, *John Steinbeck*, 39–40; Anita Virginia Rish Yancy, "*Winesburg, Ohio* and *The Pastures of Heaven*: A Comparative Analysis of Two Stories on Isolation," dissertation, University of Southern Mississippi, 1971, 171; Owens, *Steinbeck's Re-Vision*, 78.

9. Richard F. Peterson, "The Turning Point: *The Pastures of Heaven* (1932)," in *A Study Guide to Steinbeck: A Handbook to His Major Works*, ed. Tetsumaro Hayashi (Metuchen, N.J.: Scarecrow Press, 1974), 90.

10. Watt, *Steinbeck*, 35.

11. Fontenrose, *Steinbeck's Unhappy Valley*, 11–12.

12. Owens, *Steinbeck's Re-Vision*, 81; French, *John Steinbeck*, 44; Fontenrose, *Steinbeck's Unhappy Valley*, 15.

13. See Yancy, "What Setting Reveals," in "*Winesburg, Ohio* and *The Pastures of Heaven*."

14. Mitchell, "Steinbeck's Strong Women," 104.

15. Levant, *The Novels of John Steinbeck*, 49.

16. Astro, *Steinbeck and Ricketts*, 103–4.

17. Fontenrose, *Steinbeck's Unhappy Valley*, 43.
18. Owens, *Steinbeck's Re-Vision*, 82; Astro, *Steinbeck and Ricketts*, 103; Peterson, "The Turning Point," 98; Timmerman, *John Steinbeck's Fiction*, 62.
19. Peterson, "The Turning Point," 99; Fontenrose, *Steinbeck's Unhappy Valley*, 18–19.
20. Letter to Mavis McIntosh, 8 May 1931, *A Life in Letters*, 42–43.
21. Owens, *Steinbeck's Re-Vision*, 83.
22. See Astro, *Steinbeck and Ricketts*, 99.
23. Fontenrose, *Steinbeck's Unhappy Valley*, 11.
24. Astro, *Steinbeck and Ricketts*, 100; Fontenrose, *Steinbeck's Unhappy Valley*, 19.
25. Peterson, "The Turning Point," 95–96.
26. Benson, *True Adventures*, 96; Peterson, "The Turning Point" 97.
27. Peterson, "The Turning Point," 96; Lisca, *Wide World*, 68; Astro, *Steinbeck and Ricketts*, 101.
28. Fontenrose, *John Steinbeck*, 24; Lisca, *Wide World*, 69.
29. Fontenrose, *Steinbeck's Unhappy Valley*, 19.
30. Owens, *Steinbeck's Re-Vision*, 85.
31. Levant, *The Novels of John Steinbeck*, 43; Owens, *Steinbeck's Re-Vision*, 85; Fontenrose, *Steinbeck's Unhappy Valley*, 15.
32. Robert E. Morseberger, "Steinbeck's Happy Hookers," in *Steinbeck's Women: Essays in Criticism*, ed. Hayashi, 41; Mimi Reisel Gladstein, "Female Characters in Steinbeck: Minor Characters of Major Importance?" in *Steinbeck's Women: Essays in Criticism*, 18.
33. French, *John Steinbeck*, 44–45; see Moore, *Novels of Steinbeck*, 30; Astro, *Steinbeck and Ricketts*, 81–83; and Levant, *The Novels of John Steinbeck*, 43–44, n. 31.
34. Levant, *The Novels of John Steinbeck*, 44.
35. Fontenrose, *John Steinbeck*, 27.
36. French, *John Steinbeck*, 45.
37. Fontenrose, *Steinbeck's Unhappy Valley*, 14; Peterson, "The Turning Point," 100; Lisca, *Wide World*, 65.
38. Fontenrose, *Steinbeck's Unhappy Valley*, 15.
39. Ibid., 10.
40. Lisca, *Wide World*, 63–64.
41. Fontenrose, *John Steinbeck*, 22; French, *John Steinbeck*, 45; Owens, *Steinbeck's Re-Vision*, 86. Levant, *The Novels of John Steinbeck*, 45.
42. French, *John Steinbeck*, 45.
43. Fontenrose, *Steinbeck's Unhappy Valley*, 22.
44. Levant, *The Novels of John Steinbeck*, 45; Fontenrose, *Steinbeck's Unhappy Valley*, 13.

Part 1. The Short Fiction: A Critical Analysis

45. Fontenrose, *Steinbeck's Unhappy Valley*, 13–14, and *John Steinbeck*, 22; Timmerman, *John Steinbeck's Fiction*, 69.
46. Lisca, *Wide World*, 62.
47. Astro, *Steinbeck and Ricketts*, 102–3; Fontenrose, *John Steinbeck*, 25; DeMott, in *Steinbeck's Reading*, discusses Steinbeck's own interest in these classical texts (see items 386, 799, 928); Fontenrose, *Steinbeck's Unhappy Valley*, 24.
48. French, *John Steinbeck*, 45.
49. Ibid.; Owens, *Steinbeck's Re-Vision*, 86–88; Fontenrose, *Steinbeck's Unhappy Valley*, 15–16, 24.

Part 2

THE WRITER:
AUTOBIOGRAPHICAL
STATEMENTS ON SHORT
STORY WRITING

Introduction

In his letters to his friends, agents, and publisher, Steinbeck makes numerous observations about his art in the short story. This section contains a representative selection of these autobiographical observations. In a 8 March 1962 letter to Edith Mirrielees, his former English teacher at Stanford University, Steinbeck recalls Mirrielees's unsettling revelation that there is no magic formula for writing good stories. Yet, as he makes clear in the letter, Steinbeck did learn at least one basic rule from Mirrielees that helped to shape his career. In other letters, Steinbeck discusses his beliefs about writing, the place of poetry and music in his prose, how he deals with writer's block, and more. Tetsumaro Hayashi, in "John Steinbeck: His Concept of Writing," painstakingly extracts the most pertinent of these statements from *Steinbeck: A Life in Letters* (1975). Hayashi reveals Steinbeck to be a conscious and excessively devoted artist, who was willing to share his ideas with others.

[Letter to Edith Mirrielees]*

DEAR EDITH MIRRIELEES:

Although it must be a thousand years ago that I sat in your class in story writing at Stanford, I remember the experience very clearly. I was bright-eyed and bushy-brained and prepared to absorb from you the secret formula for writing good short stories, even great short stories. You canceled this illusion very quickly. The only way to write a good short story, you said, is to write a good short story. Only after it is written can it be taken apart to see how it was done. It is a most difficult form, you told us, and the proof lies in how very few great short stories there are in the world.

The basic rule you gave us was simple and heartbreaking. A story to be effective had to convey something from writer to reader, and the power of its offering was the measure of its excellence. Outside of that, you said, there were no rules. A story could be about anything and could use any means and any technique at all—so long as it was effective. As a subhead to this rule, you maintained that it seemed to be necessary for the writer to know what he wanted to say, in short, what he was talking about. As an exercise we were to try reducing the meat of a story to one sentence, for only then could we know it well enough to enlarge it to three or six or ten thousand words.

So there went the magic formula, the secret ingredient. With no more than that you set us on the desolate, lonely path of the writer. And we must have turned in some abysmally bad stories. If I had expected to be discovered in a full bloom of excellence, the grades you gave my efforts quickly disillusioned me. And if I felt unjustly criticized, the judgments of editors for many years afterwards upheld your side, not mine. The low grades on my

---

* Edith Ronald Mirrielees, a Stanford University professor, taught English 136, "Short Story Writing," in which Steinbeck enrolled in 1924. This letter is reprinted by permission of McIntosh and Otis, Inc.

college stories were echoed in the rejection slips, in the hundreds of rejection slips.

It seemed unfair. I could read a fine story and could even know how it was done, thanks to your training. Why could I not then do it myself? Well, I couldn't, and maybe it's because no two stories dare be alike. Over the years I have written a great many stories and I still don't know how to go about it except to write it and take my chances.

If there is a magic in story writing, and I am convinced that there is, no one has ever been able to reduce it to a recipe that can be passed from one person to another. The formula seems to lie solely in the aching urge of the writer to convey something he feels important to the reader. If the writer has that urge, he may sometimes but by no means always find the way to do it. And if your book, Edith, does nothing more, it will teach many readers to perceive the excellence that makes a good story good or the errors that make a bad story. For a bad story is only an ineffective story.

It is not so very hard to judge a story after it is written, but, after many years, to start a story still scares me to death. I will go so far as to say that the writer who is not scared is happily unaware of the remote and tantalizing majesty of the medium.

I wonder whether you will remember one last piece of advice you gave me. It was during the exuberance of the rich and frantic 'twenties, and I was going out into that world to try to be a writer.

You said, "It's going to take a long time, and you haven't any money. Maybe it would be better if you could go to Europe."

"Why?" I asked.

"Because in Europe poverty is a misfortune, but in America it is shameful. I wonder whether or not you can stand the shame of being poor."

It wasn't too long afterward that the depression came down. Then everyone was poor and it was no shame any more. And so I will never know whether or not I could have stood it. But surely you were right about one thing, Edith. It took a long time—a very long time. And it is still going on, and it has never got easier. You told me it wouldn't.

JOHN STEINBECK
March 8, 1962

John Steinbeck: His Concept of Writing

*Tetsumaro Hayashi**

I. Introduction

One of the most indispensable sources for Steinbeck studies is *Steinbeck: A Life in Letters,*[1] a selected, partly annotated collection of Steinbeck's letters edited by Elaine Steinbeck and Robert Wallsten. A labor of love, this book reflects, as the editors aptly put it, "the many moods of a moody man" (*SLL,* p. ix); it also, however, enlightens the reader on Steinbeck's obsessive devotion to the craft of writing. Steinbeck candidly reveals himself through many of his letters as a conscious artist, sharing with his friends his concept of writing, giving them advice on their own writing, and telling them about the ordeal of "trying to be the best writer in the world" (*SLL,* p. 753).

II. Steinbeck's Concept of Writing

In letters to his friends, Steinbeck defines the role of the writer. For instance, in a letter dated February 21, 1957, Steinbeck advises John Murphy, the father of a young friend, Dennis Murphy (author of *The Sergeant*), about his writer-son:

> Dennis is not only a writer but a very good one. . . . Don't expect to understand him because he doesn't understand himself. Don't, for God's sake, judge him by ordinary rules of human virtue or vice or failings. Every man has his price, but the price of a writer, a real one, is very hard to find and almost impossible to implement. My best advice to you is to stand aside, to roll with the punches and particularly to protect your belly. . . . (*SLL,* p. 550)

* Reprinted by permission of Gaku Shobo Press and Shigeharu Yano, editor, *John Steinbeck: From Salinas to the World* (Tokyo: Gaku Shobo Press, 1986), 34–44.

John Steinbeck: His Concept of Writing

Although Steinbeck is advising his friend's father about the inexplicable difficulties of a writer's life, he also reveals the extraordinary nature of writing, which cannot be judged by ordinary standards.

In a letter written in 1956 to Pascal Covici, his editor at the Viking Press, Steinbeck offers another more simplistic reason why he is a writer. In a humorous anecdote, he explains:

> As an answer I recall a beautiful lady of my acquaintance who was asked by her two young daughters where babies come from. Very patiently she explained the process to them and at the end asked—"Now—do you understand?"
>
> After a whispered conference, the older girl reported—"We understand *what* you do, but *why* do you do it?"
>
> My friend thought for a moment and then retired into the simple truth—"Because it is fun," she said.
>
> And that's the reason for this book [*The Short Reign of Pippin IV*]. Because it is fun. (*SLL*, p. 537)

Steinbeck's early burning desire to write appears in a letter dated October 26, 1948 to Mr. and Mrs. Joseph Henry Jackson:

> It [the desire to write] just seemed to creep in from under the door. I suppose the best thing was to write it and the next was to burn it. (*SLL*, p. 337)

In fact, Steinbeck saw this impulse as his destiny—such as he describes it in his letter dated November 19, 1948 to Bo Beskow, his Swedish friend and portrait painter:

> I have so much work to do. As soon as my Zapata script [*Viva Zapata!*] is finished I shall get to the large work of my life— The Salinas Valley [*East of Eden*]. I don't care how long it takes. . . . My blood bubbles when I think of that [work project] and I get a feeling like silent weeping. (*SLL*, p. 343)

In a letter dated June 8, 1949 he writes to John O'Hara:

> For myself there are two things I cannot do without. Crudely stated they are work and women, and more gently—creative effort in all directions. Effort and love. (*SLL*, p. 359)

Part 2. The Writer

In the same letter, Steinbeck reiterates his faith in the value of the individual imagination:

> In think I believe one thing powerfully—that the only creative thing our species has is the individual, lonely mind. Two people can create a child but I know of no other thing created by a group. The group ungoverned by individual thinking is a horrible destructive principle. . . . The individual soul was very precious. (*SLL*, p. 359)

This declaration of the individual's free, creative, but lonely soul was made again three years later in *East of Eden* (1952) itself:

> And this I believe: that the free, exploring mind of the individual human is the most valuable thing in the world. And this I would fight for: the freedom of the mind to take any direction it wishes, undirected. And this I must fight against: any idea, religion, or government which limits or destroys the individual. (*East of Eden*, p. 132)

In a sense Steinbeck is defending the value of the imagination within the context of a democracy, while denouncing systems which deny the right of the individual.

In the letter to O'Hara, Steinbeck also reveals the darker side, the frustration and alienation of being a creative writer:

> Being married to me is a very hard thing. I am kind and loving and generous but there is always the rival (work) and to most women that is worse than another woman (mistress). They can kill or eliminate another woman but that rival they cannot even get close to no matter how you try to make them a part of it. And there's the necessity for being alone—that must be dreadful to a wife. (*SLL*, p. 360)

Often a writer turns to one of his own characters to express his views and perhaps to counter his loneliness and frustration. For instance, on April 26, 1957 he writes to Elizabeth Otis, his life-long agent and friend, and to Chase Horton, who later edited Steinbeck's posthumously published book, *The Acts of King Arthur and His Noble Knights:*[2]

> A novel may be said to be the man who writes it. Now it is
> nearly always true that a novelist, perhaps unconsciously, iden-
> tifies himself with one chief or central character in his novel. In
> this character he puts not only what he thinks he is but what
> he hopes to be. We can call this spokesman the self-character.
> You will find one in every one of my books and in the novels
> of everyone I can remember. . . . I suppose my own symbol
> character has my dream wish of wisdom and acceptance. (*SLL*,
> p. 553)

Thus he defines a novel as the extension and fulfillment of his
dreams and vision as well as a reflection of the writer's "soul"
and his philosophy of life.

In his letter dated June 27, 1958 to Professor and Mrs. Eugene
Vinaver, his mentors in Arthurian studies, Steinbeck defines the
role of the novelist in relation to tradition:

> I, as a novelist, am a product not only of my own time but of
> all the flags and tatters, the myth and prejudice, the faith and
> filth that preceded me. (*SLL*, p. 591)

Here he confirms that the novelist affects his own unique voice,
but within the context of his culture, history, and race. Although
he is an individual, he also is a product of history and culture
at the same time.

Steinbeck discusses another dimension of the writer with Carlton
A. Sheffield in his letter dated December 1952: "The process of
writing a book is the process of outgrowing it. I am just as scared
now as I was 25 years ago" (*SLL*, p. 462). Thus every book he
writes reflects not only what the author is but what he is becoming.
Writing, to Steinbeck, invariably means a new, daring beginning—
a painful, even soul-shaking, fearful, creative experience.

III. Poetry and Music
in Steinbeck's Fiction

Steinbeck, while a novelist, is also a poet in prose or a writer
whose writing is "poetic" in that it appeals to the aesthetic sense.
William Appleman Williams goes as far as to say that "There is

141

a poetic wholeness in it all—and perhaps Steinbeck was inherently a poet who mistakenly chose to write prose."[3] Although Steinbeck's choice to become a novelist was deliberate, he always was a "minstrel" interested in poetry and music in his prose writings.

In his letter dated January 1, 1939 to Pascal Covici, Steinbeck defends the political value of *The Grapes of Wrath,* but in poetical terms:

> The point is this—the fascist crowd will try to sabotage this book because it is revolutionary. They try to give it the communist angle. However, the Battle Hymn is American and intensely so. Further, every American child learns it and then forgets the words so if both words and music are there the book is keyed into the American scene from the beginning. (*SLL*, p. 174)

A little later, in a letter dated February 1939, which accompanied the galleys of *The Grapes of Wrath,* Steinbeck tells Covici about the importance of poetry and music in fiction—the emotive quality of his language:

> I mean, Pat, to print *all all all* the verses of The Battle Hymn. They're all pertinent and they're all exciting. And the music if you can. (*SLL*, p. 175)

For Steinbeck, as Peter Lisca has perceptively noted in *The Wide World of John Steinbeck,*[4] both poetry and music in his fiction remained indispensable ingredients of his art.

Earlier, he had discussed the poetic language of the common worker with his agent. Mavis McIntosh, in a letter dated February 4, 1935:

> There are curious things about the language of working men. I do not mean the local idioms, but the speech which is universal in this country among traveling workers. Nearly every man uses it individually, but it has universal rules. It is not grammatical error but a highly developed speech form. (*SLL*, p. 105)

Here Steinbeck honors the colloquial tradition celebrated by Mark Twain and Walt Whitman. He further defends the value of the migrant workers' language in the same letter:

> The speech of working men may seem a little bit racy to the ladies' clubs, but, since the ladies' clubs won't believe that such things go on anyway, it doesn't matter. I know this speech and I'm sick of working men being gelded of their natural expressions until they talk with a fine Oxonian flavor. (*SLL*, p. 105)

Even earlier, Steinbeck had written about the oral and musical roots of his writing in a letter dated December 1929 to A. Grove Day, a Stanford classmate:

> I put my words down for a matter of memory. They are made to be spoken more than to be read. I have the instincts of a minstrel rather than those of a scrivener. . . . When my sounds are all in place, I can send them to a stenographer who knows *his* trade and he can slip the commas about until they sit comfortably. . . . There are millions of people who are good stenographers but there aren't so many thousands who can make as nice sounds as I can. . . . I have not lost the love for sounds nor for pictures. (*SLL*, p. 19)

Thus Steinbeck reveals to us his love of voices and sound that inspired musical rhythms and qualities of poetry in fiction. Words, to Steinbeck, mean voices speaking in the music of the common men. Hamlet's "Words, words, and words" truly exemplifies one of Steinbeck's preoccupations. As a "minstrel," he sings his words into poetry and music and creates the emotional core of his fictional world.

IV. Steinbeck's Advice on Writing and His Further Discussion of Craftsmanship

Just as Steinbeck was extremely loyal to his friends, he was often willing to advise other writers candidly on the craft of writing. Once in a letter dated April 13, 1956 he gave Pascal Covici, Jr., son of Steinbeck's editor, advice on writing:

> Make your point and make it angrily. . . . It is usual that the moment you write for publication—I mean one of course—one stiffens in exactly the same way one is being photographed. The simplest way to overcome this is to write it *to* someone, like

me. Write it as a letter aimed at one person. This removes the vague terror of addressing the large and faceless audience and it also, you will find, will give a sense of freedom and a lack of self-consciousness. (*SLL*, pp. 527–28)

In the ledger of *The Unknown God [To a God Unknown]*, Steinbeck had earlier written on the concept of telling a story, not to a faceless and generalized audience, but to one person. As the editors of *SLL* point out, "It would be his practice for the rest of his life" (*SLL*, p. 64). Steinbeck also stressed this storytelling technique to his Stanford classmate, Carlton A. Sheffield, in 1932: "I address all my writing to you, whether or not you know it" (*SLL*, p. 65).

As for artistic inspiration, Steinbeck gives one of his favorite bits of advice in a letter dated February 19, 1960:

I hear via a couple of attractive grapevines, that you are having trouble writing. God! I know this feeling so well. I think it is never coming back—but it does—one morning, there it is again. . . . [The best remedy is] to write poetry—not for selling—not even for seeing—poetry to throw away. For poetry is the mathematics of writing and closely kin to music. And it is also the best therapy because sometimes the troubles come tumbling out. (*SLL*, p. 661)

In his letter dated February 13–14, 1962, Steinbeck advises Wallsten in far greater detail on how to overcome writer's block:

1. Abandon the idea that you are never going to finish. Lose track of the 400 pages and write just one page for each day, it helps. Then when it gets finished, you are always surprised.

2. Write freely and as rapidly as possible and throw the whole thing on paper. Never correct or rewrite until the whole thing is down. Rewriting in process is usually found to be an excuse for not going on. It also interferes with the flow and rhythm which can only come from a kind of unconscious association with the material.

3. Forget your generalized audience. In the first place, the nameless audience will scare you to death and in the second place, unlike the theatre, it doesn't exist. In writing, your audience is one single reader. I have found that sometimes it helps to pick out one person—a real person you know, or an imagined person—and write to that one.

4. If a scene or a section gets the better of you and you still want it—bypass it and go on. When you have finished the whole you can come back to it and you may find that the reason it gave trouble is because it didn't belong there.

5. Beware of a scene that becomes too dear to you, dearer than the rest. It will usually be found that it is out of drawing.

6. If you are using dialogue, say it aloud as you write it. Only then will it have the sound of speech.

Well, actually that's about all. (*SLL,* pp. 736–37)

Steinbeck's advice is both specific and practical. He first stresses that the writer should worry about a page at a time only to avoid being overwhelmed by the immensity of the novelist's task. His next pieces of advice establish those invaluable Steinbeck principles that the writer be a poet and a storyteller. What follows is practical advice regarding the importance of understanding structure, of avoiding an obsession with a particular scene. His final advice returns to the oral tradition—he recommends the proper sound of a human voice—an indispensable element of storytelling.

Also concerned with the creative problem of finding a theme, Steinbeck writes to Carlton A. Sheffield on June 21, 1933:

Until you can put your theme in one sentence, you haven't it in hand well enough to write a novel. . . . The process is this— one puts down endless observations, questions and remarks. The number grows and grows. Eventually they all seem headed in one direction and then they whirl like sparks out of a bonfire. And then one day they seem to mean something. When they do, it is the most exciting time in the world. (*SLL,* p. 74)

Earlier, in a letter dated the winter of 1926 to Webster F. Street, another important Stanford classmate, Steinbeck shares a similar view of theme:

> I have been working slowly but deliciously on one thing. There is something so nice about being able to put down a sentence and then look it over and then change it, sometimes taking half an hour over two lines. And it is possible here because there seems to be no reason for rush. (*SLL,* p. 4)

As always, Steinbeck takes "delicious" delight in craftsmanship. He remains a proud writer who takes the creative process seriously and deliberately as storyteller and disciplined self-critic.

V. Steinbeck as a Workaholic: His Concept of Work as a Writer

Elaine Steinbeck and Robert Wallsten state in the "Preface" to *SLL* that "Steinbeck was an austere self-editor of works intended for publication" (*SLL,* p. x). Steinbeck was both a demanding writer and a severe self-critic. He was a disciplined writer, a dedicated "workaholic." He writes in 1931 to George Albee about his work: "I throw myself into work. . . . Our poverty is tiresome, but I can see no change in it. Only work" (*SLL,* p. 50); and in 1934 he tells Albee, "I just work all the time" (*SLL,* p. 93). To Elizabeth Otis, Steinbeck writes on March 19, 1949: "[I am] very hard at work now which is a saving thing. It would be dreadful if I didn't have work" (*SLL,* p. 350). On February 22, 1949 Steinbeck confides in Pascal Covici, his editor, "Work is pouring out of me" (*SLL,* p. 349).

Thus, work to Steinbeck is not only his obsession and passion, but it becomes a life-sustaining therapy. As he tells Bo Beskow, in September 1950: "My work is very important to me because I am an animal conditioned to this kind of work . . ." (*SLL,* p. 411). Earlier in 1930, Steinbeck had written to Carl Wilhelmson about this tireless attitude toward working:

> I take everything I write seriously; unless one does take his work seriously there is very little chance of its ever being good work. (*SLL,* p. 30)

John Steinbeck: His Concept of Writing

Steinbeck obviously was a perfectionist, as he reveals to Pascal Covici in a letter dated Monday, April 9, 1951:

> I have taken perhaps too long with her [Cathy] but I intend to take as much time as I need with everyone and everything. This is one book [*East of Eden*] in which I intend to indulge every instinct I have. And believe me I shall.[5]

All his life Steinbeck was not only active, productive, prolific, and daring: he found his life as a workaholic exhilarating. He confides in George Albee in a letter in 1931:

> You see, my letters are bound to be tiresome because I can talk of nothing but the work I am doing. Monomania! (*SLL,* p. 48)

To Amasa Miller, Steinbeck writes, on February 16, 1932, about his obsessive desire to continue writing fiction:

> I wonder you don't lose faith in my future. Everyone else does. For myself, I haven't brains enough to quit. . . . Thirty years hence I'll still be working. I am very happy when I'm working. (*SLL,* p. 54)

Steinbeck was still telling about the joy of work on March 30, 1959 in a letter to Elizabeth Otis:

> And I have so much joy in the work. . . . Instead, the words that gather to my pen are honest sturdy words. There are many more than I will ever need. And they arrange themselves in sentences that seem to me to have a rhythm as honest and unshaken as a heart beat. The sound of them is sweet in my ears so that they seem to me to have the strength and sureness of untroubled children or fulfilled old men. (*SLL,* p. 622)

Steinbeck even finds security and safety in writing. He tells of this experience to Pat Covici on June 19, 1941:

> I am working as hard and as well as I can and I don't dare do anything else. . . . I find safety in work and that is the only safety I do find. (*SLL,* p. 230)

Part 2. The Writer

For all his joy, Steinbeck was a painstakingly slow writer with exceptionally high standards for himself as a writer. He tells Carlton A. Sheffield in his letter in 1932:

> I do not write easily. Three hours of writing require twenty hours preparation. Luckily I have learned to dream about the work, which saves me some working time. (*SLL*, p. 64)

Twenty years later, he tells the same story to Sheffield:

> I cut 90,000 words [360 pp.] out of my most recent book [*East of Eden*] but I think it's a pretty good book. It was a hard one. But they're all hard. (*SLL*, p. 456)

Yet Steinbeck always enjoyed the idea and experience of writing, a feeling which he shares with Carl Wilhelmson in his letter dated August 9, 1933:

> I work because I know it gives me pleasure to work. It is as simple as that and I don't require any other reason. . . . I have a book to write. I think about it for a while and then I write it. There is nothing more. When it is done I have little interest in it. By the time one comes out I am usually tied up in another. (*SLL*, p. 87)

Steinbeck further articulated what his work has meant to him in a letter to Joseph Henry Jackson in 1935:

> The work has been the means of making me feel that I am living richly, diversely, and, in a few cases and for a few moments, even heroically. . . . But sometimes in my own mind at least I can create something which is larger and richer than I am. In this aspect I suppose my satisfaction is much like that of a father who sees his son succeed where he has failed. Not being brave I am glad when I can make a brave person whom I believe in. (*SLL*, p. 119)

Finally Steinbeck reveals the ecstasy of creative writing and its creative process in his letter dated April 1, 1959 to Elia Kazan:

148

And I watch the words of my translation go down and goddamn, I think they are good. They are clean, hard accentless English prose, exquisitely chosen and arranged and I am overwhelmed with joy because something in me has let go and the clear blue flame of my creativeness is released. I am uplifted but not humbled because I have paid for this with the currency of confusion and little sufferings and it is mine, sealed and registered. And on that whole stack under me, no one could do it as I am doing it. It makes me want to scream with a kind of orgiastic triumph. (*SLL,* pp. 627–28)

Thus Steinbeck finally comes to regard his work as a life-saver— a spiritually triumphant way of life. He was an obsessed workaholic—a first class monomaniac. Work was indeed a way of life for him; he could have it no other way.

Notes

1. *Steinbeck: A Life in Letters* (New York: Viking Press, 1975). Hereafter this source will be identified as *SLL* (paperback edition), followed by page numbers in parentheses.
2. Tetsumaro Hayashi, "Recent Steinbeck Studies in the United States," *Steinbeck and the Sea,* eds. Richard Astro and Joel W. Hedgpeth (Newport, Oregon: Oregon State University Sea Grant College Program, 1975), p. 11.
3. William Appleman Williams, "Steinbeck and the Spirit of the Thirties," Ibid., p. 43.
4. *The Wide World of John Steinbeck* (New Brunswick, New Jersey: Rutgers University Press, 1958), pp. 161–65.
5. *Journal of a Novel: The "East of Eden" Letters* (New York: Viking Press, 1969), p. 53.

Part 3

THE CRITICS

Introduction

During the last thirty years, a vigorous critical industry has sprung up around the work of John Steinbeck. Although his novels were at first the primary interest of critics, in recent years Steinbeck's short fiction has become increasingly the subject of critical commentary. This section contains a selection of these critical responses. In her ground-breaking essay, "Steinbeck's Strong Women: Feminine Identity in the Short Stories," Marilyn H. Mitchell shows that some Steinbeck female protagonists have remarkable "strength of will" and an "ambiguous combination of traditionally masculine and feminine traits." In "Myth and Mystery in Steinbeck's 'The Snake': A Jungian View," Charles E. May reveals the bizarre snakelike woman in the story to be a Jungian archetype representing unconscious, primordial forces. M. R. Satyanarayana, in "'And Then the Child Becomes a Man': Three Initiation Stories by John Steinbeck," illuminates the diverse patterns of initiation employed by Steinbeck in "The Raid," *The Red Pony,* and "Flight." And in "Thematic Rhythm in *The Red Pony,*" Arnold L. Goldsmith explains how Steinbeck uses cyclical imagery to suggest the omnipresent themes of life and death.

Steinbeck's Strong Women: Feminine Identity in the Short Stories

*Marilyn H. Mitchell**

Most writers of the first half of this century concentrated on characterizations of men and the problems and motivations of men. Perhaps that is because most writers of anything other than romantic novels or popular magazine stories were men. Two notable exceptions to the pattern were John Steinbeck and D. H. Lawrence, who tried to release woman from the pasteboard, shawdowy role she generally assumed in fiction. Today, Lawrence's portraits of aggressive and often neurotic women have come under attack by certain feminist critics, while Steinbeck's contributions to American literature in any sense are ignored or dismissed. Mention of Steinbeck recalls only *The Grapes of Wrath,* a powerful social work but not his best literary achievement, nor the one in which he demonstrated greatest sensitivity to female characters. True, Ma Joad and Rose of Sharon are unforgettable women, but both clearly fall into the "earthmother" category which is a stereotype, however flattering. Rather than in this novel or his others from the thirties, it is in his short stories that Steinbeck's understanding of his craft and of women is to be found.

Two of John Steinbeck's more intricate and memorable stories in *The Long Valley* are "The Chrysanthemums" and "The White Quail." Both examine the psychology and sexuality of strong women who must somehow express themselves meaningfully within the narrow possibilities open to women in a man's world. In each case the woman chooses a traditional feminine activity, gardening, as a creative outlet, yet the dedication with which each undertakes her project is of the sort traditionally considered masculine. It is the conflict between society's view of what constitutes masculinity and its view of what constitutes femininity as well as the conflict between the women and men depicted which carries the action

* Reprinted by permission from *Steinbeck's Women: Essays in Criticism,* ed. Tetsumaro Hayashi, Steinbeck Monograph Series, no. 9 (Muncie, Ind.: Steinbeck Society, Ball State University, 1979), 26–35.

and determines the development of character. In addition, Steinbeck reveals fundamental differences between the way women see themselves and the way they are viewed by men. For example, both husbands relate primarily to the physical attributes of their wives, making only meager attempts to comprehend their personalities. Consequently, a gulf of misunderstanding exists between the marriage partners which creates verbal as well as sexual blocks to communication. In each marriage at least one of the spouses is aware of some degree of sexual frustration, although dissatisfaction is never overtly articulated. Furthermore, the propensity of the men to see their wives as dependent inferiors, while the women perceive themselves as being equal if not superior partners, creates a strain within the marriage which is partially responsible for the isolation of each of the characters.

Both Elisa Allen of "The Chrysanthemums" and Mary Teller in "The White Quail" display a strength of will usually identified with the male but which, in these cases, the husbands are not shown to have. Steinbeck's women, with their rather bisexual identities, naturally recall certain female characters created by D. H. Lawrence, notably Gudrun Brangwen in *Women in Love* and March in "The Fox." Critics Richard F. Peterson and Peter Lisca have also noted the similarity between Steinbeck and Lawrence in the "psychological portraits of frustrated females,"[1] but decline to draw parallels between specific characters. They imply, however, that such frustration is due to an incapacity for sexual response on the part of the women.

Elisa Allen demonstrates a very earthly sensuality in "The Chrysanthemums," though not in the presence of her husband, indicating that their failure as a couple may be as much his fault as hers. Mary Teller, on the other hand, is frigid, yet she responds orgasmically to the sight of the white quail: "A shiver of pleasure, a bursting of pleasure swelled in Mary's breast. She held her breath. . . . A powerful ecstacy quivered in her body" (38). But Mary's response is really triggered by the experience of seeing herself in another form and is therefore autoerotic:

> "Why," Mary cried to herself, "She's like me! . . . She's like
> the essence of me, an essence boiled down to utter purity. She
> must be the queen of the quail. She makes every lovely thing
> that ever happened to me one thing. . . . This is the me that

was everything beautiful. This is the center of me, my heart."
(38–39)

Mary has a physical dimension, but she does not respond to that which is foreign to her, i.e., the male, her husband, who in turn tolerates her coldness, assuming that good women are naturally a bit repelled by sex. He understood that "there were things Mary didn't like to talk about. The lock on her bedroom door was an answer to a question, a clean, quick, decisive answer" (36). Because he cannot force his will on her—she had married him for that reason—his frustration in the marriage will remain unvoiced, to be given expression only symbolically in his deliberate murder of her surrogate self, the white quail.

"The White Quail" is as fabulous and ethereal in dialogue and setting as "The Chrysanthemums" is naturalistic. Furthermore, Steinbeck has created in Elisa Allen a warm, three-dimensional character with whom the reader can identify, just as he has made Mary Teller a virtual caricature of the selfish, castrating female who inspires animosity. The only obvious connection one woman has with the other is the superficial but significant detail that Mary and Elisa are childless women who have transferred maternal impulses to a garden. In addition, however, both women are trapped between society's definition of the masculine and the feminine and are struggling against the limitations of the feminine. That struggle is more apparent in the life of Elisa Allen than in that of Mary Teller, who is more physically fragile. Yet Mary is one of the most ruthless and egotistical of all Steinbeck's characters, although outwardly she conforms to the stereotype of feminine weakness. Her mythic depiction in a story that is practically a fable in modern dress leads one to conclude that Steinbeck is using her to refute outmoded conceptions of what a woman should be. Mary is not Steinbeck's model of the wife; she is merely Elisa's opposite who serves to show the real human beauty beneath Elisa's rough and somewhat masculine exterior.

Steinbeck introduces the reader to the narrow world of Mary Teller's garden through a dormer window composed of leaded, diamond-shaped panes. The convex curvature of the window and the fragmentation of its space indicate that the vision of the person within, Mary Teller, is distorted. Having been thoroughly acquainted with the landscaping and contents of the garden, we are finally, in the third paragraph, introduced to Mary, "Mrs. Harry E. Teller," that is. In the last paragraph of Part 1, Steinbeck again uses Mary's name, followed by her husband's, to show that it is her vision which controls the story. For five years she had looked for the man who would construct the garden she had so meticulously planned. "When she met Harry Teller, the garden seemed to like him" (28). Personification of the garden reveals that to Mary it is a "child" whose "step-father" she must carefully select with only a secondary interest in the man's desirability as a husband.

Harry, of course, has no understanding of Mary's personality or motivations, nor does he believe any is necessary. Just as she is attracted to him for his passivity and his income, so he is attracted to her for her apparent delicacy and beauty: "You're so pretty. You make me kind of—hungry" (29). Her attractiveness will also make her an asset to his business: "He was proud of her when people came to dinner. She was so pretty, so cool and perfect" (31). And since he does not expect a pretty girl to have any dimension but the physical, the firm determination with which she engineers the garden's construction comes as a surprise to him: "Who could tell that such a pretty girl could have so much efficiency" (29). His misconception of women is largely responsible for Mary's success in completely dominating him, for she skillfully cloaks her aggressive manipulation in feminine frailty.

For her part, Mary is dedicated to the impossible task of creating something perfect, a beautiful reflection of herself which will remain forever unchanged. As the workmen finish landscaping, she says to her husband: "We won't ever change it, will we, Harry? If a bush dies, we'll put another one just like it in the same place. . . . If anything should be changed it would be like part of me being torn out" (30). But neither the garden nor Mary's life can be completely perfect, because there are always dangers in the world waiting to destroy the beautiful. The threat to the garden comes from the wild foliage of the hill which would destroy its order and serenity were it not for the sturdy but exotic line of fuchsias, "little symbolic trees," obviously representing Mary. The hill too is a symbol—a symbol for everything that is not Mary. It, like Harry, opposes the irrationality of feeling and happenstance to her unemotional rationality.

Ironically perhaps, Mary's love for the garden does not imply a love of nature, for she reacts violently against the natural biological order which would alter her arrangement. Harry is appointed killer of the pests that come in the night to attack her garden, but, though he does not see it, she is the one who most relishes the slaughter:

> Mary held the flashlight while Harry did the actual killing, crushing the slugs and snails into oozy, bubbling masses. He knew it must be a disgusting business to her, but the light never wavered. "Brave girl," he thought. "She has a sturdiness in back of that fragile beauty." She made the hunts exciting too. "There's a big one, creeping and creeping," she would say. "He's after that big bloom. Kill him! Kill him quickly!" They came into the house after the hunts laughing happily. (31)

Harry, however, declines to kill other animals for her sake. Although he meekly accepts her absolute refusal to let him own a dog which might "do things on the plants in her garden, or even dig in her flower beds" (36), he will not set out poison for the cat which had crept from the hill into her garden and was threatening the birds. He argues that "animals suffer terribly when they get poison" (40), and despite Mary's indifference to that argument, he insists that an air rifle will work as an effective deterrent once the cat has been stung by a pellet. Harry may realize subconsciously that the cat is symbolic of him just as the white quail is of Mary. It is evident that Mary, at least, sees the cat as a threat to her: "That white quail was *me*, the secret me that no one can ever get at, the me that's way inside. . . . Can't you see, dear? The cat was after me. It was going to kill me. That's why I want to poison it" (41).

Throughout the story, Harry's threat as husband to Mary's perfection has been made obvious. She locks her bedroom door against his advances to prevent his getting at "the me that's way inside" (41). Of course, the phrase also applies to her actual personality, which he is equally unable to penetrate. Mary does not like dirt, rust, disorder, and slimy things like the slugs, all of which she perceives as concomitants of the sex act. Since her range of emotional expression is circumscribed by the limitations of the self, Harry's person and that which emanates from him are beyond her appreciation. Harry is as much an outsider in her world as the animals and the hill. To her, sex is not a sharing of physical and emotional energy, but rather a price she must pay for the garden. Four times, in describing Mary's response to Harry's advances, Steinbeck writes that "she let him." The phrase is used three times describing their courtship, and only once following the wedding, after which the locked door is mentioned on two occasions. Furthermore, it is significant that "the lot was bought and the house was built, and they were married" (29), in that order. Afterward, Harry is not invited into the garden except on those occasions when he is to protect it from harm. He may admire it but not enjoy it in the twilight hours which are "almost a sacred time" (37) for her. "When Harry came home from the office, he stayed in the house and read his paper until she came in from the garden, star-eyed. It made her unhappy to be disturbed" (37). How she in any way, in fact, functions as wife to Harry is unclear, because even their dinner is prepared by another person, a high-school girl.

Just as Mary, inside, perceives the garden through a distorted glass, so her perception of the home, and the marriage is distorted when she is outside looking in. She sees the living room "like a picture, like the set of a play that was about to start" (33), and having noticed Harry, in passing, reading the paper, she conjures a vision of herself sitting in the firelight's glow in quiet perfection:

> She could almost see herself sitting there. Her round arms and long fingers were resting on the chair. Her delicate, sensitive face was in profile, looking reflectively into the firelight. "What is she thinking about?" Mary whispered. "I wonder what's going on in her mind. Will she get up? No, she's just sitting there. The neck of that dress is too wide, see how it slips sideways over the shoulder. But that's rather pretty. It looks careless, but neat and pretty. Now—she's smiling. She must be thinking something nice." (33)

Harry is but a financial necessity in Mary Teller's world. In begging him to poison the cat, which opposes her will, she is obliquely threatening him as well, and he responds to her challenge by deliberately, though surreptitiously, killing the white quail with which she so strongly identified. This act of destruction, F. W.

Watt writes in his *Steinbeck* (1967), is the result of the "sexual and intellectual gulf between a husband and wife." Although Harry has temporarily forsaken his passive role for action, it is not a constructive one and will bring no resolution. His last words in the story are, "I'm lonely. . . . Oh, Lord, I'm so lonely" (42). In a sense, he has become the white quail, a pitiful victim, while the garden, the cat, and Mary continue to survive.

In this story, as in "The Chrysanthemums," Steinbeck proposes no solutions for the psychological conflicts which plague human interactions. There will always be predators and victims in life which is comprised of mere plateaus of contentment between joy and despair. Although Mary Teller, at story's end, is ignorant of the death of the quail, her period of happiness is nonetheless predestined to dissolution as are all the works of man. She cannot prevent the physical deterioration of her body or of the garden; then what will become of her self-admiration and her husband's love?

Elisa Allen of "The Chrysanthemums," whom Joseph W. Beach calls "one of the most delicious characters ever transferred from life to the pages of a book,"[2] is a vastly more sympathetic figure than Harry Teller but more akin to him in her loneliness and frustration than to his wife, Mary. Still she, like Mary, "mothers" a garden, a chrysanthemum bed, and takes great pride in her ability to nurture life and beauty. She says of her flowers, as if they were children, that "it's the budding that takes the most care" (17). A similarity of setting is also notable. Elisa's house and garden, though not as spatially restricted as Mary Teller's, are proscribed areas of beauty and security which she maintains against the wilderness, yet without losing an appreciation for the wild beauty beyond her yard. Physically as well as emotionally, however, Elisa and Mary are almost complete opposites. Steinbeck continually refers to Mary as "pretty," but he describes Elisa's face as "eager and mature and handsome" (10), interesting masculine adjectives. Mordecai Marcus is correct in saying in "The Lost Dream of Sex and Childbirth in 'The Chrysanthemums' " that Elisa's pervasive combination of femininity and masculinity is an element "central to the story."

Another contrast is that, while Mary Teller's selfish refusal to compromise her ambitions recalls Gudrun Brangwen of *Women in Love,* who eventually destroyed her lover Gerald Crich, Elisa

Marilyn H. Mitchell

Allen's strength coupled with her vulnerability is reminiscent of March in "The Fox." This is Lawrence's description of March: "When she was out and about, in her puttees and breeches, her belted coat and loose cap, she looked almost like some graceful, loose-balanced young man, for her shoulders were straight, and her movements easy and confident, even tinged with a little indifference, or irony." In his presentation of Elisa, Steinbeck's imagery is strikingly similar:

> She was thirty-five. Her face was lean and strong and her eyes were as clear as water. Her figure looked blocked and heavy in her gardening costume, a man's black hat pulled low over her eyes, clod-hopper shoes, a figured print dress almost completely covered by a big corduroy apron with four big pockets . . . her work with the scissors was over-eager, over-powerful. The chrysanthemum stems seemed too small and easy for her energy. (10)

Of course it is mere speculation whether, or to what extent, Steinbeck was influenced by one or another of Lawrence's "masculine" women. What the women do share, and importantly so, is an intense strength of personality which sets them apart from so many of their retiring sisters in the literature of the twenties and thirties.[3]

Elisa is essentially different from March, however, in the frustration she feels in her role as a rancher's wife; and part of Elisa's sense of frustration stems from the fact that her work, even the dirty work of gardening, remains "woman's work." When we first meet her she is tending the flower bed and watching her husband Henry discussing business with two men. "The three of them stood by the tractor shed, each man with one foot on the side of the little Fordson. They smoked cigarettes and studied the machine as they talked" (9–10). Theirs is a sphere of money, tobacco, and machines from which she is deliberately excluded, although their conversation concerns the ranch and is therefore her affair as much as Henry's. Later, when Henry comes by to tell her about the transaction, he praises her for her gardening skills. "I wish you'd work out in the orchard and raise some apples that big," he comments; and she replies as to a challenge: "Maybe I could do it, too. I've got a gift with things, all right" (11). But Henry

161

obviously takes neither his remark nor her response seriously, for he says: "Well, it sure works with flowers" (11). The fact that she strongly believes in her ability to perform paid work emerges again in her conversation with the itinerant pot-mender who boasts of his skill in the trade. She responds to this with a more positive challenge: "You might be surprised to have a rival some time. I can sharpen scissors, too. And I can beat the dents out of little pots. I could show you what a woman might do" (19). But he tells her that his life, which she views romantically, "ain't the right kind of life for a woman" (19).

Elisa may know nothing of the world beyond her valley, but she believes in her talents and in the possibility of a life more rewarding than her own. As the man and his equipage move on down the road, she stands at the fence watching him: "Her lips moved silently, forming the words 'Good-bye—good-bye.' Then she whispered, 'That's a bright direction. There's a glowing there' " (20). At the conclusion when the man's disregard for her and her work has been revealed by his callous disposal of her gift of the plants, she grasps at adventure on a smaller scale: wine with dinner. She acknowledges the fact that a man's freedom is denied her by agreeing with her husband that she would, after all, probably dislike the prizefights, saying: "It will be enough if we can have wine. It will be plenty" (23).

Elisa's ambiguous combination of traditionally masculine and feminine traits, more apparent than Mary Teller's, has a great deal to do with making her a plausible character. It is also fully half the concern of the story. The second major theme of "The Chrysanthemums" is related to the first in its revelation of Elisa's sensuality and the apparent sexual frustration she experiences in her marriage. While she and her husband appear to be friends, there is a definite failure of communication between them in the exchange of ideas; therefore, it is reasonable to assume a similar malfunction of sexual communication. The exchange of dialogue following her meeting with the tinker and prior to the couple's evening in town is a typical example of Henry's capacity for understatement and his embarrassment in her presence. Elisa has just dressed in the garment "which was the symbol of her prettiness" (21) and is waiting on the porch for Henry to appear. As he emerges from the house,

Marilyn H. Mitchell

Elisa stiffened and her face grew tight. Henry stopped short and
looked at her. "Why—why, Elisa. You look so nice!"
"Nice? You think I look nice? What do you mean by 'nice'?"
Henry blundered on. "I don't know. I mean you look different,
strong and happy."
"I am strong? Yes, strong. What do you mean 'strong'?"
He looked bewildered. "You're playing some kind of a game,"
he said helplessly. "It's a kind of a play." (21)

In the tinker, though, Elisa finds a man whose strength seems
to match hers, although she later discovers his emotional poverty.
Their brief encounter reveals an aspect of Elisa which is not seen
in her dealings with Henry—her erotic potential.

At first, she reacts to the tinker with firm sales resistance but
is brought into sympathy with him by the interest he expresses
in her flowers. At last he shatters her resistance by asking for a
pot of the young shoots to give a customer of his who has no
chrysanthemums. It is at this point that Elisa begins to respond
to him in a sexual fashion and shifts rapidly into the feminine,
passive role. Steinbeck's imagery builds to Elisa's orgasmic speech
to the tinker, then recedes in the afterglow of her bathing.

The first sign of change in Elisa is her desire to appear womanly
for the man: "She tore off the battered hat and shook out her
dark pretty hair" (16). As she eagerly begins the transplanting,
her gloves are discarded and she feels the rich earth between her
bare fingers, an obviously sensual image. In the process she finds
herself "kneeling on the ground looking up at him. Her breast
swelled passionately" (18). She is now below him in the traditional
female position for intercourse. "Elisa's voice grew husky" as she
tried to express for them both the feeling one has, alone, at night,
beneath the stars:

"Why, you rise up and up! Every pointed star gets driven into
your body. It's like that. Hot and sharp and—lovely."
Kneeling there, her hand went out toward his legs in the greasy
black trousers. Her hesitant fingers almost touched the cloth.
Then her hand dropped to the ground. She crouched low like a
fawning dog. (18)

Elisa is subconsciously contrasting him with her husband as a
potential sexual partner. Ray B. West, Jr., says in *The Short Story*

163

in America, 1900–1950 (1952) that Elisa's vigorous bathing, following the tinker's departure, is an attempt on her part to maintain the physical vitality which he had aroused. It is equally probable that Elisa is attempting to wash away the taint of her own sensual approach to a stranger, whether or not he recognized her passion. The very idea that she might, even for a moment, have contemplated disloyalty toward the kind, if obtuse, Henry would impel her to scrub "legs and thighs, loins and chest and arms, until her skin was scratched and red" (20). Steinbeck enumerates these parts of her body, the sexual ones, omitting mention of her face and hands which he had previously described as dirt-smudged. It is clear that he means this passage to be part of the story's sexual focus, and that he uses it as another detail which shows Elisa to be sexually repressed.

Despite whatever guilt Elisa feels as a result of the afternoon's experience, she also feels renewed confidence in her spiritual strength and in her physical attractiveness. Following the bath, she lingers awhile before the mirror appraising her body from different angles. Then she dresses slowly, luxuriously in her finest, newest clothing and expends a considerable amount of effort on her makeup.

Possibly because Elisa identifies so strongly with the male, at least in terms of a desire for adventure, she is vulnerable to the sexual appeal of a man. For whatever reasons, her husband does not stimulate her latent eroticism, so she has indulged herself in a fantasy involving a stranger. Her fantasy, however, is cruelly shattered by the tinker's deceit. She had believed they shared common emotions, that they actually communicated, but now she sees his talk as the saleman's trick that it was. In fact, he hadn't even the sensitivity to dump the plants furtively; he was too greedy to retain the pot. So she must see her small and broken flowers in the highway, a symbol of her broken dreams. Intuitively, she knows that her life will not change substantially, that the seasons will follow each other inexorably, and that only the birds will be migratory. Steinbeck says: "She turned up her coat collar so he [Henry] could not see that she was crying weakly—like an old woman" (23). Indeed, part of the vision she must be seeing is herself as an old woman. Her dream of something in life beyond mere existence is crushed at this moment.

Marilyn H. Mitchell

Henry is unaware of Elisa's suffering, nor could he offer effective consolation were he to notice her change of mood. Like the Tellers, the Allens are separated from one another by sexual, temperamental, and intellectual differences which they seem incapable of bridging. The women have certain needs of the spirit, the abstract nature of which keeps happiness forever elusive. The men are more practical, with greater involvement in physical concerns; but confronted by women whose malaise is partially due to a confusion of sexual identity, the men retreat from the masculine role of leadership, leaving the women to flounder between aggression and submission. Undoubtedly, part of the attraction the tinker holds for Elisa is his independence and the confidence of his manner which her husband apparently lacks. Likewise, Harry Teller, in his indulgence of Mary's whims, encourages her selfish dictation of their lives to the detriment of both partners. Steinbeck is not advocating that wives be submissive to their husbands; if his opinion on male-female relations can be interpreted at all from the two stories, it would seem to support a sharing of interests determined through real communication between people, so that none can say with Harry Teller: "Oh, Lord, I'm so lonely" (42).

Notes

1. Peter Lisca, *The Wide World of John Steinbeck* (New Brunswick, N.J.: Rutgers University Press, 1958), p. 95; Richard F. Peterson, "The God in the Darkness: A Study of John Steinbeck and D. H. Lawrence," in *Steinbeck's Literary Dimension: A Guide to Comparative Studies,* ed. Tetsumaro Hayashi (Metuchen, N.J.: Scarecrow Press, 1973), p. 68. Peter Lisca sees in these stories from *The Long Valley* "a certain resemblance to the preoccupations of D. H. Lawrence, for whom Steinbeck has expressed some admiration" (p. 95). Unfortunately, neither Lisca nor Peterson reveals what of Lawrence's Steinbeck read. Peterson, however, does say that Mary Teller functions toward her husband in somewhat the same fashion as Mrs. Morel does toward the men in her family *(Sons and Lovers),* and that Harry Teller's eventual isolation resembles that of Anton Skrebensky *(The Rainbow)* and Gerald Crich *(Women in Love).*

2. Joseph W. Beach, quoted in *Steinbeck and His Critics,,* eds. E. W. Tedlock, Jr. and C. V. Wicker, (Albuquerque: University of New Mexico Press, 1969), p. 83.

3. An alternate model for Elisa Allen, especially for her frustration, could also have been Steinbeck's first wife, Carol Henning, to whom he was married at the time this story was written. During the period of

their marriage, Steinbeck was in the most active phase of his career as writer, explorer, and observer of California and the surrounding territory. This meant long absences from his wife and hours of solitary writing while at home. According to Warren French, *John Steinbeck* (New York: Twayne, 1961), p. 26, she divorced him in 1942, "on the grounds that she was too much alone at Pacific Grove." Such an action at least indicates firmness of decision; it would be interesting to investigate her further as a possible model for Steinbeck's characterizations of women.

Myth and Mystery in Steinbeck's "The Snake": A Jungian View
Charles E. May*

John Steinbeck's short story about a woman who buys a rattlesnake and then pays to watch it eat a white rat has been a mystery to readers since it was published in *The Long Valley* in 1938.[1] According to Steinbeck it was a mystery to him as well, one of the mysteries that were constant at the laboratory of his friend Ed Ricketts. "I wrote it just as it happened. I don't know what it means and do not even answer the letters asking what its philosophic intent is. It just happened." Summarizing the actual incident, Steinbeck says that the frightening thing was that as the snake unhinged its jaws before swallowing the rat, "the woman, who watched the process closely, moved her jaws and stretched her mouth as the snake was doing. After the rat was swallowed, she paid for a year's supply of rats and said she would come back. But she never did come back. Whether the woman was driven by a sexual, a religious, a zoophilic, or a gustatory impulse we never could figure."[2]

The few readers who have commented in passing on the story seem satisfied that the mystery stems from the psychological problems of the woman. Most of them agree that the story is a

* From *Criticism* 15, no. 4 (1973): 322–35. Reprinted by permission of Wayne State University Press. Copyright 1973, Wayne State University Press.

tale of sex perversion about a neurotic woman who intrudes into a zoological garden of Eden and objectifies her frustration by watching a male rattlesnake eat a white rat.[3] Edmund Wilson has singled the story out as characteristic of Steinbeck's tendency to present human life in animal terms, not those "aspects of animals that seem most attractive to humans, but rather the processes of life itself." Such a subject is a limited one, Wilson says. "This tendency on Steinbeck's part to animalize humanity is evidently one of the causes of his relative unsuccess at creating individual humans."[4] Only Warren French has suggested that the central focus of the story is not so much the woman as it is "what she allows us to learn about another." Steinbeck's sympathy, French says, "lies not with those who give free rein to irrational drives, but those who seek knowledge of the world they live in."[5] However, French's assumption—that the scientific method is the only way to gain knowledge of the world—is not born out by the story. In fact, just the opposite is true; the inadequacy of scientific knowledge is the essential subject of "The Snake."

The critics' failure to understand the story is symptomatic of a general failure of readers to understand the short story form itself, to distinguish from the novel the short story's characteristic subject, technique, and aesthetic intent. The basic distinction critics have failed to note (as indicated by their sole concern with what drives the woman to her strange compulsion in "The Snake") is between how we respond to character in the two forms. Edmund Wilson's comments are central, for his criticism of Steinbeck's focus on the "processes of life itself" instead of individual human beings is based on the assumption that fiction must present individualized characters with whom the reader can identify. However, Frank O'Connor has suggested that while such individualizing may be true for the novel, it is not necessarily true for the short story. The novel, O'Connor says, is "bound to a process of identification between the reader and the character. . . . And this process of identification invariably leads to some concept of normality—hostile or friendly—with society as a whole." However, there is usually no character with whom the reader can identify in short fiction and no form of society a character can regard as normal.[6] Northrop Frye makes a similar distinction between the novel and the romance which may offer, if not an aesthetic, at least an historical explanation of the difference between the novel and the short story. The generic roots of twentieth-century short fiction are in the nineteenth-century romance, as Frye defines it:

> The romancer does not attempt to create "real people" so much as stylized figures which expand into psychological archetypes. It is in the romance that we find Jung's libido, anima, and shadow reflected in the hero, heroine, and villain respectively. That is why the romance so often radiates a glow of subjective intensity that the novel lacks, and why a suggestion of allegory is constantly creeping in around its fringes.[7]

Once we readjust our generic expectations and see that the woman in Steinbeck's story is a psychological archetype instead of a psychologically abnormal individual, the mystery of the story becomes, not allegorically evident, but mythically significant. Within the short story form, related as it is to the romance, Steinbeck is not bound to create individual human beings. What Edmund Wilson refers to as characteristics of animal in the woman may be better understood as characteristic of her role as anima, that personification of the feminine which Jung says has " 'occult' connexions with 'mysteries,' with the world of darkness in general." When in "dreams or other spontaneous manifestation," Jung says, we meet with an ambivalent, unknown female figure, "it is advisable to let her keep her independence and not reduce her arbitrarily to something known. . . . In all [such] accounts the anima . . . is a being that belongs to a different order of things."[8]

And because the woman belongs to a different order of things, so does the story embody a different level of activity than either the practical or the theoretical. It embodies rather that lower substratum, which Ernst Cassirer says we are prone to forget, that lies beneath them both—the level of mythical activity. In fact, the mysterious incident recounted in "The Snake" is a reaction of the mythic world against the efforts of science to obliterate it. The anima force embodied in the woman rises out of the primeval sea, disrupts the doctor's methodical scientific process, upsets his calm and ordered existence, and then goes back to her sea home never to be seen by him again. Critics have failed to respond to the story because they have failed to distinguish between the theoretical world and properties and the mythical world which Cassirer says is more fluid and fluctuating.

In order to grasp and to describe this difference we may say
that what myth primarily perceives are not objective but *physiognomic* characters. . . . The world of myth is a dramatic
world—a world of actions, of forces, of conflicting powers. In
every phenomenon of nature it sees the collision of these powers.
Mythical perception is always impregnated with these emotional
qualities. Whatever is seen or felt is surrounded by a specific
atmosphere—an atmosphere of joy or grief, of anguish, of excitement, of exultation or depression.[9]

For various complex historical and aesthetic reasons (which I
intend to examine in detail at another time) such physiognomic
characters and emotional qualities have always played a more
important role in short fiction than they have in the novel. Several
fiction writers have suggested but failed to explore or substantiate
this characteristic of the form. Elizabeth Bowen has said that the
short story must have the emotion and spontaneity of the lyric;
Alberto Moravia says it is the product of lyrical institutions rather
than philosophic ideas as the novel is; and Joyce Carol Oates
recently suggested that the short story is a "dream verbalized"
and that its most interesting characteristic is its mystery.[10] Eudora
Welty, in an article that predates Oates' observation by over twenty
years, has also said that the first thing we notice about a story is
its mystery. The cause of this mystery, as she describes it, sounds
quite similar to the emotional qualities of myth that Cassirer
notes. "The first thing we notice about our story is that we can't
really see the solid outlines of it—it seems bathed in something
of its own. It is wrapped in an atmosphere."[11] Finally, we need
only to turn to one more great story teller, Joseph Conrad, to
grasp the relationship between Oates' suggestion that the story is
a dream verbalized and Welty's idea that it is wrapped in an
atmosphere. For Marlowe, Conrad's story-telling surrogate, the
meaning of an episode is a mythic not a theoretical one, to be
found "not inside like a kernel, but outside enveloping the tale
which brought it out only as a glow brings out a haze." In his
attempt to convey to his listeners the significance of the story of
Kurtz, Marlowe understands the difficulty of verbalizing those
physiognomic characters which inhabit the heart of darkness. "Do
you see the story? Do you see anything? It seems to me I am
trying to tell you a dream—making a vain attempt, because no

relation of a dream can convey the dream sensation, that commingling of absurdity, surprise, and bewilderment in a tremor of struggling revolt, that notion of being captured by the incredible which is the very essence of dreams. . . ."

In the following discussion I hope to show that "The Snake" is a paradigmatic example of this quality of short fiction; for in describing a thing that "just happened," Steinbeck conveys that very commingling of absurdity, surprise, and bewilderment of the young Dr. Phillips' being captured by the incredible forces of the mythic realm. And because the story is an account of dream reality rather than phenomenal reality its meaning is not to be found in a kernel within but in the atmosphere which surrounds it, in the emotional qualities which impregnate it.

The forces which oppose each other in the story are suggested in the first paragraph by the juxtaposition of the laboratory and the tide pool: the one a "tight little building" closed off from nature yet built for the purpose of observing nature, the other the primal source of life itself where the mysteries of nature truly take place.[12] The action that opens the story—Dr. Phillips' leaving the tide pool for the laboratory—creates an atmosphere that echoes with ominousness. We need only think of the pervasive stereotype of the misguided scientist—Hawthorne's Rappaccini and Mary Shelley's Dr. Frankenstein come immediately to mind—to recognize this first scene. In the growing darkness the doctor swings a sack over his shoulder, squashes through the street until he enters a laboratory where rats scamper in their cages and captive cats mew for milk; he turns on a light over a dissection table, dumps his clammy sack on the floor, and goes over to glass cages where rattlesnakes "recognize" him and pull in their forked tongues.

Even when we discover that the clammy sack is filled only with common starfish and that the dissection table is used for small animals, we are still apprehensive that something is not "natural" about the laboratory or the young doctor who has the "preoccupied eyes of one who looks through a microscope a great deal" and whose bedroom is a book-lined cell containing an army cot, a reading light and an uncomfortable chair." The imagery is too much that of one who, having withdrawn from life, is content merely to look on, of one who does not live life but experiments with it.

Charles E. May

A central and recurring element of the conflict between the laboratory and the sea, one that reminds us that the doctor may not be completely safe in his "tight little building," is the sound of the waves that wash quietly about the piles underneath. For the laboratory, as might be expected in a story that deals with the conflict between primal reality and everyday reality, stands "partly on piers over the bay water and partly on the land." Until the woman enters and symbolically embodies the sound of the sea, the washing of the waves are counterpointed against the homey, everyday hum of the doctor's kettle boiling water for his dinner. This sound then establishes another juxtaposition of the doctor's normal activity of preparing and eating his meal with the instruments of his "abnormal" scientific experiments. He lifts the can of beans out of the boiling water with a pair of forceps and eats his meal out of one of the specimen watch-glasses. "While he ate he watched the starfish on the table. From between the rays little drops of milky fluid were exuding." With the same disinterestedness he takes a cat out of a cage, strokes her for a moment, and then places her in "the killing chamber" and turns on the gas. "While the short soft struggle went on in the black box he filled the saucers with milk." The short soft struggle of the cat echoes the sound of the waves which become "little sighs" as the doctor begins his work on the starfish and hears "quick steps on the wooden stairs and a strong knocking at the door."

Most of the description of the woman clearly and simply establishes her physical identity with the snake. Tall and lean, dressed in a severe dark suit, she has straight black hair growing low on a flat forehead. "He noted how short her chin was between lower lip and point." Her dark eyes, "veiled with dust," look at him without seeming to see him. As she waits to talk to him, she seems completely at rest. "Her eyes were bright but the rest of her was almost in a state of suspended animation. He thought, 'Low metabolic rate, almost as low as a frog's, from the looks.'" However, other details and actions of the woman are not so clearly related to the snake. She does not want to look into the microscope although the doctor thinks, "People always wanted to look through the glass." Her eyes do not center on him; "rather they covered him and seemed to see in a big circle around him." When the doctor goes over to the rattlesnake cage, he turns to find her standing beside him. "He had not heard her get up from the

171

chair. He had heard only the splash of water among the piles and the scampering of rats on the wire screen." Later, when the doctor puts the rat into the snake cage, the room becomes very silent. "Dr. Phillips did not know whether the water sighed among the piles or whether the woman sighed." Finally, when the woman leaves, the doctor hears her footsteps on the stairs but "could not hear her walk away on the pavement." These details do not identify the woman with the snake so much as they identify her with the sea itself. The yoking of the sounds she makes with the sound of the waves underneath the laboratory makes this clear. The doctor does not hear her walk away on the pavement because she does not walk away; she goes back to the tide pool that she came from, back to the "deep pool of consciousness" out of which she awakens when the doctor is ready to talk to her.

She does not wish to look in to the microscope because, being a mythic creature, an embodiment of mana, her vision is a mythical one that sees not narrowly but in a large circle that is all-encompassing. These images which identify her with the sea as well as those that identify her with the snake, such as swaying as it sways and opening her mouth when it does, are, of course, the primary ones. Since both these identifications are inherently related, the mythic significance of the snake and the sea and their connection with the mysterious anima force deserve more detailed exploration.

We can certainly believe Steinbeck when he says that he wrote "The Snake" just as it happened, that he was conscious of no philosophical intent. The very success of the story is proof of this just as the failure of *Of Mice and Men* is proof of his deliberate manipulation there. Although, as Harry Thornton Moore tells us, apropos of *The Long Valley,* Steinbeck had been for a long time working out a theory of subconscious symbolism, "by which certain elements of the rhythm and certain hidden symbols prepare the reader's unconsciousness for the ultimate effect of the story," we can see that the rhythm and symbols of "The Snake" are too integrated to have been the result of Steinbeck's conscious aesthetic theories.[13] More helpful in understanding the nature and origin of the woman in the story are Steinbeck's tentative notions of a racial unconscious developed by analogy to biology and the sea in *The Log from the Sea of Cortez.* This account of his scientific expedition with Ed Ricketts has been rightfully termed as important to Steinbeck's art and thought as *Death in the Afternoon* is to Hemingway's.[14]

In his account of the Old Man of the Sea, a phenomenon seen by many people in Monterey, Steinbeck says he hopes it is never photographed, for if it turns out to be a great malformed Sealion, "a lot of people would feel a sharp personal loss—a Santa Claus loss. And the ocean would be none the better for it. For the ocean, deep and black in the depths, is like the low dark levels of our minds in which the dream symbols incubate and sometimes rise up to sight like the Old Man of the Sea. And even if the symbol vision be horrible, it is there and it is ours."[15] Developing the analogy between the sea as primal source of man and source of the dream symbols of man's unconsciousness even further, Steinbeck gives us a basis for understanding that the strange woman in "The Snake" comes from the tide pool of the sea at the same time that she comes from the unconscious of the young doctor and all men:

> And we have thought how the human fetus has, at one stage of its development, vestigial gill-slits. If the gills are a component of the developing human, it is not unreasonable to suppose a parallel or concurrent mind or psyche development. If there be a life-memory strong enough to leave its symbol in vestigial gills, the preponderantly aquatic symbols in the individual unconscious might well be indications of a group psyche-memory which is the foundation of the whole unconscious. And what things must be there, what monsters, what enemies, what fears of dark and pressure, and of prey![16]

Surely the woman is one of these monsters—an entity from the mythic realm which persists always in dreams.

Since Steinbeck's formulations here are so similar to Jung's theories of the Collective Unconscious, we might better understand what kind of dream symbol the woman is and why she rises out of the doctor's unconscious to confront him if we turn to Jung's compilation of such archetypes in *Symbols of Transformation*.[17] Jung says that in dreams and fantasies, the snake is an excellent symbol to express the sudden and unexpected manifestations of the unconscious, "its painful and dangerous interventions in our affairs, and its frightening aspects" (p. 374). According to Jung, the snake is a representation of the world of instinct. "Snake dreams always indicate a discrepancy between the attitude of the conscious mind and instinct, the snake being a personification of the threatening aspect of that conflict" (p. 396). To understand why the snake-woman or instinctual force has risen abruptly from the doctor's unconscious to confront him, we do not have to try to understand the "personal" contents of his unconscious any more than we have to try to understand or postulate a particular sexual neurosis for the woman. Indeed, the story gives us no basis for trying to understand either as individual characters. The doctor, embodying as he does a scientific and therefore detached existence, is simply intolerable in his one-sidedness. As Jung might say, he is one who has rejected the unconscious to such an extent that the instinctual forces rise up in opposition (p. 294). The woman is a threatening force to the doctor because he refuses to recognize and integrate the archetypal contents of his unconscious which she embodies.

The chthonic message the woman brings the doctor is the essential message of the mythic world. By her very existence she challenges the doctor's scientific realm of being and his Cartesian mode of knowing, both of which separate him from life and make him an observer only. Accustomed to dividing life into the two spheres of practical and theoretical activity the doctor, like most men, has forgotten that primitive substratum which underlies them both. As Ernst Cassirer says, primitive man's feelings are still embedded in this lower substratum.

> His view of nature is neither merely theoretical nor merely practical; it is *sympathetic*. . . . Primitive man by no means lacks the ability to grasp the empirical differences of things. But in his conception of nature and life all these differences are obliterated by a stronger feeling: the deep conviction of a fundamental and indelible *solidarity of life* that bridges over the multiplicity and variety of single forms.[18]

And just as the woman challenges the doctor's level of being in the world, she also challenges his mode of apprehending the world. Warren French is right when he says that Steinbeck's sympathy is with those who seek knowledge of the world they live in, but he is surely mistaken when he assumes that Steinbeck's sympathy is with scientific knowledge in this story. Steinbeck affirms a deeper level of being and knowing in *The Log from the Sea of Cortez:*

> The whole is necessarily everything, the whole world of fact and fancy, body and psyche, physical fact and spiritual truth, individual and collective, life and death, macrocosm and microcosm (the greatest quanta here, the greatest synapse between these two), conscious and unconscious, subject and object. The whole picture is portrayed by *is,* the deepest word of deep ultimate reality, not shallow or partial as reasons are, but deeper and participating, possibly encompassing the Oriental concept of *being.*[19]

The doctor's sense of reality, based on reason and science, is determined by what Jung calls "directed thinking"; he has no concern with "fantasy thinking" or what Cassirer calls mythic or sympathetic perception. This mode of thought, often called "poetic" or "religious," has always been associated in myth with woman's connections with the mysterious source of life. Karl Stern has suggested that it stems from woman's biological connections with the life processes:

> One of the reasons why we associate all praeter-rational thinking with womanhood is that the knowledge by connaturality originates in the child-mother relationship. All *knowledge by union;* all knowledge by incorporation (incorporating or being incorporated); and all knowledge through love has its natural fundament in our primary bond with the mother. The skeptic warns the believer not to "swallow" things and not "to be taken in." And from his point of view he is right. Faith, the most sublime form of nonscientific knowledge, is a form of swallowing or of being taken in.[20]

Stern's metaphor of swallowing also helps us understand the imagery in Steinbeck's story of the snake's unhinging its jaws to swallow the rat and the woman's identification with this act as well as her general identification with the snake. The centrality of this action (it is the action which originally caught Steinbeck's imagination in the actual incident) in the story is obvious: the climax of the story, it is so intense and frightening the doctor cannot bring himself to look at it. "Dr. Phillips put his will against his head to keep from turning toward the woman. He thought, 'If she's opening her mouth, I'll be sick. I'll be afraid.' " And because the scene is so central, it explains what the doctor cannot explain even though he says he has read much about psychological sex symbols. If he has done his reading in Freudian psychology and thus associates the snake with the phallus, then perhaps, as he says, "it doesn't seem to explain." Jung, however, does not restrict himself to such allegorical or anatomical explanations; he is often concerned more with the androgynous nature of the symbols in myth and dream he says we must understand not anatomically but psychologically as libido symbols. In the realm of the libido, according to Jung, the fixed meaning of things comes to an end. "We take mythological symbols much too concretely and are puzzled at every turn by the endless contradictions of myths" (p. 222). Moreover, Jung notes that the serpent often has a vaginal as well as a phallic meaning. It symbolizes the "Terrible Mother, the voracious maw, the jaws of death" (p. 251).

The feminine sexuality of the snake/woman parallel now becomes clearer; the archetype here is related to the pervasive and frightening myth of the *vagina dentata,* the vagina with teeth, which often represents man's fear of woman's sexuality. The gaping open of the snake's mouth and the corresponding gaping open of the mouth of the woman represent the female sex as a voracious mouth which threatens to devour the penis. Dr. Phillips realizes that the snake making its kill and eating it has symbolic significance. "I think because it is a subjective rat. The person is the rat. Once you see it the whole matter is objective. The rat is only a rat and the terror is removed." The doctor's confidence that once you see it the terror is removed is shaken in the story just as his other scientific perceptions are. He rejects as simply "sport" those activities which perhaps might give him "poetic" rather than scientific knowledge. When he agrees to feed the snake for the woman he says, "It's better than a bullfight if you look at it one way, and it's simply a snake eating his dinner if you look at it another." But when the doctor says this his tone has become acid, for he hates people "who made sport of natural processes. He was not a sportsman but a biologist. He could kill a thousand animals for knowledge, but not an insect for pleasure. He'd been over this in his mind before." However, the act of killing and swallowing the rat is not only death by devouring; it is representative of life and knowledge by swallowing and being swallowed as well. Suggesting death which is necessary for a deeper level of life, it is the kind of experience which the doctor calls "the most beautiful thing in the world . . . the most terrible thing in the world." Yet the doctor is unable to integrate and accept this necessity into his experience. The only way his conscious mind will allow him to see the process is that of a snake eating its dinner.

The woman who has come to confront the doctor with this conflict and make him aware of mythic being and perception is the universal goddess who has appeared in myth in various guises. Two of her best known embodiments, both of which find echoes in "The Snake," are the Hebrew Lilith and the Greek Lamia. Both these figures, Jung says, are related to the Terrible Mother, for both are personifications of death that precedes rebirth. However, in Steinbeck's story, instead of allowing himself to be drawn into the mythic aura of the woman, the doctor, like the philosopher Appolonius in Keats' "Lamia," exerts his conscious will and refuses. All charms fly at the mere touch of cold science as well as cold philosophy.

The implications of the doctor's refusal to be devoured by the voracious mother, to "die" so that he might be born again, are made clear in the dénouement of the story. After the climactic moment, as the snake begins to engulf the rat with slow peristaltic pulsing, the doctor turns angrily to his work table because he has missed one of the series of starfish germination. Having forgotten the time, having forgotten time altogether in the momentary primal atmosphere of the mysterious woman, his attempt to control the process of gestation has been spoiled.

> He put one of the watch-glasses under a low-power microscope and looked at it, and then angrily he poured the contents of all the dishes into the sink. The waves had fallen so that only a wet whisper came up through the floor. The young man lifted a trapdoor at his feet and dropped the starfish down into the black water. He paused at the cat, crucified in the cradle and grinning comically into the light. Its body was puffed with embalming fluid.

Images of life and death are closely integrated here to fulfill our ominous suspicions about the doctor at the beginning of the story. More importantly, they reveal the implications of his refusal to perform the heroic task of integration by suggesting not death and consequent rebirth, but rather death in the very process of birth—the abortion of life. The flushing of the fertilizing sperm and ova from the bisexual starfish down the drain and the dumping of their bodies down through the trapdoor is the most obvious such image. The death of life in its very gestation is also reflected in the grotesque image of the cat's puffed body. Swollen with embalming fluid, it is literally pregnant with death. However, the most startling image of death in the very process of life is that of the cat "crucified in the cradle." In a single phrase it telescopes the whole history of Christ—that one born in the manger so that he might die on the cross. That the image reflects neither Christ's life nor his rebirth suggests the doctor's refusal of both. According to Jung, Christ signifies the "self" psychologically; "he represents the projection of the most important and most central of archetypes" (p. 368). Moreover, the crucifixion represents the successful establishing of a relationship between the ego and the unconscious. On the cross, Christ unites himself with the mother in death so that he might be reborn again (p. 263). That the Christ image in Steinbeck's story is grotesque and sardonic, sticking its tongue out in derision, however, does not suggest Jung's heroic Christ, but rather Yeats' "rough beast."

After the woman leaves, the doctor sits in front of the snake cage and tries to "comb out his thought," but the only explanation he has, and perhaps the only explanation possible is: "Maybe I'm too much alone." Indeed, the doctor has been visited by the mythic force because he is alone. Cut off from life by his sole attention to the observation of life, cut off from any spiritual realm by his concern for the scientific, the doctor remains outside that "solidarity of life" which ultimately is religious. Perhaps realizing this, yet helpless to do anything about it, the doctor admits, "If I knew—no, I can't pray to anything."

The theoretical scientist mystified by the strange woman might be seen as a reflection of the critical reader who, although he may have little difficulty with the novel, finds the short story often mysterious and strange. The most fundamental feature of short fiction is perhaps similar to what Ernst Cassirer says is the fundamental feature of myth. Instead of springing from a special direction of thought it is "an offspring of emotion and its emotional background imbues all its productions with its own specific color."[21] The meaning of short fiction, because it is a product of emotion, because it is the "dream verbalized," is therefore not to be found inside like a kernel, but outside, "enveloping the tale which brought it out only as a glow brings out a haze, in the likeness of one of these misty halos that sometimes are made visible by the spectral illumination of moonshine."

Notes

1. Peter Lisca tells us that Steinbeck tried several times without success to get the story published. Finally he had it printed in *The Monterey Beacon* in 1936, a small magazine run in conjunction with a stable. Steinbeck's payment for the story was six month's use of a big bay horse. The following year when Steinbeck tried to get the story published again, it was rejected by both *Atlantic Monthly* and *Harper's*. "Steinbeck: A Literary Biography," in *Steinbeck and His Critics: A Record of Twenty-Five Years,* eds. Ernest W. Tedlock, Jr., and C. V. Wicker (Albuquerque: University of New Mexico Press, 1957), p. 11.

2. "About Ed Ricketts," *The Log from the Sea of Cortez* (New York: Viking Press, 1951), pp. xxiii–xxiv.

3. See Peter Lisca, *The Wide World of John Steinbeck* (New Brunswick, N.J.: Rutgers University Press, 1958), p. 95; Joseph Fontenrose, *John Steinbeck: An Introduction and Interpretation* (New York: Barnes and Noble, Inc., 1963), p. 63; Lincoln R. Gibbs, "John Steinbeck: Moralist," in Tedlock and Wicker, p. 93; Frederick Bracher, "Steinbeck and the Biological View of Man," in Tedlock and Wicker, p. 184.

4. The Boys in the Back Room," in *Classics and Commercials: A Literary Chronicle of the Forties* (New York: Farrar, Straus and Co., 1950), pp. 38, 41.

5. *John Steinbeck* (New York: Twayne Publishers, Inc., 1962), p. 82.

6. *The Lonely Voice: A Study of the Short Story* (Cleveland, Ohio: World Publishing Co., 1963), p. 17.

7. *Anatomy of Criticism* (New York: Atheneum, 1957), p. 304.

8. "The Psychological Aspects of the Kore," in C. G. Jung and C. Kerenyi, *Essays on the Science of Mythology,* Bollingen Series, XXII (New York: Pantheon Books, 1949), pp. 150–51.

9. *An Essay on Man* (New Haven, Conn.: Yale University Press, 1944), p. 76.

Part 3. The Critics

10. Elizabeth Bowen, "The Faber Book of Modern Short Stories," in *Collected Impressions* (New York: Alfred A. Knopf, Inc., 1950), p. 43; Alberto Moravia, "The Short Story and the Novel," in *Man as End: A Defense of Humanism,* trans. Bernard Wall (New York: Farrar, Straus and Giroux, Inc., 1969), p. 182; Joyce Carol Oates, "The Short Story," *Southern Humanities Review,* 5 (Summer 1971), 214.

11. "The Reading and Writing of Short Stories," *Atlantic Monthly,* 183 (Feb. 1949), 56.

12. In *Classics and Commercials,* Edmund Wilson says that the laboratory is one of the key images in all of Steinbeck's fiction. Stanley Edgar Hyman suggests that it is the tide pool which is the central metaphor of *The Sea of Cortez,* and perhaps much of Steinbeck's fiction as well. "Some Notes on John Steinbeck," in Tedlock and Wicker, p. 184.

13. *The Novels of John Steinbeck: A First Critical Study* (Chicago: Normandie House, 1939), p. 52.

14. Freeman Champney, "John Steinbeck, Californian," in Tedlock and Wicker, p. 146.

15. *The Log from the Sea of Cortez,* p. 21.

16. Ibid., p. 32.

17. Carl G. Jung. *Symbols of Transformation: An Analysis of the Prelude to a Case of Schizophrenia,* trans. R. F. C. Hull, Bollingen Series, XX (New York: Pantheon Books, 1956). All subsequent references to Jung are from this edition of *Symbols of Transformation.* Page numbers follow the citation in the text.

18. *An Essay on Man,* p. 82.

19. *The Log from the Sea of Cortez,* pp. 150–51.

20. *The Flight from Woman* (New York: Farrar, Straus and Giroux, 1965), p. 54.

21. *An Essay on Man,* p. 82.

M. R. Satyanarayana

"And Then the Child Becomes a Man": Three Initiation Stories of John Steinbeck

*M. R. Satyanarayana**

In his introduction to *John Steinbeck* (New York, 1965) Joseph Fontenrose observes: "Myth has been a more consistent factor, profoundly affecting the form and content of all his (Steinbeck's) novels since 1929. In most of them we see a palimpsest upon which Steinbeck has inscribed a realistic tale of contemporary men."[1] Yet, in his actual interpretation of the works, Fontenrose makes no reference to the use of myth in three stories from *The Long Valley:* "The Raid," *The Red Pony* cycle, and "Flight." He considers only *The Red Pony* as a story of initiation in which the hero passes from "naive childhood to the threshold of adulthood through knowledge of birth, old age, and death, gained through experience with horses."[2] As a matter of fact all the three works are about the growth of boys into men, each different from the others, in its use of myth. "The Raid" is an excellent example of a sociological initiation, in which the boy hero is initiated to an altogether new social order. In *The Red Pony* the hero's initiation is brought about within the same social order into which he is born, with a view to preserving the traditions cherished by that order. Further, the hero is also introduced to the existential aspects of pain, age, and death. "Flight" is somewhat complex as an initiation story. It deals with the improper initiation of the hero leading to tragedy as in the myth of Phaëton; and at the same time it is a story of the hero's magic flight and the mystic return to the origin.

I

The structure of "The Raid" falls neatly into four parts: (1) the hero's severance from the mother, (2) the revelation of the mystery

* From *Indiana Journal of American Studies* 1 (1971): 87–92. Reprinted by permission from M. R. Satyanarayana.

of adult experience, (3) the ordeal, and (4) the symbolic death and rebirth. Root, the hero goes through all the well-known rites of passage except the change of name.

The story begins with Dick, the initiator, and Root, the novice, walking away from the well-lit streets to a dark and lonely place where they expect to hold a radical meeting. Severance from the mother has already taken place for the boy, he having been thrown out by the father for his radical views. The boy looks back in regret at his childhood innocence, and is at the same time anxious to experience a new life. This state of confusion, typical of all the novices, is symbolically expressed by an old tune, "Come to me my melancholy baby," which haunts the boy, and try as he might, he is unable to get it out of his head. Passing through the dark streets he observes that "it's a good night to get away if anything happens."[3] The dark night is the mother whose protection the boy seeks. The novice is quickly pulled back to the road by Dick (father-surrogate) who holds out the threat of a denial of the much desired new experience. He warns Root that his party would have nothing to do with cowards.

In the second part we find Dick and Root in a lonely store lit by a small kerosene lamp. They put up the picture of their leader on the wall, along with a certain red symbol on a white background. As they wait for their audience Root becomes more and more nervous. He asks for the time of the night thrice in three quarters of an hour. He keeps on pestering the senior man as to how it would be to face a group of vigilantes. He is scared of them and the cops, having heard of their brutality. Although annoyed and irritated by the boy's questions Dick allays his fears by kind words. With the picture of the leader presiding over the ceremony, the initiator passes on the magic formula (the *mantra*) to the novice, a formula he himself had been taught in similar circumstances: "The men of little spirit must have an example of stead—steadfastness. The people at large must have an example of injustice" (103–104). And therefore no sacrifice is too much and the initiate must remember that "If some one busts you, it isn't him that's doing it, it's the System. And it isn't you he's busting. He's taking a crack at the Principle" (104). This initiatory ceremony is observed on the lines followed by secret societies like the Free Masons.

The tension caused by anxiety and suspense is itself an ordeal. But the real test for the initiate is physical torture which includes bleeding also. Just as the male adults of the Australian tribes surround the initiate and beat him up, Root is buffeted by the vigilantes when they raid the place. As he begins the prepared text of his speech he is knocked down by a blow on the side of the head. When he struggles to his feet, "his split ear spill[ing] a red stream down his neck," he is no longer a boy. "His breath burst passionately. His hands were steady now, his voice sure and strong. His eyes were hot with an ecstasy." (107) As he goes down again under a wave of violence he cries, "You don't know what you're doing" (107).

When Root falls unconscious he goes through the last phase of the initiatory rites, symbolic death, from which he emerges a new being. The last words of the boy before he falls down unconscious, add a new dimension to the story. His death and rebirth become a re-enactment of Christ's death and resurrection. Later, in the hospital, Root recalls how he felt like saying those words of Christ to his killers. Written in 1934, "The Raid" reveals Steinbeck's interest in some of the most devoted radicals he knew. Root is also a symbol of all the good Christians, who in the 1930's looked toward Russia for an answer to the economic questions which the democratic Europe had failed to solve. This same Root, who appears as Jim in *In Dubious Battle*, "grows" to become the radical Christ, Jim Casy in *The Grapes of Wrath*.

II

In *The Red Pony* the boy Jody Tiflin is initiated to the chores of an agrarian life on his father's ranch. Here there is no sudden severence from the childhood links for the boy. It is a slow transition from childhood innocence to experience, and the transition takes place without a change of scene. His initiators are his parents and Billy Buck, the ranch hand. And because it is a transitional type of initiation the ordeal is spread over a considerable length of time. Jody's loss of innocence occurs when the shock of realization of death comes upon him. "Perhaps this is the first adulthood of any man or woman," as Steinbeck puts it.

"The first tortured question 'why?' and then acceptance, and then the child becomes a man."[4]

In "The Gift," Jody's initiation begins with the gift of a pony by his father. The boy's curiosity is excited. But severe restrictions are laid down to thwart his enthusiasm to ride the pony. He must scrub the pony, polish the saddle, and feed the animal, but he should not ride him yet. In the course of his training under Billy Buck the boy experiences pain and horror, which invariably accompany the rites of passage. When the pony catches a severe cold an operation becomes necessary. To help the animal breathe a hole is drilled in his throat. Jody is made to watch and help in the operation. He keeps a close watch over the ailing pony and witnesses his futile struggle against death. With the death of the pony, Jody is entrusted with greater responsibility. In "The Promise," he is placed in charge of the mare Nellie. He is asked to get her bred, and to take good care of the mare during the gestation period, if the newborn colt is to be his. Once again an operation becomes necessary. To save the colt the mare has to be killed. The boy is made to watch Billy Buck take a hammer and knock down the animal, saw through her belly, and bring out a dripping bundle of a colt. With this ritualistic killing of the mare the novice realises that birth and death are only phases in a continuous process of life.

The horse is the central symbol in *The Red Pony,* as in D. H. Lawrence's "St. Mawr." All knowledge of pain, suffering, old age, death, and even the knowledge of sex comes to Jody through the three horses in the story. The proud red pony gives him the first glimpse of death, which is repeated in the death of the mare Nellie. The mating of the mare and the stallion provides a vicarious lesson in sex for the boy. In "The Great Mountains," there is the horse Easter, which had served the master faithfully for years, but is now disliked by the master Tiflin for being old and useless. Tiflin equates the old horse with Gitano, an old paisano, who seeks shelter on the ranch. Tiflin is not impressed by the fact that the paisano was born on the ranch long before he bought it and now wishes to die on the place. He has no feeling for either the old horse or the old man. Luckily for Jody he has, as models, the defence of the old horse by Billy Buck and his mother's sympathy for the paisano. It is through Billy Buck and his mother that Jody gets a proper initiation to the right understanding of others' sorrows. For there is a repetition of the father's rudeness and the compassionate response of Jody's mother and Billy Buck in the fourth section of the story cycle. It is here, in "The Leader of the People," that Jody shows signs of growth. In the teeth of his father's opposition he asks his grandfather to tell stories about "Injuns" (Indians), which he had told a number of times. Tiflin considers his father-in-law a bore. The story ends with the efforts of the boy in consoling the grandfather who has been insulted by his father. It is as though Jody were the grown-up man, and the grandfather a child. (He offers to get a lemonade for the old man). The growth of Jody to adult experience is suggested by a humorous change of his name into Mr. Big Britches.

III

Unlike the initiation of Root and Jody the initiation of Pepé takes place overnight. It is actually a case of improper initiation, and reflects "the pathos of inverted emphasis" in the United States where, as Joseph Campbell observes, "The goal is not to grow old, but to remain young; not to mature away from Mother, but to cleave to her."[5] Although nineteen years old and the father dead, Pepé is not called upon to shoulder the responsibility of the adult male. An early initiation would have been the most natural thing in his case. Instead we find Mama Torres dismissing her son's claim to manhood as that of a "foolish chicken." Yet, it is not as though she is unaware of the need for boys to grow up in time. For she tells her second son (after Pepé rides away for the first time by himself) that "A boy gets to be a man when a man is needed. Remember this thing. I have known boys forty years old" (50). But, in spite of this wisdom she goes on waiting for a need to arise. Initiation rites are meant to prevent precisely this sort of danger, men of forty remaining boys, by preparing the boys to be ready for adult life well in advance. What actually happens is that Pepé finds himself unprepared when the need at last arises.

Pepé rides to town. He has been allowed to use his father's saddle. He carries with him his father's knife, which has always been with him. In Monterey he drinks wine with some people. Some one calls him names and makes a gesture of attack. And

185

Pepé throws the knife at him as unerringly and as thoughtlessly as he had been throwing at a redwood post in a playful manner. The knife "went almost by itself. It flew, it darted before Pepé knew it" (51–52). Like Phaëthon he is ignorant of the proper use of the weapon (the bridle of Phoebus), and he has to pay for it with his life. Taken by surprise at his own action Pepé rushes back to the protective mother. Mama Torres ruefully realises that the son has attained manhood. She prepares him for his flight into the mountains. With the severance of her son from her imminent, she takes on the role of an initiator for a brief time. She gives Pepé her husband's black coat, and rifle. She gives him food and water. And she gives good advice concerning the dangers on the way and how to surmount them. When at last he rides away she raises a formal death wail: "Our beautiful—our brave, he is gone" (54). With this Pepé completes the rite of severance from the mother, and a symbolic death, and enters upon the next stage of the great ordeal.

So far it has been a story of maturation. With the commencement of the hero's ordeal the story gathers a new dimension. Pepé's ordeal is his flight; and the flight becomes the magic flight of the mythical hero.[6] In his flight (ordeal) Pepé does not encounter the elders of the tribe or a father-surrogate in person. The hurdles he crosses and the physical torture he undergoes are not due to any human agency. (The flight itself is caused by human pursuers, who are not on the scene of action). For three days and nights he flees, gradually losing his hat, horse, the coat, and the rifle. He is incapacitated by hunger, thirst, and a poisonous wound. Finally, he gives up the struggle and stands up to welcome death. In all his ordeals Pepé is alone, without a sympathetic initiator. The initiator, if there is one, is his dead father, represented by his black coat, the hat, the rifle, and the saddle. When all these articles are lost the hero is ready to die. The unseen but ever-present father, then, puts his son to a severe ordeal after the severance from the mother. At the end of the ordeal the son becomes himself the father. There is no return to the normal world for him who achieves an atonement with the father.[7] Having shed all "infantile illusions of 'good' and 'evil' " the hero is purged of hope and fear, and at peace in the understanding of the revelation of being."[8]

Pepé's flight is an inversion of the mythical hero's magic flight. In the latter's flight the hero discards objects which grow in size and delay the pursuers. For instance, a discarded hairbrush grows to be a huge wooded mountain. But here Pepé leaves behind him, quite unintentionally, articles which are of great use. The coat or the hat or the rifle, instead of delaying his pursurers, serve only as clues in the chase. This is so because the hero is not fleeing *from* anything. He is only making "a return to the origin."

Steinbeck's use of the symbolic *regressus ad uterum* lends a third dimension to the story "Flight." According to Mercea Eliade the mythical hero is swallowed by a sea monster and re-emerges breaking through the monster's belly; or the hero goes through an "initiatory passage through a *vagina dentata,* or the dangerous descent into a cave or a crevice assimilated to the mouth or the uterus of Mother Earth."[9] Pepé's passage belongs to the latter type. But unlike the adventures of the mythical hero, which are accomplished physically, Pepé's adventures are symbolic in the oriental tradition. Pepé descends into narrow dark valleys three times, and when he meets his death, he rolls down the mountain and is covered over by an avalanche of rocks, thus entering the womb of the Mother Earth. Further these initiatory adventures of the spiritual type do not end in the hero becoming, even spiritually, a new being; they end in the searcher becoming one with "the Primordial Great-One," as visualized by the oriental mystics for whom "the goal ceased to be beginning a new life again here below, on earth, and became 'going back' and reconstituting the Primordial Great-One."[10]

I believe there are many ways of looking at this most interesting story. It is possible to see in it the murderer, pursued by his sense of guilt and failing to shake it off, finally welcome death as proper wages for his sin. It is also possible to see in it "the emergence of Man from the primeval darkness."[11]

Notes

1. *John Steinbeck* (New York, 1963), p. 6.
2. Ibid., p. 64.
3. *The Long Valley* (New York, 1956), p. 97. All subsequent references in the text are to this edition.

4. John Steinbeck, "My Short Novels," *Steinbeck and His Critics,* ed. E. W. Tedlock Jr., and C. V. Wicker (Albuquerque, N. M., 1957), p. 38.

5. *The Hero with a Thousand Faces* (New York, 1949), p. 11.

6. See Campbell pp. 196–207.

7. The concept of atonement with the father is underscored by the similarity in the circumstances of the death of both father and son. Pepé's father trips over a stone, falls on a rattlesnake which strikes him dead. Wounded by a splinter of a stone Pepé develops gangrene, and is struck by a bullet.

8. Campbell, p. 137.

9. *Myth and Reality* (New York, 1963), p. 81.

10. Ibid., p. 88.

11. John Antico, "A Reading of Steinbeck's 'Flight,' " *Modern Fiction Studies,* XI (Spring 1965), p. 45.

Thematic Rhythm in The Red Pony
*Arnold L. Goldsmith**

Underlying Steinbeck's four short stories which make up *The Red Pony* are thematic rhythms, structural balance, and a seasonal symbolism which skillfully integrate the whole work and relate it to his Emersonian mysticism found in later books such as *The Grapes of Wrath* (1939) and *Sea of Cortez* (1941). "The Leader of the People," added by Steinbeck in 1938 to the three stories first published as *The Red Pony* in 1937, is an integral part of the whole work, but readers of college anthologies usually find one of the stories published separately or the first three as a unit, and thus miss a good opportunity to study Steinbeck's subtle extension of the themes expressed in "The Gift," "The Great Mountains," and "The Promise."

The central figure unifying all four stories is Jody Tiflin. Like Hemingway's early hero Nick Adams, Jody is being initiated into

* From *College English* 26, no. 5 (February 1965): 391–94. Copyright 1965, National Council of Teachers of English. Reprinted by permission.

a violent world where danger lurks everywhere, pain and death are imminent, and the best laid plans of mice and boys often go astray. In the first story Jody is ten, in the next apparently a year older, and in the third and fourth, probably twelve. The adventures of both youths are intended to teach them the need for stoic endurance in order to survive in an imperfect and cruel world. In this sense, Hemingway's stories and *The Red Pony* can be considered bildungsromans, but there are some significant differences. Because of Jody's age, sex plays much less a part of his initiation than it does in Nick's, whose experiences are not just vicarious. And violence, which explodes all around Nick and finally wounds him in the war, destroys only the things Jody loves, not harming him physically. Where Nick's wounds are both physical and psychic, Jody's are only psychic, and we do not know whether they have a permanent effect on him. The third story ends with Jody's thrill at the birth of his new colt, but even this thrill is dampened by pain: "He ached from his throat to his stomach. His legs were stiff and heavy. He tried to be glad because of the colt, but the bloody face, and the haunted, tired eyes of Billy Buck hung in the air ahead of him."[1] The last story substitutes the tired face of Jody's grandfather for that of Billy Buck, but the optimism implied in the title as well as Jody's kindness to the old man are adequate evidence of the kind of adjustments Jody will make in life.

More important than the above contrasts is the fact that Steinbeck composed *The Red Pony* as an integrated whole, while Hemingway wrote the Nick Adams stories sporadically at different times during his literary career. All four stories in *The Red Pony* take place in the Salinas Valley, where Steinbeck himself grew up as a boy. The stories are filled with realistic and lyric descriptions of the Valley's flora and fauna (e.g., horned toads, newts, blue snakes, lizards, buzzards, rabbits, hoot-owls, turkeys, coyotes, muskmelons, oakwoods, and black cypresses) which Steinbeck knew as intimately as Thoreau knew the woods, ponds, and fields around Concord.

The time sequence of the stories can be worked out as follows. "The Gift" begins in late summer and ends around Thanksgiving, the beginning of the winter with its rainy season in California. The reader of Hemingway's *A Farewell to Arms* is certainly familiar with the association of rain with disease, violence, and death, and such seasonal symbolism is most appropriate in the story about the death of Jody's pony suffering from pneumonia. "The Great Mountains" begins in the "heat of a midsummer afternoon" (p. 53), probably a year after the first story began. It spans less than twenty-four hours, ending the next morning. "The Promise" begins that spring and ends eleven months later, in a January rain, once again an appropriate setting for the death of the mare Nellie and the birth of her colt. "The Leader of the People" takes place a couple of months later, in March, probably the same year that the mare died. The same unity of time and place found in the second story is evident here also. As in "The Great Mountains," the story begins on an afternoon and ends the next morning.

This analysis of the time sequence helps illuminate the structural symmetry of the stories. Just as Hemingway in *A Farewell to Arms* alternates a book of war with a romantic interlude for dramatic contrast, Steinbeck follows the violence of the first story with the tragic quiet of the second, with this same pattern repeated in the third and fourth sections. Where the first and third stories are about the violent deaths of horses, the second and fourth are about the twilight years of two old men.

The basic thematic rhythm unifying the four stories in *The Red Pony* is the life-death cycle. This organic theory of life ending in death which in turn produces new life is the major theme of Hemingway's "Indian Camp," where Nick Adams witnesses the Caesarean delivery of an Indian baby and the violent death of the father. It is the same cycle of life and death implicit in Whitman's image of the "cradle endlessly rocking."

In *The Red Pony* we see this rhythm in the cycle of the seasons, the buzzards flying overhead, the life and death of Jody's pony Galiban, the death of the buzzard Jody kills with his bare hands, the approaching death of the paisano Gitano and the old horse Easter (his very name suggesting life in death), and the two opposing sets of mountains: Galiban (jolly, populated, suggesting life) and the Great Ones (ominous, mysterious, suggesting death, a place where we must all go eventually), the little bird Jody kills with his slingshot and then beheads and dissects, the death of Nellie and the birth of her colt, and the approaching death of Jody's old grandfather, the old leader of the people, with the implication that Jody is to be the new one. All of these objects and incidents represent the never-ending rhythm of life and death to which Jody is continually exposed. The subtle expression of this theme can even be found at the beginning of "The Leader of the People," when Billy Buck rakes the last of the old year's haystack, an action which implies the end of one season and the beginning of the next. In terms of the story, life is ending for the grandfather, but it is just beginning for Jody.

The most obvious example of Steinbeck's conscious effort to present this theme in *The Red Pony* is the sharp contrast he develops in "The Promise" between the black cypress tree by the bunkhouse and the water tub. Where the cypress is associated with death, the never-ending spring water piped into the old green tub is the symbol of the continuity of life. The two paragraphs where Steinbeck explains the effect these things have on Jody should be given in full:

> Jody traveled often to the brush line behind the house. A rusty iron pipe ran a thin stream of water into an old green tub. Where the water spilled over and sank into the ground there was a patch of perpetually green grass. Even when the hills were brown and baked in the summer that little patch was green. The water whined softly into the trough all the year round. This place had grown to be a center-point for Jody. When he had been punished the cool green grass and the singing water soothed him. When he had been mean the biting acid of meanness left him at the brush line. When he sat in the grass and listened to the purling stream, the barriers set up in his mind by the stern day went down to ruin.
>
> On the other hand, the black cypress tree by the bunkhouse was as repulsive as the water-tub was dear; for to this tree all the pigs came, sooner or later, to be slaughtered. Pig killing was fascinating, with the screaming and the blood, but it made Jody's heart beat so fast that it hurt him. After the pigs were scalded in the big iron tripod kettle and their skins were scraped and white, Jody had to go to the water-tub to sit in the grass until his heart grew quiet. The water-tub and the black cypress were opposites and enemies. (pp. 91–92)

As Jody daydreams about his colt, he finds himself under the black cypress and superstitiously moves over to the green grass near the trilling water. "As usual the water place eliminated time and distance" (p. 93).

Jody's communion with nature, a semimystical experience in which time and place are eliminated, is not very different from the withdrawal into the wilderness of Jim Casy in *The Grapes of Wrath*. Casy adds a religious dimension to the experience when he says, "There was the hills, an' there was me, an' we wasn't separate no more. We was one thing. An' that one thing was holy."[2] The most explicit statement Steinbeck has made on this mystical feeling of oneness of the animate and inanimate is in *Sea of Cortez*, where he wrote:

> groups melt into ecological groups until the time when what we know as life meets and enters what we think of as non-life: barnacle and rock, rock and earth, earth and tree, tree and rain and air. And the units nestle into the whole and are inseparable from it . . . And it is a strange thing that most of the feeling we call religious, most of the mystical outcrying which is one of the most prized and used and desired reactions of our species, is really the understanding and the attempt to say that man is related to the whole thing, related inextricably to all reality, known and unknowable. This is a simple thing to say, but the profound feeling of it made a Jesus, a St. Augustine, a St. Francis, a Roger Bacon, a Charles Darwin, and an Einstein. Each of them in his own tempo and with his own voice discovered and reaffirmed with astonishment the knowledge that all things are one thing and that one thing is all things.[3]

Throughout his literary career John Steinbeck has attempted to render dramatically his passionate belief in the oneness of all life, and *The Red Pony* is no exception, as the life-death cycle and Jody's romantic communion with nature will attest. But there is one final example which should be mentioned because of its effective fusion of character, theme, and setting. It occurs in "The Great Mountains." To Jody, these mountains represent the mystery of the unknown, unlived life, but to the old man they stand for the mystery of death. Beyond them lies the sea—eternity. As Gitano rides off into the mountains, he carries a long rapier with a golden basket hilt, a family heirloom passed down to him by his father. This rapier adds just the right touch of myth and folklore to the ancient legend of an old man returning to his birthplace to die. It echoes the classic tradition of such weapons as the magical sword of King Arthur and Beowulf, the shield of

Achilles, even the long rifle of Natty Bumppo. To Jody, Gitano is "mysterious like the mountains. There were ranges back as far as you could see, but behind the last range piled up against the sky there was a great unknown country. And Gitano was an old man, until you got to the dull dark eyes. And in behind them was some unknown thing" (p. 68). Thus the mountains are an extension of Gitano, and Gitano is an extension of the old horse with its ribs and hip-bones jutting out under its skin. All three objects blend into one as Jody watches them disappear in the distance, lying in the green grass near the water-tub, the symbol of timelessness:

> For a moment he thought he could see a black speck crawling up the farthest ridge. Jody thought of the rapier and Gitano. And he thought of the great mountains. A longing caressed him, and it was so sharp that he wanted to cry to get it out of his breast. He lay down in the green grass near the round tub at the brush line. He covered his eyes with his crossed arms and lay there a long time, and he was full of a nameless sorrow. (p. 72)

Notes

1. John Steinbeck, *The Red Pony* (New York, The Viking Press, 1945), p. 104. Hereafter, all references to *The Red Pony* will be to this edition and page numbers will be enclosed in parentheses.

2. John Steinbeck, *The Grapes of Wrath* (New York, Random House, 1939), p. 110.

3. John Steinbeck, *The Log from the Sea of Cortez* (New York, The Viking Press, 1951), pp. 216–217.

Chronology

1902   Born Salinas, California, 27 February, third of four children and only son of John Ernst Steinbeck, Sr., and Olive Hamilton.

1919   Graduates from Salinas High School; writes (but does not publish) stories during high school years; enrolls at Stanford; attends sporadically for six years.

1924   "Fingers of Cloud" and "Adventures in Arcademy" appear in *Stanford Spectator;* takes story writing class taught by Edith Mirrielees.

1925   Leaves Stanford permanently without degree; lives briefly in New York City where he writes as many as a dozen stories, only six of which survive.

1927   "The Gifts of Iban," first story to appear in a national magazine.

1929   *Cup of Gold,* first novel.

1930   Marries Carol Henning; moves to Pacific Grove; meets Ed Ricketts.

1932   *The Pastures of Heaven,* short story cycle.

1933   "The Red Pony (retitled "The Gift") and "The Great Mountains," first stories published by prominent magazine *(North American Review); To a God Unknown.*

1934   "The Murder" wins O. Henry Prize; "The Raid"; writes numerous stories published in subsequent years; mother dies.

1935   "The White Quail" and "The Snake"; *Tortilla Flat.*

1936   "The Leader of the People," "The Vigilante," "Breakfast," and "Saint Katy the Virgin"; *In Dubious Battle;* father dies.

1937   *The Red Pony* (first three parts), "Johnny Bear," and "The Chrysanthemums"; *Of Mice and Men.*

1938   "The Promise" wins O. Henry Prize; *The Long Valley,* fifteen collected stories including all four *Red Pony* tales.

1939   *The Grapes of Wrath* (Pulitzer Prize); elected to National Institute of Arts and Letters.

1940   Visits Gulf of California (Sea of Cortez) with Ed Ricketts; films *The Forgotten Village* in Mexico.

1941   "How Edith McGillcuddy Met R. L. S."; *The Sea of Cortez;* films of *Of Mice and Men* and *The Grapes of Wrath.*

1942   "How Edith McGillcuddy Met R. L. S." wins O. Henry Prize; *Bombs Away; The Moon Is Down* (novel and play); divorced from Carol Henning.

1943   Marries Gwyn Conger; visits the European war zone for the New York *Herald Tribune.*

1944   Writes script for Alfred Hitchcock film *Lifeboat;* first son, Thom, born 2 August.

1945   *The Red Pony* republished in four parts; *Cannery Row;* "The Pearl of the World"; *A Medal for Benny* (film).

1946   Second son, John IV ("Catbird") born on 10 June.

1947   "The Time the Wolves Ate the Vice-Principal"; *The Pearl* (book and film); *The Wayward Bus;* trip to Russia.

1948   "Miracle of Tepayac"; *A Russian Journal;* divorced from Gwyn Conger; Ed Ricketts dies.

1949   "His Father"; *The Red Pony* (film).

1950   *Burning Bright* (novel and play); *Viva Zapata!* (film); marries Elaine Scott.

1951   *Log from the Sea of Cortez,* including "About Ed Ricketts."

1952   *East of Eden;* sends reports to *Collier's* from Europe.

1954   *Sweet Thursday.*

1955   "Affair at 7, Rue de M——," "The Summer Before," and "We're Holding Our Own" (retitled "The Short-Short Story of Mankind"); *Pipe Dream* (Rogers and Hammerstein musical based on *Sweet Thursday*).

1956   "Affair at 7, Rue de M——" wins O. Henry Prize; "How Mr. Hogan Robbed a Bank."

1957   "Case of the Hotel Ghost . . ." (retitled "Reunion at the Quiet Hotel"); *The Short Reign of Pippin IV.*

1958   *Once There Was a War.*

1961 *Flight* (film); *Winter of Our Discontent.*

1962 Writes preface to Edith Mirrielees's textbook, *Story Writing; Travels with Charley;* Nobel Prize for Literature.

1963 Tours Europe for U.S. Cultural Exchange program.

1964 Awarded United States Medal of Freedom by President Johnson.

1966 *America and Americans;* the John Steinbeck Society organized.

1968 Dies in New York City, 20 December.

1969 *Journal of a Novel: The "East of Eden" Letters.*

1974 Boyhood home in Salinas opens as a museum and restaurant on his 72d birthday.

1975 *Steinbeck: A Life in Letters.*

1976 *The Acts of King Arthur and His Noble Knights.*

Bibliography

Primary Sources

Published Stories (Chronological)

"Fingers of Cloud: A Satire on College Protervity." *Stanford Spectator* 2 (February 1924): 149, 161–64.

"Adventures in Arcademy: A Journey into the Ridiculous." *Stanford Spectator* 2 (June 1924): 279, 291.

[John Stern, pseud.]. "The Gifts of Iban." *The Smokers Companion* 1 (March 1927): 18–19, 70–72.

"The Red Pony." *North American Review* 236 (November 1933): 421–38. (appeared in *The Long Valley* as "The Gift.")

"The Great Mountains." *North American Review* 236 (December 1933): 492–500.

"The Murder." *North American Review* 237 (April 1934): 305–12.

"The Raid." *North American Review* 238 (October 1934): 299–305.

"The White Quail." *North American Review* 239 (March 1935): 204–11.

"The Snake." *Monterey Beacon* 1 (22 June 1935): 10–11, 14–15.

"The Leader of the People." (London) *Argosy* 20 (August 1936): 99–106.

"The Lonesome Vigilante," *Esquire* 6 (October 1936): 35, 186A–186B. (Appeared in *The Long Valley* as "The Vigilante.")

"Breakfast." *Pacific Weekly* 5 (9 November 1936): 300.

"Saint Katy the Virgin." Covici-Friede monograph, Christmas, 1936.

"The Promise." *Harper's Magazine* 175 (August 1937): 243–52.

"The Ears of Johnny Bear." *Esquire* 8 (September 1937): 35, 195–200. (Appeared in *The Long Valley* as "Johnny Bear.")

"The Chrysanthemums." *Harper's Magazine* 175 (October 1937): 513–19.

"The Harness." *Atlantic Monthly* 161 (June, 1938): 741–49.

"Flight." First published in *The Long Valley*. New York: Viking Press, 1938.

"How Edith McGillcuddy Met R. L. Stevenson," *Harper's Magazine* 183 (August 1941): 252–58.

"The Time the Wolves Ate the Vice-Principal." *'47, the Magazine of the Year* 1, no. 1 (March 1947): 26–27. (Rejected interchapter from *Cannery Row*.)

"Miracle of Tepayac." *Collier's* 122 (25 December 1948): 22–23.

"His Father." *Reader's Digest* 55 (September 1949): 19–21.

"The Affair at 7, Rue de M____." *Harper's Bazaar,* no. 2921 (April 1955): 112, 202, 213.

198

"The Summer Before." *Punch* 128 (25 May 1955): 647–51.
"We're Holding Our Own." *Lilliput* 37 (November 1955): 18–19. (Appeared later in *Playboy* 5 (April 1958) as "The Short-Short Story of Mankind.")
"How Mr. Hogan Robbed a Bank." *Atlantic Monthly* 197 (March 1956): 58–61.
"Case of the Hotel Ghost—Or . . . What Are You Smoking in That Pipe, Mr. S.?" *Louisville Courier-Journal,* 30 June 1957, sec. 4, p. 3. (Appeared later in the (London) *Evening Standard,* 25 January 1958, p. 9, as "Reunion at the Quiet Hotel.")

Unpublished Stories (by Date of Composition)
"The Days of Long Marsh," ca. 1926, TS. The Houghton Library, AL 3523.20.16.
"East Third Street," ca. 1926, TS. The Houghton Library, AL 3523.20.21.
"The Nail," ca. 1926, TS. The Houghton Library, AL 3523.20.58.
"The Nymph and Isobel," ca. 1926, TS. The Houghton Library, AL 3523.20.62.
"The White Sister of Fourteenth Street," ca. 1926, TS. The Steinbeck Collection, Department of Special Collections, Stanford University Libraries.
[Untitled Christmas story], ca. 1926, TS. The Steinbeck Collection, Department of Special Collections, Stanford University Libraries.
"Unnamed Narrative," ca. 1926, MS. The Steinbeck Collection, Department of Special Collections, Stanford University Libraries.
"Case History," ca. 1934, MS. Steinbeck Research Center, San Jose State University.

Books by Steinbeck Containing Short Fiction
Cannery Row. New York: Viking Press, 1945.
The Grapes of Wrath. New York: Viking Press, 1939.
The Long Valley. New York: Viking Press, 1938.
Once There Was a War. New York: Viking Press, 1958.
The Pastures of Heaven. New York: Brewer, Warren, and Putnam, 1932.
Sweet Thursday. New York: Viking Press, 1954.
Tortilla Flat. New York: Covici-Friede, 1935.

Secondary Sources

Bibliographies
Goldstone, Adrian H., and John R. Payne. *John Steinbeck: A Bibliographical Catalogue of the Adrian H. Goldstone Collection.* Austin: University of Texas, 1974.

Bibliography

Gross, John, and Lee Richard Hayman, eds. *John Steinbeck: A Guide to the Collection of the Salinas Public Library.* Salinas, Calif.: Salinas Public Library, 1979.

Hayashi, Tetsumaro, ed. *John Steinbeck: A Concise Bibliography (1930–1965).* Metuchen, N.J.: Scarecrow Press, 1967.

———. *John Steinbeck: A Guide to the Doctoral Dissertations (a Collection of Dissertation Abstracts, 1946–69). Steinbeck Monograph Series, no. 1.* Muncie, Ind.: John Steinbeck Society of America, Ball State University, 1971.

———. *A New Steinbeck Bibliography, 1929–1971.* Metuchen, N.J.: Scarecrow Press, 1973.

———. *Steinbeck Criticism: A Review of Book-Length Studies (1939–1973). Steinbeck Monograph Series, no. 4.* Muncie, Ind.: John Steinbeck Society of America, Ball State University, 1974.

———. *A New Steinbeck Bibliography, 1971–1981.* Metuchen, N.J.: Scarecrow Press, 1983. (See pp. 35–39 for an extensive list of Steinbeck bibliographies and bibliographical essays.)

Biographies

Bennett, Robert. *The Wrath of John Steinbeck: Or, St. John Goes to Church.* Los Angeles: Albertson Press, 1939.

Benson, Jackson J. *The True Adventures of John Steinbeck, Writer: A Biography.* New York: Viking Press, 1984.

Champney, Freeman. "John Steinbeck, Californian." In *Steinbeck: A Collection of Critical Essays,* edited by Robert Murray Davis. Englewood Cliffs, N.J.: Prentice-Hall, 1972.

Gannett, Lewis. "John Steinbeck's Way of Writing" and "Biographical and Bibliographical Note." In *The Portable Steinbeck,* vii–xxx. New York: Viking Press, 1957.

Jackson, Joseph Henry. "John Steinbeck, a Portrait." *Saturday Review of Literature* 16 (25 September 1937): 11–12, 18.

Kiernan, Thomas, *The Intricate Music: A Biography of John Steinbeck.* Boston: Little, Brown, 1979.

Lisca, Peter. "John Steinbeck: A Literary Biography." In *Steinbeck and His Critics,* edited by E. W. Tedlock, Jr., and C. V. Wicker. Albuquerque: University of New Mexico Press, 1957.

Moore, Harry Thornton. "A Biographical Sketch." In *The Novels of John Steinbeck, a First Critical Study,* 2d ed. 73–96. Port Washington, N.Y.: Kennikat Press, 1968.

Valjean, Nelson. *John Steinbeck, an Intimate Biography of His California Years.* San Francisco: Chronicle Books, 1975.

(See Tetsumaro Hayashi, *A New Steinbeck Bibliography, 1971–1981,* pp. 39–42, for an extensive list of biographical books and essays on Steinbeck.)

Bibliography

Letters

Letters to Elizabeth: A Selection of Letters from John Steinbeck to Elizabeth Otis. Edited by Florian J. Shasky and Susan F. Riggs. San Francisco: The Book Club of California, 1978.

Steinbeck: A Life in Letters. Edited by Steinbeck and Elaine and Robert Wallsten. New York: Viking Press, 1975.

Criticism: Books and Dissertations

Astro, Richard. *John Steinbeck and Edward F. Ricketts: The Shaping of a Novelist.* Minneapolis: University of Minnesota Press, 1973.

DeMott, Robert J. *Steinbeck's Reading: A Catalogue of Books Owned and Borrowed.* New York: Garland Publishing, 1984.

Ditsky, John. *John Steinbeck: Life, Work, and Criticism.* Fredericton, Canada: York Press, 1985.

Fontenrose, Joseph. *John Steinbeck: An Introduction and Interpretation.* New York: Barnes and Noble, 1963.

———. *Steinbeck's Unhappy Valley.* Berkeley, Calif.: Albany Press, 1981. Discusses *The Pastures of Heaven.*

French, Warren. *John Steinbeck.* Twayne United States Authors Series, no. 2. New York: Twayne Publishers, 1961.

———. *John Steinbeck.* Twayne United States Authors Series, no. 2, 2d. rev. ed. Boston: Twayne Publishers, 1975.

Gajewski, Antoni. "Nowelistyka Johna Steinbecka w latach miedzwojennych." Diss. Institute of English Philology at Adam Michiewicz University, Poznon, Poland, 1970.

Gladstein, Mimi Reisel. *The Indestructible Woman in Faulkner, Hemingway, and Steinbeck.* Ann Arbor, Mich.: UMI Research Press, 1986.

Gray, James. *John Steinbeck.* Pamphlets on American Writers Series, no. 94. Minneapolis: University of Minnesota Press, 1971.

Hughes, R. S. *Beyond the Red Pony: A Reader's Companion to Steinbeck's Complete Short Stories.* Metuchen, N.J.: Scarecrow Press, 1987.

———. "Steinbeck's Short Stories: A Critical Study." Dissertation Indiana University, Bloomington, Indiana, 1981.

Levant, Howard. *The Novels of John Steinbeck: A Critical Study.* Columbia: University of Missouri Press, 1974.

Lisca, Peter. *John Steinbeck: Nature and Myth.* New York: Thomas Y. Crowell, 1978.

———. *The Wide World of John Steinbeck.* New Brunswick, N.J.: Rutgers University Press, 1958.

McCarthy, Paul. *John Steinbeck.* New York: Ungar, 1980.

Marks, Lester Jay. *Thematic Design in the Novels of John Steinbeck.* The Hague, Netherlands: Mouton, 1969.

Bibliography

Moore, Harry Thornton. *The Novels of John Steinbeck: A First Critical Study.* 2d ed. Port Washington, N.Y.: Kennikat Press, 1968.
O'Connor, Richard. *John Steinbeck.* New York: McGraw-Hill, 1970.
Owens, Louis. *John Steinbeck's Re-Vision of America.* Athens: University of Georgia Press, 1985.
Pratt, John Clark. *John Steinbeck.* Contemporary Writers in Christian Perspective Series. Grand Rapids, Mich.: William B. Eerdmans, 1970.
Timmerman, John H. *John Steinbeck's Fiction: The Aesthetics of the Road Taken.* Norman: University of Oklahoma Press, 1986.
Watt, F. W. *Steinbeck.* Edinburgh: Oliver and Boyd, 1962.
Yancy, Anita Virginia Rish. "*Winesburg, Ohio* and *The Pastures of Heaven:* A Comparative Analysis of Two Stories on Isolation." Dissertation University of Southern Mississippi, 1971.

Criticism: Articles, Collections, and Parts of Books

Anderson, Hilton. "Steinbeck's 'Flight.'" *Explicator* 28 (October 1969), item 12.
Antico, John. "A Reading of Steinbeck's 'Flight.'" *Modern Fiction Studies* 11 (1965): 45–53.
Astro, Richard. "Something That Happened: A Non-Teleological Approach to 'The Leader of the People.'" *Steinbeck Quarterly* 6 (1973): 19–23. Reprinted in *A Study Guide to Steinbeck's "The Long Valley,"* edited by Tetsumaro Hayashi, 105–11. Ann Arbor, Mich.: Pierian Press, 1976.
Astro, Richard, and Tetsumaro Hayashi, eds. *Steinbeck: The Man and His Work.* Corvallis: Oregon State University Press, 1971.
Autrey, Max L. "Men, Mice, and Moths: Gradation in Steinbeck's 'The Leader of the People.'" *Western American Literature* 10 (1975): 195–204.
Barbour, Brian. "Steinbeck as a Short Story Writer." In *A Study Guide to Steinbeck's "The Long Valley,"* edited by Tetsumaro Hayashi, 113–28. Ann Arbor, Mich.: Pierian Press, 1976.
Beach, Joseph Warren. *American Fiction, 1920–1940.* New York: MacMillan, 1941, 309–47.
Benton, Robert M. "Breakfast." In *A Study Guide to Steinbeck's "The Long Valley,"* edited by Tetsumaro Hayashi, 33–40. Ann Arbor, Mich.: Pierian Press, 1976.
———. "Realism, Growth, and Contrast in 'The Gift.'" *Steinbeck Quarterly* 6 (1973): 3–9. Reprinted in *A Study Guide to Steinbeck's "The Long Valley,"* 81–88. Ann Arbor, Mich.: Pierian Press, 1976.
———. "Steinbeck's *The Long Valley.*" In *A Study Guide to Steinbeck: A Handbook to His Major Works,* edited by Tetsumaro Hayashi, 69–86. Metuchen, N.J.: Scarecrow Press, 1974.

Bibliography

Caldwell, Mary Ellen. "A New Consideration of the Intercalary Chapters in *The Grapes of Wrath.*" *Markham Review* 3 (1971–72): 115–19.

Chapin, Chester, F. "Pepé Torres: A Steinbeck 'Natural.' " *College English* 23 (1962): 676.

Court, Franklin E. "A Vigilante's Fantasy." *Steinbeck Quarterly* 5 (1972): 98–101. Reprinted in *A Study Guide to Steinbeck's "The Long Valley,"* edited by Tetsumaro Hayashi, 53–56. Ann Arbor, Mich.: Pierian Press, 1976.

Cox, Matha Heasley. "Remembering John Steinbeck: An Interview with Webster F. Street." *San Jose Studies* 1, no. 3 (1975): 108–27.

———. "The Steinbeck Collection in the Steinbeck Research Center, San Jose State University" *Steinbeck Quarterly* 11 (1978): 96–99.

Davis, Elmer. "The Steinbeck Country." Review of *The Long Valley.* *Saturday Review* 18 (24 September 1938): 11.

Davis, Robert Murray. "Steinbeck's 'The Murder.' " *Studies in Short Fiction* 14 (1977): 63–68.

Delgado, James P. "The Facts behind John Steinbeck's 'The Lonesome Vigilante.' " *Steinbeck Quarterly* 16 (1983): 70–79.

Ditsky, John. "Steinbeck's 'Flight': The Ambiguity of Manhood." In *A Study Guide to Steinbeck's "The Long Valley,"* edited by Tetsumaro Hayashi, 17–24. Ann Arbor, Mich.: Pierian Press, 1976.

Fadiman, Clifton. Review of *The Long Valley. New Yorker* 14 (24 September 1938): 72.

Folsom, James K. "John Steinbeck." In *Critical Survey of Short Fiction,* edited by Frank N. Magill, 2274–279. Englewood Cliffs, N.J.: Salem Press, 1981.

Fontenrose, Joseph. "The Harness." *Steinbeck Quarterly* 5 (1972): 94–98. Reprinted in *A Study Guide to Steinbeck's "The Long Valley,"* edited by Tetsumaro Hayashi, 47–52. Ann Arbor, Mich.: Pierian Press, 1976.

Friedman, Norman. "What Makes a Short Story Short?" *Modern Fiction Studies* 4 (1958): 103–17.

French, Warren. " 'Johnny Bear': Steinbeck's 'Yellow Peril' Story." *Steinbeck Quarterly* 5 (Summer–Fall 1972): 101–7. Reprinted in *A Study Guide to Steinbeck's "The Long Valley,"* edited by Tetsumaro Hayashi, 57–64. Ann Arbor, Mich.: Pierian Press, 1976.

———. "Steinbeck's Winter Tale." *Modern Fiction Studies* 11 (1965): 66–74.

Garcia, Reloy. "Steinbeck's 'The Snake': An Explication." *Steinbeck Quarterly* 5 (1972): 85–90.

Gierasch, Walter. "Steinbeck's *The Red Pony* II: 'The Great Mountains.' " *Explicator* 4 (March 1946), item 39.

Girard, Maureen. "Steinbeck's 'Frightful' Story: The Conception and Evolution of 'The Snake.' " *San Jose Studies* 8 (1982): 33–40.

Bibliography

Gladstein, Mimi Reisel. "Female Characters in Steinbeck: Minor Characters of Major Importance?" In *Steinbeck's Women: Essays in Criticism,* edited by Tetsumaro Hayashi, 17–25. Steinbeck Monograph Series, no. 9. Muncie, Ind., John Steinbeck Society of America, Ball State University, 1979.

Goldsmith, Arnold L. "Thematic Rhythm in *The Red Pony.*" *College English* 26 (1965): 391–94. Reprinted in *Steinbeck: A Collection of Critical Essays,* edited by Robert Murray Davis, 70–74. Englewood Cliffs, N.J.: Prentice-Hall, 1972.

Gordon, Walter K. "Steinbeck's 'Flight': Journey to or from Maturity?" *Studies in Short Fiction* 3 (1966): 453–55.

Greet, T. V., et al., eds. "The Snake." In *The World of Fiction: Stories in Context,* 370–75. Boston: Houghton Mifflin, 1964.

Groene, Horst. "The Themes of Manliness and Human Dignity in Steinbeck's Story, 'Flight.' " *Die Neueren Sprachen* 72 (1973): 278–84.

Grommon, Alfred H. "Who *Is* the 'Leader of the People'?: Helping Students Examine Fiction." *English Journal* 48 (1959): 449–56.

Gullason, Thomas A. "Revelation and Evolution: A Neglected Dimension of the Short Story." *Studies in Short Fiction* 10 (1973): 347–56. Discusses "The Chrysanthemums."

Hamby, James A. "Steinbeck's Biblical Vision: 'Breakfast' and the Nobel Prize Acceptance Speech." *Western Review* (Western New Mexico University) 10, no. 1 (Spring 1973): 57–59.

Hayashi, Tetsumaro, ed. *Steinbeck's Women: Essays in Criticism.* Steinbeck Monograph Series, no. 9. Muncie, Ind.: John Steinbeck Society of America, Ball State University, 1979. Includes essays on female characters in Steinbeck's stories.

———. *A Study Guide to Steinbeck: A Handbook to His Major Works.* Metuchen, N.J.: Scarecrow Press, 1974. Includes essay on *The Long Valley.*

———. *A Study Guide to Steinbeck's "The Long Valley."* Ann Arbor, Mich.: Pierian Press, 1976. Contains essays on individual stories; see separate entries herein.

Houghton, Donald E. " 'Westering' in 'The Leader of the People.' " *Western American Literature* 4 (Summer 1969): 117–24.

Hughes, Robert S., Jr. "Steinbeck Stories at the Houghton Library: A Case for Authenticity of Four Unpublished Texts." *Harvard Library Bulletin* 30 (1982): 87–95.

———. "Steinbeck's Uncollected Stories." *Steinbeck Quarterly* 18 (1985): 79–93. See also Clifford L. Lewis, "Four Dubious Steinbeck Stories."

Johnston, Kenneth G. "Teaching the Short Story: An Approach to Steinbeck's 'Flight.' " *Kansas English* 58 (1973): 4–11.

Jones, Lawrence W. "A Note on Steinbeck's Earliest Stories." *Steinbeck Quarterly* 2 (1969): 59–60.

———. "An Uncited Post-War Steinbeck Story: 'The Short-Short Story of Mankind.' " *Steinbeck Quarterly* 3 (1970): 30–31.

Jones, William M. "Steinbeck's 'Flight.' " *Explicator* 18 (November 1959), item 11.

Levant, Howard. "John Steinbeck's *The Red Pony:* A Study in Narrative Technique." *Journal of Narrative Technique* 1 (May 1971): 77–85.

Lewis, Clifford L. "Four Dubious Steinbeck Stories." *Steinbeck Quarterly* 5 (1972): 17–19. See also Roberts Hughes, "Steinbeck Stories at the Houghton Library."

Lisca, Peter. " 'The Raid' and *In Dubious Battle.*" *Steinbeck Quarterly* 5 (Summer–Fall 1972): 90–94. Reprinted in *A Study Guide to Steinbeck's "The Long Valley,"* 41–46.

Review of *The Long Valley. Springfield Weekly Republican* (Springfield, Mass.), 6 October 1938, 8.

McMahan, Elizabeth E. " 'The Chrysanthemums': Study of a Woman's Sexuality." *Modern Fiction Studies* 14 (Winter 1968–69): 453–58. See also Gerald Noonan, "A Note on 'The Chrysanthemums.' "

Madeo, Frederick. " 'Flight'—An Allegorical Journey." *English Record* 14 (1964): 55–58.

Mandlebaum, Bernard. "John Steinbeck's 'The Snake': The Structure of a Dream." *English Record* 16 (1966): 24–26.

Marcus, Mordecai. "The Lost Dream of Sex and Childbirth in 'The Chrysanthemums.' " *Modern Fiction Studies* 11 (1965): 54–58.

Marovitz, Sanford E. "The Cryptic Raillery of 'Saint Katy the Virgin.' " In *A Study Guide to Steinbeck's "The Long Valley,"* edited by Tetsumaro Hayashi, 73–80. Ann Arbor, Mich.: Pierian Press, 1976.

Martin, Bruce. " 'The Leader of the People' Reexamined." *Studies in Short Fiction* 8 (1971): 423–32.

Matsumoto, Fusae. "Steinbeck's Women in *The Long Valley.*" In *John Steinbeck: East and West.* Steinbeck Monograph Series, no. 8, edited by Tetsumaro Hayashi et al., 48–53. Muncie, Ind.: John Steinbeck Society of America, Ball State University, 1978.

Mawer, Randall R. "Takashi Kato, 'Good American': The Central Episode in Steinbeck's *The Pastures of Heaven.*" *Steinbeck Quarterly* 13 (1980): 23–31.

May, Charles E. "Myth and Mystery in Steinbeck's 'The Snake': A Jungian View." *Criticism* 15 (1973): 322–25.

Miller, William V. "Sexual and Spiritual Ambiguity in 'The Chrysanthemums.' " In *A Study Guide to Steinbeck's "The Long Valley,"* edited by Tetsumaro Hayashi, 1–10. Ann Arbor, Mich.: Pierian Press, 1976.

Mitchell, Marilyn H. "Steinbeck's Strong Women: Feminine Identity in the Short Stories." In *Steinbeck's Women: Essays in Criticism.* Steinbeck Monograph Series, no. 9, edited by Tetsumaro Hayashi, 26–35.

Bibliography

Muncie, Ind.: John Steinbeck Society of America, Ball State University, 1979.

Mizener, Arthur. "Does a Moral Vision of the Thirties Deserve a Nobel Prize?" *New York Times Book Review,* 9 December 1962, 4, 43–45.

Morsberger, Katherine M., and Robert E. Morsberger. " 'The Murder': Realism or Ritual?" In *A Study Guide to Steinbeck's "The Long Valley,"* edited by Tetsumaro Hayashi, 65–71. Ann Arbor, Mich.: Pierian Press, 1976.

Morsberger, Robert E. "In Defense of 'Westering.' " *Western American Literature* 5 (Summer 1970): 143–46.

———. "Steinbeck's Happy Hookers." In *Steinbeck's Women: Essays in Criticism.* Steinbeck Monograph Series, no. 9, edited by Tetsumaro Hayashi, 36–48. Muncie, Ind.: John Steinbeck Society of America, Ball State University, 1979.

Noonan, Gerald, "A Note on 'The Chrysanthemums.' " *Modern Fiction Studies* 15 (1969): 542. Reply to Elizabeth E. McMahan, " 'The Chrysanthemums': Study of a Woman's Sexuality."

Osborne, William R. "The Education of Elisa Allen: Another Reading of John Steinbeck's 'The Chrysanthemums.' " *Interpretations* 8 (1976): 10–15.

———. "The Texts of Steinbeck's 'The Chrysanthemums.' " *Modern Fiction Studies* 12 (1966): 479–84.

Owens, Louis D. " 'The Murder': Illusions of Chivalry." *Steinbeck Quarterly* 17 (1984): 10–14.

———. "Steinbeck's 'Flight': Into the Jaws of Death." *Steinbeck Quarterly* 10 (1977): 103–8.

Review of *The Pastures of Heaven. Booklist* 29 (1 December 1932): 116.

Review of *The Pastures of Heaven. New York Evening Post,* Saturday, 29 October 1932, 7.

Review of *The Pastures of Heaven. Saturday Review of Literature,* 26 November 1932, 275–76.

Pearce, Howard D. "Steinbeck's 'The Leader of the People': Dialectic and Symbol." *Papers on Language and Literature* 8 (Fall 1972): 415–26.

Peterson, Richard F. "The Grail Legend and Steinbeck's 'The Great Mountains.' " *Steinbeck Quarterly* 6 (1973): 9–15.

———. "The Turning Point: *The Pastures of Heaven* (1932)." In *A Study Guide to Steinbeck: A Handbook to His Major Works,* edited by Tetsumaro Hayashi, 87–106. Metuchen, N. J.: Scarecrow Press, 1974.

Piacentino, Edward J. "Patterns of Animal Imagery in Steinbeck's 'Flight.' " *Studies in Short Fiction* 17 (Fall 1980): 437–43.

Raess, John. "Steinbeck Used San Jose Hangings for Short Story with Lynching Theme." *Spartan Daily* (San Jose State University), 26 April 1978, 1, 8. Discusses "The Vigilante."

Reich, Charles R. "Study Questions for *The Red Pony*." *Exercise Exchange* 9 (April 1962): 3–4.

Renner, Stanley. "Mary Teller and Sue Bridehead: Birds of a Feather in 'The White Quail' and *Jude the Obscure*." *Steinbeck Quarterly* 18 (1985): 35–45.

————. "Sexual Idealism and Violence in 'The White Quail.' " *Steinbeck Quarterly* 17 (1984): 76–87.

Riggs, Susan F. "The Steinbeck Collection in the Department of Special Collections, Stanford University Libraries." *Steinbeck Quarterly* 11 (1978): 102–3.

Rohrberger, Mary [on Steinbeck's short stories]. In *The American Short Story, 1900–1945: A Critical History*, edited by Philip Stevick, 178–82. Boston: Twayne Publishers, 1984.

Satyanarayana, M. R. "And Then the Child Becomes a Man: Three Initiation Stories of John Steinbeck." *Indian Journal of American Studies* 1 (1971): 87–92.

Sheffield, Carlton A. Introduction to *Letters to Elizabeth: A Selection of Letters from John Steinbeck to Elizabeth Otis*. Edited by Florian J. Shasky and Susan F. Riggs. San Francisco: The Book Club of California, 1978, vii–xix.

Simmonds, Roy S. "The First Publication of Steinbeck's 'The Leader of the People.' " *Steinbeck Quarterly* 8 (1975): 13–18.

————. "John Steinbeck, R. L. Stevenson, and Edith McGillcuddy." *San Jose Studies* 1 (November 1975): 29–39.

————. "The Original Manuscripts of Steinbeck's 'The Chrysanthemums.' " *Steinbeck Quarterly* 7 (1974): 102–11.

————. "Steinbeck's 'The Murder': A Critical and Bibliographical Study." *Steinbeck Quarterly* 9 (1976): 45–53.

Simpson, Arthur L. " 'The White Quail': A Portrait of an Artist." In *A Study Guide to Steinbeck's "The Long Valley,"* edited by Tetsumaro Hayashi, 11–16. Ann Arbor, Mich.: Pierian Press, 1976.

Street, Webster. "John Steinbeck: A Reminiscence. In *Steinbeck: The Man and His Work*, edited by Richard Astro and Tetsumaro Hayashi, 35–41. Corvallis: Oregon State University Press, 1971. See also Martha Heasley Cox, "Remembering John Steinbeck: An Interview with Webster F. Street."

Sullivan, Ernest W., II. "The Cur in 'The Chrysanthemums,' " *Studies in Short Fiction* 16 (1979): 215–17.

Sweet, Charles A., Jr. "Ms. Elisa Allen and Steinbeck's 'The Chrysanthemums.' " *Modern Fiction Studies* 20 (1974): 210–14.

Tedlock, E. W., Jr., and C. V. Wicker. *Steinbeck and His Critics: A Record of Twenty-Five Years*. Albuquerque: University of New Mexico Press, 1957.

Bibliography

Vogel, Dan. "Steinbeck's 'Flight': The Myth of Manhood." *College English* 23 (1961): 225–26.

Walton, Eda Lou. "The Simple Life." Review of *The Long Valley*. *Nation* 147 (1 October 1938): 331–32.

West, Philip J. "Steinbeck's 'The Leader of the People': A Crisis in Style." *Western American Literature* 5 (1970): 137–41.

Whipple, T. K. "Steinbeck: Through a Glass, Though Brightly." Review of *The Long Valley*. *New Republic* 96 (12 October 1938): 274–75.

Wilson, Edmund, "The Californians: Storm and Steinbeck." *New Republic* 103 (9 December 1940): 784–87.

——. *Classics and Commercials: A Literary Chronicle of the Forties*. New York: Farrar, Straus, 1950, 35–45.

Woodward, Robert H. "John Steinbeck, Edith McGillcuddy, and *Tortilla Flat*." *San Jose Studies* 3 (1977): 70–73.

——. "The Promise of Steinbeck's 'The Promise.'" In *A Study Guide to Steinbeck's "The Long Valley,"* edited by Tetsumaro Hayashi, 97–104. Ann Arbor, Mich.: Pierian Press, 1976.

Work, James C. "Coordinate Forces in 'The Leader of the People.'" *Western American Literature* 16 (1982): 279–89.

Young, Stanley. "The Short Stories of John Steinbeck." Review of *The Long Valley*. *New York Times Book Review*, 25 September 1938, 7.

Theory and Criticism of the Short Story

Allen, Walter. *The Short Story in English*. New York: Oxford University Press, 1981.

Aycock, Wendell M., ed. *The Teller and the Tale: Aspects of the Short Story*. Lubbock, Texas: Texas Tech, 1982.

Bates, H. E. *The Modern Short Story: A Critical Survey*. London: Thomas Nelson and Sons, 1941.

Beachcroft, T. O. *The Modest Art: A Survey of the Short Story in English*. London: Oxford University Press, 1968.

Current-García, Eugene, and Walton R. Patrick, eds. *What Is the Short Story?* Rev. ed. Glenview, Ill.: Scott, Foresman and Co., 1974.

Grabo, Carl H. *The Art of the Short Story*. New York: Charles Scribner's Sons, 1913.

Hanson, Clare. *Short Stories and Short Fictions, 1880–1980*. London: Macmillan, 1985.

Ingram, Forrest L. *Representative Short Story Cycles of the Twentieth Century: Studies in a Literary Genre*. The Hague: Mouton Press, 1971.

"The International Symposium on the Short Story." *Kenyon Review*. Pt. 1: 30, no. 4 (1968): 443–90; pt. 2: 31, no. 1 (1969): 58–94; pt. 3: 31, no. 4 (1969): 450–503.

Bibliography

Joselyn, Sister M. "Edward Joseph O'Brien and the American Short Story." *Studies in Short Fiction* 3 (1965): 1–15.

Lieberman, Elias. *The American Short Story: A Study of the Influence of Locality in Its Development.* 1912. Reprint. New York: AMS Press, 1970.

Lohafer, Susan. *Coming to Terms with the Short Story.* Baton Rouge: Louisiana State University, 1983.

Magill, Frank, ed. *Critical Survey of Short Fiction.* Englewood Cliffs, N.J.: Salem Press, 1981, 2274–79. Discusses Steinbeck as a story writer.

Matthews, Brander. *The Philosophy of the Short-Story.* 1901. Reprint. New York: Peter Smith, 1931.

May, Charles E. *Short Story Theories.* Athens: Ohio University Press, 1976.

Mirrielees, Edith Ronald. "The American Short Story." *Atlantic Monthly,* June 1941, 714–22.

————. "Short Stories, 1950." *College English* 12 (May 1951): 425–32.

————. *The Story Writer.* Boston: Little, Brown, 1939.

————. *Story Writing.* Boston: The Writer, 1947.

————. *Story Writing.* Preface by John Steinbeck. New York: Viking Press, 1962.

O'Brien, Edward J. *The Advance of the American Short Story.* Rev. ed. New York: Dodd, Mead, 1963.

————. *The Dance of the Machines; The American Short Story and the Industrial Age.* New York: Macaulay, 1929.

O'Connor, Frank. *The Lonely Voice: A Study of the Short Story.* Cleveland: World Publishing Co., 1963.

O'Faolain, Sean. *The Short Story.* London: Collins, 1948.

Pattee, Fred Lewis. *The Development of the American Short Story: An Historical Survey.* New York: Harper & Brothers, 1923.

Peden, William. *The American Short Story: Continuity and Change, 1940–1975.* 2d ed. Boston: Houghton Mifflin, 1975.

Reid, Ian. *The Short Story.* New York: Barnes & Noble, 1977.

Ross, Danforth. *The American Short Story.* Minnesota Pamphlets on American Writers, no. 14. Minneapolis: University of Minnesota Press, 1961.

Stevick, Philip, ed. *The American Short Story, 1900–1945: A Critical History.* Boston: Twayne Publishers, 1984.

Summers, Hollis. *Discussions of the Short Story.* Boston: Heath, 1963.

Thurston, Jarvis, et al., eds. *Short Fiction Criticism: A Checklist of Interpretation since 1925 of Stories and Novelettes (American, British, Continental), 1800–1958.* Denver: Alan Swallow, 1960.

Voss, Arthur. *The American Short Story: A Critical Survey.* Norman: University of Oklahoma, 1973.

Bibliography

Walker, Warren S. *Twentieth-Century Short Story Explication: Interpretations, 1900–1975, of Short Fiction since 1800.* 3d. ed. Hamden, Conn.: Shoe String Press, 1977.

Weaver, Gordon, ed. *The American Short Story, 1945–1980: A Critical History.* Boston: Twayne Publishers, 1983.

Weixlmann, Joe. *American Short Fiction Criticism and Scholarship, 1959–1977: A Checklist.* Chicago: Swallow Press, 1982.

West, Ray B., Jr. *The Short Story in America: 1900–1950.* Freeport, N.Y.: Books for Libraries Press, 1968.

Index

211

Index

Index

Index

Index

About the Author

R. S. Hughes received his Ph.D. in American literature from Indiana University and is an associate professor of English at the University of Hawaii. His writings on Steinbeck include *Beyond the Red Pony: A Reader's Companion to Steinbeck's Complete Short Stories* (1987), and he has published numerous essays and reviews in the *Steinbeck Quarterly, Harvard Library Bulletin,* and other journals and books. He was the 1985 recipient of the Richard and Dorothy Burkhardt Best *Steinbeck Quarterly* Article of the Year Award.

About the Editor

General editor Gordon Weaver earned his B.A. in English at the University of Wisconsin-Milwaukee in 1961; his M.A. in English at the University of Illinois, where he studied as a Woodrow Wilson Fellow, in 1962; and his Ph.D. in English and creative writing at the University of Denver in 1970. He is the author of several novels, including *Count a Lonely Cadence, Give Him a Stone, Circling Byzantium,* and most recently *The Eight Corners of the World* (Vermont: Chelsea Green Publishing Company, 1988). Many of his numerous short stories are collected in *The Entombed Man of Thule, Such Waltzing Was Not Easy, Getting Serious, Morality Play,* and *A World Quite Round.* Recognition of his fiction includes the St. Lawrence Award for Fiction (1973), a National Endowment for the Arts Fellowship (1974), and the O. Henry First Prize (1979). He edited *The American Short Story, 1945-1980: A Critical History.* He is a professor of English at Oklahoma State University and serves as an adjunct member of the faculty of the Vermont College Master of Fine Arts Writing Program. Married, and the father of three daughters, he lives in Stillwater, Oklahoma.